Education and Rehabilitation Techniques

Education and Rehabilitation Techniques

James S. Payne, Ed.D.
Assistant Professor
Department of Special Education
University of Virginia

Cecil D. Mercer, M.S.
Assistant Professor
Department of Special Education
University of Florida

Michael H. Epstein, M.Ed.
Doctoral Fellow
Department of Special Education
University of Virginia

Behavioral Publications
New York

Library of Congress Catalog Number 74-6176
ISBN: 0-87705-255-5 (paper)
       0-87705-163-1 (cloth)
Copyright 1974 by Behavioral Publications, Inc.

BEHAVIORAL PUBLICATIONS, Inc.
72 Fifth Avenue
New York, New York 10011

Printed in the United States of America
456789 987654321

Library of Congress Cataloging in Publication Data

Payne, James S   1931-
    Education and rehabilitation techniques.

    Bibliography: p.
    1. Rehabilitation. 2. Rehabilitation counseling. 3. Handicapped children—Education. I. Mercer, Cecil D., joint author. II. Epstein, Michael H., joint author. III. Title.
HD7255.P39   362.8'5   74-6176

Dedicated to. . .

Clare W. Graves,
for theory

Jerry D. Chaffin,
for application

Lao Russell,
for inspiration

CONTENTS

PREFACE

This book was created and developed on the premise that education and rehabilitation programs represent to many handicapped individuals the link which spans the gap between debilitating dependence and livelihood. Its purpose springs from the philosophy that all honorable work has dignity and that a nation should afford all of its members extensive opportunities to participate in such a humanizing and worthwhile activity as work. In essence, each country needs to foster the development of its most precious resource--its people.

This book is divided into three sections. Section I, Developing Human Resources, begins with a discussion covering education and rehabilitation. Maximizing human potential is recognized as a common goal of the total rehabilitation process. In order to facilitate human development it was determined that persons in the helping professions must operate from a realistic theory concerning the nature of man. The theories of Riesman, Heath, Maslow, Shostrom, and Schein are reviewed and incorporated into a comprehensive theory of man developed by Dr. Clare Graves. Graves' theory is presented as a viable operational base for effecting education and rehabilitation. The rehabilitation counselor's job is discussed in terms of using Graves' theory to grow people. Finally Graves' theory is presented as an operational base for managers to use to get people to do their job and enjoy it.

Section II, Vocational Adjustment of the Handicapped, focuses on the practical skills needed for securing and maintaining vocational resources for the handicapped. Practical techniques are described which demonstrate how the rehabilitation counselor can survey the community for training and placement resources, develop and maintain these resources, and evaluate the adjustment of the client. A summation chapter presents a model which enables the counselor to evaluate the client in the work environment.

Section III, Overview of Services, reviews services afforded in the education and rehabilitation processes. The rationale for education is illustrated from the perspective of early intervention and career education for young children. Rehabilitation delivery systems are described under the rubric of career education, rehabilitation facilities, and vocational rehabilitation services. The humanist and behaviorist viewpoints are discussed as major influences on the delivery of services to handicapped individuals.

This book is specifically developed for use as a primary text for introductory courses in rehabilitation, e.g., Rehabilitation Techniques. Since the book does not use the traditional labels which categorize areas of exceptionality (mental retardation, emotional disturbance, etc.), it provides a noncategorical approach to special education and would be suitable for supplementary reading for introductory courses in special education, e.g., Survey of Exceptional Children. As a resource book it can be used by vocational counselors, special education teachers, teachers interested in career education, school principals, directors and supervisors of vocational programs, employers, and work study personnel.

The authors wish to express specific appreciation to the three outstanding individuals to whom this book is dedicated. First, we are indebted to Clare W. Graves, Professor of Psychology, Union College, Schenectady, New York, for his theory of man and work. Graves' theory, in addition to influencing our thinking through-

out the book, provided a foundation for Section I.   Next we are indebted to Jerry D.
Chaffin, Associate Professor, Department of
Special Education, University of Kansas, Lawrence, Kansas, for his gift of applying ideology and theory to the real world.   Chaffin's
practicality makes the ideas contained in this
book usable.   Finally we are indebted to Lao
Russell, President of the University of Science
and Philosophy, Swannanoa, Waynesboro, Virginia,
for her inspiration.   Her graciousness consistently generated renewed life into the
authors.

Special acknowledgement goes to Ann R.
Mercer for editing and typing the manuscript.
Without her conscientious, consistent, and
diligent work, the manuscript would never have
been completed.

Section I

DEVELOPING HUMAN RESOURCES

1. I HOPE THIS BOOK ...

Several years ago I was hired as a vocational rehabilitation counselor and I can readily recall my first day on the job. I was assigned a caseload of handicapped clients and my major responsibilities were too numerous and varied to list. My duties ranged from providing transportation for dental services to evaluation of clients on jobs. New, green, young, excited, and somewhat nervous I was introduced to the vocational rehabilitation staff. I was instructed how to fill out the travel form for reimbursement and where to put the coffee money. Next I was handed a multi-paged manual and taken to my own office. I opened the door to see a barren room, for it had been stripped of anything that resembled life. There was an empty metal book case which looked as if it had come from an army surplus warehouse. There was a green metal desk, swivel chair, and a regular chair for clients and visitors. On top of the desk was a stack of client folders over a foot high. I was instructed to read the policy manual and find the clients.

"What do you mean, 'find the clients'?" I responded.

"The last counselor left unexpectedly and the first thing you need to do is find out who and where your clients are," I was matter-of-factly told.

1

This is what is referred to as preservice training. Although preservice training has improved somewhat over the past few years, I hope this book will help a person to understand something about rehabilitation <u>beyond</u> the policy manual and stack of client folders.

I read the manual and was confused by many of its terms and codes, and I had never seen so many forms. There were big forms, little forms, pink forms, green forms, yellow forms, lavender forms, forms for purchasing false teeth, canes, wheelchairs, transportation .... There were forms for everything-- one hundred and three forms in all, not counting the sign-in and sign-out forms. I sure hope this book <u>doesn't</u> have many forms in it.

When I asked questions about the various forms, I was told that I probably would understand them better as I worked with individual clients. Talking about forms in and of themselves isn't very interesting or meaningful. However, if I had a client to work with and he needed some type of service, such as dental service, then the forms for securing specific services would acquire meaning. Therefore, I decided to do what I was told and go find a client. I picked the folder lying on top and arbitrarily chose this person to be my first client. After reading the folder, I decided to go to the restaurant where the client was listed as working. I pulled up to the restaurant in a state car and entered the place of business to find I had arrived at a busy time. Since the manager wasn't available to talk, I decided to have lunch. After eating, I was approached by the manager who informed me that the client had walked off the job four months ago. I hope this book will help counselors to understand business routine, <u>schedule</u>, and business thinking.

It took me four days to find the client. He was at home, unshaven, watching television,

and feeling sorry for himself. He was living
in a place which smelled like urine and looked
like a pigsty. I hope this book talks about
people.

Within a year under my counseling and
guidance, this client was placed on, and
walked off of, five different jobs. I hope
this book mentions something about evaluation
and training.

One time I remember driving around the
block three times to build up enough courage
to talk with a hostile employer. He was mad
and he had a right to be. My client lost his
temper and broke the front window in the store.
I hope this book talks about how to approach
an employer.

I once knew an eager counselor who placed
six clients on jobs in one day. He thought he
really had done something. During a follow-up
session one month later, he couldn't find any
of them--they all had been fired. I hope this
book has something in it about follow-up.

I heard of a client placed at the local
humane society to care for animals. During
the second week he felt sorry for the caged
up animals and went around opening up all the
pens. There were dogs all over the county.
It took over two weeks to round up the dogs.
Yes, I hope this book talks about people's
feelings.

I once worked with a client who had spent
considerable time in jail for stealing bicy-
cles. I took him to a grocery store to be
interviewed for a job. Things were going
fairly well until he spotted a bicycle shop
across the street. I couldn't get his nose
away from the window. He just kept muttering,
"I want to work in a bicycle shop." I gave
up at the grocery store, grabbed his arm, and
quickly went across the street to inquire

about a job in the bicycle shop. I don't
know how, but the client somehow got a job
that very day and worked there for several
years before he was sent to prison for breaking into houses. You know, I hope this book
really does talk about people, all types of
people.

I have had clients hug me, laugh with me,
cry with me, curse me, throw things at me, and
spit on me. I have experienced joy and sorrow,
success and failure. I have worked with clients
I enjoyed seeing come into my office and I have
worked with clients I enjoyed seeing walk out
of my office. At times I really liked working
for vocational rehabilitation and at other
times I couldn't stand it.

This book was written for persons who
are working with handicapped people, plan to
work with handicapped people, or think they
might be interested in working with handicapped people. This book isn't complicated
or technical, but it is accurate and somewhat
detailed. When I was a student in my under-
graduate program, I enrolled in a course on
first aid. The instructor valued first aid
and felt it was an extremely important subject
to know as well as to apply. He didn't want
the course to get the reputation of being
easy, so he set out to complicate a rather
simple body of knowledge. He accomplished
this by devising some of the craziest tests
I have ever seen. We had to memorize all the
bones of the body. To test our bone knowledge
he placed each bone in a cloth sack. He handed
us the sacks labeled A to Z and we wrote on an
answer sheet what bone we thought was in each
sack. We weren't allowed to open the sack.
We had to determine what bone it was by feeling the outside of the sack. Later in the
semester, we had an objective examination on
the first aid manual that called for pure rote
memorization of all italicized words, headings,
and phrases. The instructor did everything

known to man to knock all of the life out of
the course. It was indeed a difficult course.
He succeeded in taking an important yet simple
subject and making it difficult. Some people
try to do the same thing with rehabilitation.
We don't want to oversimplify vocational rehabilitation, but neither do we want to project that it is too complicated for the average person to understand.

After reading this book, you should know
a little bit about rehabilitation services
and facilities. You should know something
about prevention and the recent movement of
career education. You should know something
about different types of people and ways to
approach them. Also, you should learn something about acquiring, developing, and maintaining an employer's interest in evaluating,
training, and hiring the handicapped.

We are not interested in reproducing a
policy manual nor in describing the characteristics of various handicapping conditions. We
are interested in talking about assisting
handicapped people with employment and life.
As we talk about clients, facilities, services,
trends, techniques, theories, etc., it must
constantly be kept in mind that we are talking
about people, not things nor statistics. We
are talking about real people--real people who
need help.

Handicapped people are not to be abused,
felt sorry for, or pitied. They are people
just like you and me. There is a film called
Leo Beuerman.[1] Leo was so handicapped he was
described sometimes as "grotesque" or "too
horrible to look at." He was small, weighed
less than 90 pounds, and his legs were bent

---

1. Leo Beuerman, Centron Educational
Films, 1621 West 9th Street, Lawrence, Kansas
(13 minutes, color).

out of shape so he couldn't walk. He also
had poor eyesight and was hard of hearing.
Leo lived on a farm in Kansas. Somehow he
learned to drive a tractor, and later he invented a hoist which allowed him to raise himself onto the tractor. He also invented and
built a pushcart which enabled him to get
around from place to place. He was able to
use his hoist to get his cart on the tractor.
Then he would get on the tractor and drive to
town. In town Leo would park his tractor,
lower himself and his cart down to the street,
get in the cart and propel himself down the
sidewalk to a store front where he repaired
watches and sold pencils. The reason this
movie had such an impact on me is that I can
remember buying pencils from him as a kid in
school. As a child I didn't realize how remarkable Leo really was. He just wanted to
talk to people, work, and do his own thing.
He wanted to be self-sufficient and independent. Here was a man, deformed to the point
that, for most people, he was repulsive to
see. However, he was more an individual, more
free, and more alive than most people. As he
sold his pencils, repaired his watches, and
made his small leather purses, he thought
about himself, life, and others. He was
quoted in his later years as saying, "I hope
someday I will be able to help the poor."
You know something, that's rehabilitation.

As we discuss theories about man and
work, describe preventive rehabilitation techniques via early intervention and career education, explain facilities and services, and
suggest how to acquire, develop, and maintain
employer participation and interest, it must
be remembered that we are talking about peo-
ple--real, live, warm human beings. Their
faults, their frailties, and their weaknesses
must not be allowed to masquerade their present strengths. Some handicapped people just
need an opportunity, some just an even break.
Others need support and still others need

intensive care and treatment. This book is
about people, education, rehabilitation, and
life. Don't read it for facts and figures
for memorization. Read it for understanding.

2. LIFE STYLES OF MAN

Conflicts between family members, tribes,
and nations permeate the history of civiliza-
tion. Religious views, skin color, politics,
and hair length are a few of the topics which
have traditionally ignited battles in living
rooms as well as across continents. These
conflicts between persons are encountered in
all walks of life. Myers and Myers (1973)
acknowledged the widespread existence of these
conflicts in our society by stating:

> Parents and teachers are sometimes
> distressed by the appearance and
> behavior of young people. Clergy-
> men are finding more concern with
> the here-and-now than in the here-
> after and government officials are
> encountering rebellion against bu-
> reaucratic constraints. Union lead-
> ers are losing control of their mem-
> bers, and athletic coaches are learn-
> ing that Lombardi-like charisma and
> domination no longer assure obedi-
> ence and commitment among athletes
> (in press).

This widespread conflict among people has
generated much human suffering which has ranged
from death to the retardation of personal-so-
cial growth of many people. The majority of

8

these conflicts may be viewed as resulting
from the mixing of opposing value systems.

It is possible to discuss human adjustment to a value parameter at four levels:
(a) intolerance, (b) tolerance, (c) respect,
and (d) appreciation. Hate characterizes the
intolerance level and the survival-of-the
fittest modus operandi prevails. Intolerance
leads to war and culminates in both human
suffering and destruction. The tolerance
level is the level at which the joining of
human effort from different value systems to
accomplish group objectives becomes possible.
However, this participation in a group effort
is often achieved at the expense of much emotional involvement. Persons at this level
may appear perpetually "up tight" or simply
"bent out of shape." For example, a person
can tolerate a toothache and continue to function in a socially acceptable manner, but it
does not mean the person is happy about it.
An examination of persons who function at the
intolerance and tolerance levels readily reveals that much mental and emotional energy
is dissipated in attacking and adjusting to
different value systems. This type of energy
waste can serve to retard the efforts of education and rehabilitation programs to develop
human resources.

Respect enables individuals with different values to function together to accomplish
group goals and actually enjoy it. To a degree fondness of others with different values
is obtainable at this level. The appreciation
level enables a person to become very fond of
other individuals who possess values dissimi-
lar to their own. Respect and appreciation
represent conditions which are complimentary
to the development of human resources. In
essence, it is possible to identify each respective adjustment level with the words hate,
dislike, like, and love.

Behaviorists have convincingly demonstrated that appropriate environmental conditions enhance human growth, and nonsupportive
environmental conditions retard the development or restoration of human potential. Respect and appreciation are the levels that
are characteristic of salutary environments
and may be achieved in two ways. All people
can be developed to the point that respect
and appreciation are inherent values, or people can be matched in their immediate environments so they are surrounded by values consistent with their own.

It is imperative that professional persons in the social sciences strive to respect
or appreciate persons with different values.
Although it would be desirable to have all
persons respect and appreciate different value
systems, a history of conflict suggests that
this goal is not immediately feasible. Thus,
it is important that educators, rehabilitation
counselors, and other social scientists strive
to achieve the second alternative by directing
people into environments compatible with their
values.

The psychological matching of milieus is
a viable solution, but a problem arises when
one considers that a theory of man is needed
which enables social scientists to understand
the values of man and make accurate predictions.
People make certain assumptions about others
and these assumptions operate as theory and
effect how a person deals with his superiors,
peers, and subordinates. The person's effectiveness depends on the degree that the assumptions match reality (Schein, 1970). In essence, a theory of man is needed which provides a realistic framework to guide the delivery of education and rehabilitation services.

Voluminous literature exists which describes studies designed to define the nature
of man. However, as exemplified by Schein

(1970), many of these studies culminate in
conclusions which suggest that people are so
complex that they defy categorization. This
conclusion appears warranted when a person
confines his scope to a small sample of studies
or when one model of man is sought. For example, Schein, in searching for a view of man,
documented the existence of three distinct
types of man which led him to conclude that
the development of a theory was impractical
because of the conflicting life styles. It
appears that Schein was looking for one level
to represent a theory of man, and, when one
level did not suffice, he concluded that the
complex nature of man eluded classification.

The remainder of this chapter will focus
on examining a representative sample of investigations and theories concerning the nature of man with the purpose of developing a
functional theory of man. The goal of this
functional theory is to provide a framework
for effecting human growth and development of
both handicapped and nonhandicapped individuals.

Studies on the Nature of Man[1]

In an effort to elucidate upon the nature of man, Riesman, Glazer, and Denney
(1953) studied man's adaptation to his environment and purported that individuals primarily change because of variations in social
and economic conditions. They suggested the
existence of three different directions of
personality development which are characterized
under the rubric of (a) tradition-directed,
(b) inner-directed, and (c) other-directed.
Riesman et al. acknowledged that every indi-

---

1. Adapted in part from: Pratt, G. W.,
& Mercer, C. D. Self-actualization and beyond.
Unpublished manuscript, University of Virginia,
1973.

vidual possesses some aspect of each of these
dimensions but usually selects one as a predominant mode of behavior.

The tradition-directed person develops
according to the demands, customs, and beliefs
of his social group, especially those of his
family. Since the tradition-directed person
is governed by rules and pressures of the
group, his uniqueness is repressed or sub-
merged. This individual is usually located
in preindustrialized nations or communities.
The inner-directed person is guided by internal demands and desires and thus is not at
the mercy of external forces, pressures, and
sanctions. Although he is aware of and sensitive to the social norms and customs, the
inner-directed person realizes that a modern
mobile society requires a strong self-will
or internal set of values. The other-directed
person is governed by parents and social group
membership; however, the number of relationships are considerably expanded beyond those
of the tradition-directed person. He is sensitive to others, adapts to a variety of social
situations, and is likely to join such philanthropic programs as the Peace Corps or VISTA.

Hershey and Lugo (1970) suggested a fourth
direction to add to the idea of Riesman, Glazer,
and Denney (1953). This fourth direction is
the self-directed man and is characterized by
the behavior of the self-actualized person.
This person trusts his intrinsic guidance and
is capable of directing himself.

Heath (1964) presented a study which focused on the characteristics and types of change
of a Princeton freshman class. Selected students were observed throughout their college
program and the results suggested that there
were basically four major groups which are presented in Table 1 and are called X, Y, Z, and
A.

Table 1

Heath's Characteristics of Students at Four Model Positions

	X Noncommitter	Y Hustler	Z Plunger	A Reasonable Adventurer
Reactivity	Under-reactive	Counter-reactive	Over-reactive	Appropriate
Common Defense	Denial	Reaction-formation	Apology, Res-titution	Reasoning
Attitude to Self	Unstructured	Rejecting	Alternating	Accepting
Social Motive	To belong	To be esteemed	To be noticed	To com-municate
Problem	Self-expression	Self-acceptance	Communica-tion	Frontier
Impression on Others	Bland Friendly Conforming Neutral	Aggressive Tough-minded Cold Ambitious	Scattered Direct Impulsive Moody	Independent Sensitive Playful Compassionate
Characteristic Utterance	Who me?	Yes, but ...	Why not?	If only, then ...

An individual in the X group is called
a Noncommitter and may be described as con-
servative, friendly, and noninvolved. He
prefers to maintain neutral positions and
avoids arguments. Heath (1964) referred to
a person in the second group (Y) as a Hustler
and described these individuals as very active with a great need for achievement and
success. Heath employed the terms fighter
and aggressor to explain the Hustler's nature.
Individuals in the third group (Z) are called
the Plungers. These individuals frequently
overextend themselves and thus encounter a
variability of moods. The Plunger likes to
engage in talk, has a tendency to over-react,
and does not like an orderly schedule. The
ultimate objective of personality development
is found in the A group, which Heath called
the Reasonable Adventurers. These individuals
have the ability to create situations for
their own satisfaction. They are intelligent,
independent, like close friends, tolerate
ambiguity, have many interests, and are hu-
morous.

Schein (1970) discussed the nature of
man in terms of the assumptions that organizations have historically made about man. He
presented these assumptions in chronological
order of their emergence and categorized them
under four headings: (a) rational-economic
man, (b) social man, (c) self-actualizing man,
and (d) complex man. Schein documented the
existence of each stage by citing observations
of how organizations have interacted with man
to achieve their desired goals. The rational-
economic view of man springs from the philosophy of hedonism and claims that man calcu-
lates the behaviors that will enhance his
self-interest and then responds accordingly.
At the rational-economic stage the emphasis
is on efficient task performance and people's
feelings are relegated to secondary concerns.
Rational-economic man works for material things
and responds to both intelligently administered

hard bargaining and traditional reinforcers
such as bonuses, prestigious titles, incen-
tives, and increased power. Schein cited
the Hawthorne studies as evidence in support
of the social viewpoint of man. These studies
demonstrated that the need to be accepted and
liked by fellow workers is a viable incentive
for man. Social man emphasizes the needs of
man as primary and relegates task performance
to a secondary concern. He is concerned with
feelings, acceptance, and a sense of belonging
and identity. Self-actualizing man seeks to
fulfill his potential and demands a certain
amount of autonomy and independence. He is
self-motivated, self-controlled, possesses
highly developed skills, and has great flexibility in adapting to various circumstances.
Schein introduced complex man as a combination
of all the stages. He purported that man is
too complex to be categorized within one viewpoint, and thus a theory of complex man should
be adopted. In essence, this view indicates
that man is a mixture of all three viewpoints
and different styles emerge as environmental
conditions vary.

     Another approach to describing the psy-
chological position of individuals is presented by Everett Shostrom (1968) in Man, the
Manipulator. As illustrated in Table 2,
Shostrom claimed that people are basically
manipulators or actualizors, and the life
style of manipulators is a set of learned
values and behaviors. The manipulator is
described as both needing to control others
and as needing to be controlled by others.
He often is artificial, unaware, and nontrust-
ing of others. The actualizor, in contrast,
is described as honest, aware, free, and
trusting of others. An actualizor likes his
uniqueness, is a loving person, and likes to
become involved in close, warm relationships.
The manipulator, on the other hand, likes to
use others for personal reasons. People usually have some aspect of both the manipulator

Table 2
A Comparison of Fundamental Characteristics
of Manipulators and Actualizors

Manipulators	Actualizors
Deception (Phoniness, Knavery). The manipulator uses tricks, techniques, and strategies. He plays roles to create impressions. His overt behavior is deliberately selected to fit the occasion.	Honesty (Transparency, Genuineness, Authenticity). The actualizor is honestly able to express his feelings, regardless of their nature. He is characterized by candidness and genuinely being himself.
Unawareness (Deadness, Boredom). The manipulator is unaware of the viable concerns of living. He has restricted awareness because he only attends to what he wants to hear and see.	Awareness (Responsiveness, Aliveness, Interest). The actualizor is sensitized to himself and others. He is aware of nature, art, music, and the reality of experiences.
Control (Closed, Deliberate). The manipulator approaches life in a calculated manner. He appears relaxed, yet is very systematic in controlling and disguising his motives from his competition.	Freedom (Spontaneity, Openness). The actualizor is spontaneous. He is the master of his life and feels a freedom to express himself and develop his potential.
Cynicism (Distrust). The manipulator distrusts himself and others. In essence, he does not trust human nature.	Trust (Faith, Belief). The actualizor trusts himself and others. He believes that people can cope with life in the here and now.

and the actualizor as parts of their psychological structure. Shostrom stated that "only
when we are aware of our manipulators are we
free to experience them and derive from them
actualizing behavior (p. 12)." As an individual gains awareness of his manipulations, the
manipulations decrease and actualization increases. In conjunction with this type of insight and awareness, Shostrom purported that
group dynamics activities may be helpful in
the transformation of manipulation to actualization. He suggested participation in actualization training, sensitivity groups, and
marathon groups to facilitate the development
of the actualization process.

Maslow (1968) developed a system of hierarchical needs which parallel the growth of
man. The needs of this hierarchy are listed
in ascending order:
1. Physiological needs, i.e., hunger, thirst,
oxygen.
2. Safety needs, i.e., security.
3. Belongingness and loving needs, i.e., af-
fection, identification.
4. Esteem needs, i.e., prestige, self-respect.
5. Self-actualization needs.

It is important to note that the lower
level needs must be met before the needs of
the next level emerge. Insufficient gratifi-
cation of needs at one level will keep the
individual from developing to the next level
and ultimately stifle self-actualization.
Although Maslow (1968) developed the hierarchy of needs, he dealt much more extensively
with the self-actualized person than with
persons with lower need levels. He described
this person as one who does not judge or interfere and possesses a noncondemning attitude
toward others. Maslow (1971) stated that
these people tend to be unconventional, un-
realistic, and unscientific. He claimed that
few people ever reach this level and estimated
that less than one percent of all people reach

it. An important part of the task of self-
actualization is "to become aware of what one
is, biologically, temperamentally, constitu-
tionally, ... of one's capacities, desires,
needs, and also of one's vocation, what one
is fitted for, what one's destiny is (p. 32)."

In order to help an individual grow it
appears his basic needs (needs man has in
common with animals) must be met until he
reaches the level of self-actualization.
Maslow (1971) suggested that a clinician
should help the client "to unfold, to break
through the defenses against his own self-
knowledge, to recover himself, and get to
know himself (p. 52)." One of the main values
of Maslow's theory is that it presents a comprehensive approach for human growth which
spans several levels of existence. It, however, is not precise enough to predict behavior
for each person.

Graves' Theory of Man[2]

A final approach, and one which may in
fact include all the others, is presented by
Clare W. Graves, and it is possible that
Graves' theory of man may provide the precision needed in the social sciences. Graves
(1970) used Maslow's theory as a base for a
very well organized theory of how man grows
and changes.

Using the hierarchical need theory as a
base, Dr. Clare W. Graves, Professor of Psychology, Union College, Schenectady, New York,
developed a viable theory of man. The best

---

2. Adapted from: Payne, J. S., Mercer,
C. D., Payne, R. A., & Davison, R. G. Head
Start: A tragicomedy with epilogue. New
York: Behavioral Publications, 1973, pp. 126-
139. Reprinted in part by permission.

way to comprehend Graves' theory of man is
to turn to original sources and practitioners
who use his theory. The following passages
are taken from an unpublished manuscript en-
titled, "Clare W. Graves' Theory of Levels of
Human Existence and Suggested Managerial Systems for Each Level," compiled by the staff
of the Management Center, University of Richmond, Richmond, Virginia, 1971.

> The theory advocates that the
> psychological growth of mature man
> is an unfolding process marked by
> the progressive subordination of
> older lower-level behavioral sys-
> tems to higher-level behavioral
> systems. Each successive level is
> a state of equilibrium through which
> people pass to other states of equi-
> librium. At each stage the individ-
> ual has a psychology that is unique
> to that level. Actions, feelings,
> motivations, ethic values, and
> thoughts are all behavior manifes-
> tations which are required to deal
> with problems at a particular level.
> Also, persons at each level prefer
> a particular style of management.
> That is, in different levels of
> existence, an individual acts, feels,
> thinks, judges and is motivated
> through different managerial styles.
>   A person does not mechanically
> grow to another level of existence.
> Constitutionally, he may not be
> equipped to change in an upward
> direction although the conditions
> of his environment change. A per-
> son may continue to grow, under
> certain conditions, through a sys-
> tematic series of ordered behavioral
> systems or stabilize and live a life
> at any one or a combination of levels
> in the hierarchy. Thus, persons
> live in a potentially open system

of needs, values and aspirations,
but often settle into what approxi-
mates a closed system. In order for
people and their societies to grow
they must subordinate old values
and behaviors to develop new values
and behaviors appropriate to new
states of existence. Develop and
discard, retain and rearrange, seems
to be nature's way of handling
things (pp. 1-2).

Graves (1970) indicated that there are
presently eight major systems of existence as
outlined in Table 3.

First Level of Existence: Reactive. Man
at the first level is primarily concerned with
staying alive. The physiological needs are
paramount and all energy is consumed in reducing the tension generated by these physiological needs. Virtually, it is a state of
psychological nonexistence in which man is
not aware of self and in which he exists pure-
ly as a reflex organism.

A person at level one is not capable of
productive effort and is consequently unemployable. Usually these persons exist in infancy and in severe forms of senility. Most
are located either in state mental institutions or listed on welfare as totally dependent cases. Although these individuals are
few and unemployable in the United States industrial system, businesses that emerge or
develop in underdeveloped countries must deal
with them.

Second Level of Existence: Tribalistic.
The second-level man progresses to a state beyond that of mere physiological existence.
His basic needs are for stability and safety,
and he begins a state of psychological existence in which the brain awakens, receives
stimuli, but does not comprehend or understand

Table 3

Hierarchical Development of Man's Forms for Existence,
Motivational System, and Organizational Problems

Level of Existence	Nature of Existence	Motivation	Organizational Problems at Each Stage
8	Experientialistic	Experience	?
7	Cognitive	Existence	Contributing
6	Sociocentric	Affiliation	Acceptance
5	Manipulator-Materialistic	Independence	Prestige
4	Saintly-Conformist	Security	Stability
3	Egocentric	Survival	Survival
2	Tribalistic	Assurance	Creation
1	Reactive	Physiological	---

it. This level person vaguely realizes that
he exists as an individual being separate from
an external world. He lives a life that is
strongly defended but not understood.

The magical thinking is ingrained in his
existence and greatly influences the way he
lives. Safety is an overwhelming concern, and
although he is basically passive, he will use
force readily if he feels he is threatened.
Tradition and ritualistic thinking provide
him a means which assures his safety. People
at this level are capable of productive effort,
providing it does not clash with the super-
stitions and magical beliefs that permeate
their life style. They are strongly influenced
by tradition and power exerted by authority
figures, i.e., boss, chieftain, teacher, po-
liceman, etc.

Third Level of Existence: Egocentric.
The third-level person becomes totally aware
of his existence as an individual being. The
higher brain processes begin to awaken as new
stimuli thrust on his consciousness. He realizes that he is alive and that he must die,
and this fact triggers a survival need which
is psychologically based. All external forces
are immediately interpreted as threatening,
and it is necessary to combat them through
self-assertion. Existence at this level is
characterized by competition, aggressiveness,
and a morality of the "eye for eye and tooth
for tooth" variety. Power is revered, and the
best means of obtaining it are through rugged,
aggressive, self-assertive individualism. The
egocentric-level man further realizes he has
the power to manipulate the world to the betterment of his existence and to the enhancement of his self-centered survival needs. He
readily insists that winners in this fight for
survival deserve the spoils of their victories
and that losers are relegated to a state of
submissive existence. Also, it is perceived
that the powerful man has the inalienable

right to authoritarian control over the lesser
man or the "have-nots." It is important to
note that the losers or "have-nots" in this
system hold the same values as their authoritarian counterparts but are reduced to a miserable life of trying to beat the system.

Fourth Level of Existence: Saintly and/or
Conformist. The reality of death encourages
third-level man to question the reason for his
existence since, ultimately, the powerful and
the weak face death on equal ground. Why does
an existence characterized by the reverence of
power face such a powerless ending? The enigma
of death provides the impetus for third-level
man to seek a new level of existence.

When man reaches the fourth level, the
inequality of earthly conditions is accepted,
and the problem of death is resolved. To him
there is an all-powerful external force which
determines and guides the nature of each person's existence. The will of this all-powerful force provides the fourth-level man with
a framework for establishing the guidelines
for a saintly life which esteems sacrifice as
a means to salvation. This sacrificial style
of life manifests itself through actions characterized by denial, deference, piety, modesty,
harsh self-discipline, and self-indulgence.

He is very secure in this saintly way of
life, and it usually unfolds under the guiding
authority of one of the world's great reli-
gions or philosophies. In keeping with doc-
trines the fourth-level person thrives on
rules, order, and moralistic prescriptions.
Also, it is worthwhile to note that fourth-
level man focuses on the means (sacrifice)
rather than the end (salvation).

Fourth-level man historically has presented a puzzling paradox between values and
actions. Although the sacrificial existence
is esteemed, fourth-level man has fought many

wars over whose sacrificial system will prevail. In a recent study, Myers and Myers
(1973) described the fourth-level person as
a conformist with low tolerance for both ambiguity and people with different values.

Fifth Level of Existence: Manipulator
and/or Materialistic. When fourth-level man
begins to question the value of the sacrificial life, he starts fulfilling the conditions
needed to move to the fifth level. These
fifth-level conditions focus on living a life
guided by the attainment of wealth and its
associated pleasures. Fifth-level man feels
a strong desire to be independent, and this
independence is achieved by conquering the
physical world through a positive, objective,
scientific method that simultaneously enables
him to collect wealth. Although both third-
level and fifth-level man are concerned about
conquering the world, they differ in their
method. Whereas third-level man uses force
and power with reckless abandon, the fifth-
level person rationally approaches his means
and avoids bringing the wrath of others on
him. The strong materialistic needs of fifth-
level man are reflected in his value system,
which reveres competition, gamesmanship, and
the business attitude. He seeks higher status
and strives to manipulate people and things.

Graves (1970) noted that "Fifth-level
values improve immeasurably man's conditions
for existence. They create wealth ... and
lead to knowledge which improves the human
condition (p. 150)."

This level represents the mode of existence for much of middle-class America. Although there are many persons who exist at
this level, it is interesting to note that
persons at the saintly level consider them
akin to sin.

Sixth Level of Existence: Sociocentric.
The sixth-level person has traveled through

the hierarchical order of needs concerned
with survival, safety, order, salvation, and
material gain. Predominantly, he is concerned with social matters and seeks a work
environment that is congenial. The sociocentric man strives to be accepted and liked
and is very sensitive to group standards.
The level six person's behavior always reflects the behavior of the group of which he
is a part. A level six man is very flexible
and his behavior is predictable when viewed
in conjunction with peer influence. In essence, level six persons have high affiliation needs, hate violence, and are concerned
with social issues.

The following excerpt from Graves (1970)
assists our understanding of existence at this
level.

On the surface sociocratic values
appear shallower, less serious and
even fickle in contrast to values
at other levels because the surface
aspect of them shifts as the "valued-
other" changes his preferences. But
the central core of this system is
a very solid process. It is being
with, in-with and within, the feelings of his valued other (p. 151).

Seventh Level of Existence: Cognitive.
Seventh-level man has traversed from subsis-
tence levels to a level of true being. He
has achieved an existence free of needs that
are common to animals. His cognitive self
leaps into freedom, and he dwells in an environment of abundant motivation where his
concept of existence greatly broadens. He
is uniquely human and has no fear of God, boss,
survival, or social approval. He is confident
of his ability to survive in any situation.
He is intrigued with existence itself and
dwells on the improvement of existence states
of all beings. He is concerned with man as

becoming and welcomes any alternative that
enhances existence. A person at this level
enjoys living for its sheer pleasure. To him
the means, methods, or ways are relatively
unimportant, but viable ends are extremely
important. The seventh-level man is a high
producer as long as the means to an end are
left to his personal direction. In addition
to being a producer, he possesses creative
excellence, and this combination makes him a
valuable resource in advanced technological
and professional service fields.

Eighth Level of Existence: Experientialistic. When the need to esteem life is satisfied, man grows to an experientialistic state
where he realizes that he cannot know all
about existence. A problem-solving existence
gives way to an intuitive existence level at
which man must adjust to the reality of existence and accept existential dichotomies.

He values wonder, awe, reverence, humil-
ity, fusion, integration, unity, simplicity,
the noninterfering receptive perception versus
active controlling perception, enlarging consciousness, the ineffable experience (Maslow,
1968). He insists on an atmosphere of trust
and respect and avoids domination. He is end
oriented and takes his activities very seri-
ously.

The life and work of Walter Russell as
reported by Glenn Clark (1973) provide many
illustrations of the type of thinking which
is derived from meditation and is inherent in
an eighth-level existence. For example, Russell stated,

No greater proof than my experience
is needed to prove to the doubting
world that all knowledge exists in
the Mind universe of Light--which
is God--that all Mind in One Mind,
that men do not have separate minds,

and that all knowledge can be obtained from the Universal Source
of All-Knowledge by becoming One
with that Source (p. 36).

An Integrated Theory of Man

A perusal of the myriad of theories concerning the nature of man certainly testifies
to the complexity of the problem. Manipulators, actualizors, plungers, hustlers, inner-
directed, other-directed, and conformists are
just a small sampling of terms used to define
the characteristics of man. However, a critical review of the theories reveals that an
astonishing degree of similarity exists among
them. To begin with, it is readily discern-
ible that Graves' (1970) theory is the most
comprehensive and expands a broader range of
psychological existences than do any of the
other theories. The span and framework of
Graves' theory enables us to integrate all
of the theories into a meaningful perspective.

As illustrated in Table 4, Graves (1970)
and Maslow (1971) are the only theorists to
incorporate the lower levels of existence
(Reactive, Tribalistic, and Egocentric). Although Maslow does not discuss the hierarchical stages in terms of respective life styles,
it is apparent that the existence of Graves'
reactive person originates from a concern for
physiological needs. The tribalistic and egocentric existence levels appear to spring from
a combination of the physiological and safety
needs presented in Maslow's hierarchical need
structure.

Riesman, Glazer, and Denney's tradition-
directed person and Heath's noncommitter correspond to the saintly-conformist level in
Graves' theory. This level person would originate from both the need to belong and the
survival needs in Maslow's hierarchy.

Table 4
Stages of Man: A Composite

Riesman, Glazer, & Denney	Heath	Schein	Shostrom	Maslow	Graves
				Animal Related Need Life Styles	Reactive Tribalistic Egocentric Saintly-Conformist
Tradition-Directed	Noncommitters				Materialistic-Manipulator
Inner-Directed	Hustlers	Rational-Economic Man	Manipulator		Sociocentric
Other-Directed	Plungers Reasonable Adventurers	Social Man Self-Actualizing	Actualizor	Self-Actualization	Cognitive Experientialistic

Riesman, Glazer, and Denney's inner-directed person, Heath's hustler, Schein's rational-economic man, and Shostrom's manipulator are congruent with Graves' materialistic-manipulator level. The self-esteem needs in Maslow's theory would tend to produce a life style similar to a materialistic or manipulative level of existence.

Riesman, Glazer, and Denney's other-directed person, Heath's plunger, Schein's social man, and Shostrom's actualizor are representative of Graves' sociocentric level of psychological existence. Also, it is feasible to postulate that the social and self-actualization needs as identified by Maslow would provide the psychological foundation for the sociocentric level of existence.

Heath's reasonable adventurer and Schein's self-actualizing man are the only levels which extend to the cognitive stage that Graves (1970) describes. In Maslow's (1968) discussions of the self-actualized man, he appears to mix the sociocentric level with portions of Graves' cognitive level. For example, the dimension of fear and the concern with means to an end is not present in the person functioning at Graves' cognitive level while it is in Maslow's self-actualized man.

Graves (1970) is the only theorist to incorporate the experientialistic level of psychological existence. It is possible that the popularity of this level is depressed because of its scarcity and recent emergence. According to Graves, "These eighth level experientialistic values are only beginning to emerge in the lives of some men (p. 155)." Moreover, Graves believes that if the proper conditions exist, eighth level values will someday become the dominant value system.

The open-ended aspect of the theory is important to consider since Graves (1970) sees

man continuing to grow into levels currently
unknown. For the present, Graves stated, "And
so we come, momentarily, to the end of man's
value trek (p. 155)."

Many people have a tendency to recoil
from the theory described by Graves (1970)
because it appears to be categorizing people.
However, it can be argued effectively that he
is encouraging exactly the opposite. Our
society is prone to judge by prototypes which,
in actuality, is grouping. For example, prototypes exist for nurses, doctors, ministers,
counselors, lawyers, teachers, policemen, and
countless others. Graves dispells and reveals
the illogic of this categorizing approach by
demonstrating that all of these groups may
manifest an extensive array of systems of behavior, i.e., conformist, materialistic, etc.
Furthermore, Graves (1972) acknowledged that
approximately 95 percent of the people whom
he has studied during the past 14 years operate at one of the levels most of the time but
are capable of functioning at different levels
under varying environmental conditions. As
illustrated in Figure 2-1, Graves described
these individuals as exemplifying an "open
personality." In contrast, as illustrated in
Figure 2-2, a small portion of the people he
studied exhibited what he called a "closed
personality." These individuals predominantly
adhere to the values of one level.

Conclusion

This chapter acknowledged that one of the
aims of counselors, educators, and managers is
to help an individual develop his potential.
The clashing of incongruent values was presented as a phenomena which has historically
not only generated human suffering but has retarded individual growth. Intolerance, tolerance, respect, and appreciation were discussed
as a hierarchy of conditions which characterize an individual's adjustment to different

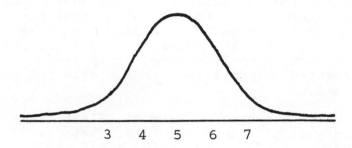

Fig. 2-1. Graves' open personality type at fifth level.

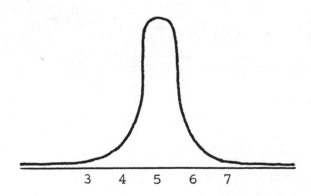

Fig. 2-2. Graves' closed personality type at fifth level.

values. Respect and/or appreciation were
established as germane to an education or
rehabilitation program. The existence of
these conditions appears to be accomplished
by: (a) manipulating the immediate environment of individuals, or (b) attempting to
develop all people to more mature disposi-
tions. The manipulation of the environment
was determined to be a feasible goal for
counselors, teachers, managers, and other
social scientists. However, the logistics
of effective environmental manipulation were
presented as contingent on a viable theory
of man.

The theories of Riesman, Glazer, and
Denney (1953), Heath (1964), Schein (1970),
Shostrom (1968), and Maslow (1968, 1971) were
reviewed as a representative sample of contemporary theories concerning the nature of
man. Graves' (1970) theory was presented as
an all-inclusive theory and the other theories
were assimilated with it to formulate a sim-
plified theory of man. It was inferred that
Graves' theory provides us with a composite
of man which enables us to operate within a
realistic framework concerning the understanding of values and the prediction of human behavior. The functional aspects of Graves'
theory are demonstrated in the next chapter
when intervention strategies for influencing
life styles are discussed.

REFERENCES

Clark, G. The man who tapped the secrets of
    the universe. Waynesboro, Va.: The
    University of Science and Philosophy,
    1973.

Graves, C. W. Levels of existence: An open
    system theory of values. Journal of
    Humanistic Psychology, 1970, 10, 131-
    155.

Graves, C. W. Levels of human existence and
    their relation to management problems.
    (Brochure). Management Center, Institute
    for Business and Community Development,
    University of Richmond, 1972.

Heath, R. The reasonable adventurer. Pitts-
    burgh, Penn.: University of Pittsburgh
    Press, 1964.

Hershey, G. L., & Lugo, J. O. Living psy-
    chology. London: Macmillan Company,
    1970.

Management Center Staff. Clare W. Graves'
    theory of levels of human existence and
    suggested managerial systems for each
    level. Unpublished manuscript, Institute
    for Business and Community Development,
    University of Richmond, 1971.

Maslow, A. H. Toward a psychology of being.
    (Rev. ed.) Princeton, N. J.: Van Nos-
    trand, 1968.

Maslow, A. H. The farther reaches of human
    nature. New York: Viking Press, 1971.

Myers, M. S., & Myers, S. S. Adapting to the
    new work ethic. Business Quarterly, 1973,
    38(4), in press.

Riesman, D., Glazer, N., & Denney, R. *The lonely crowd*. New York: Doubleday, 1953.

Schein, E. H. *Organizational Psychology*. (2nd ed.) Englewood Cliffs, N.J.: Prentice-Hall, 1970.

Shostrom, E. L. *Man, the manipulator*. New York: Bantam Books, 1968.

3. INFLUENCING LIFE STYLES

Rehabilitation counselors are constantly faced with the task of intervening in the lives of clients during crucial periods of development. Medical treatment, vocational evaluation, vocational training, job place- ment, and adjustment counseling represent some of the services that the counselor de- livers or coordinates according to the indi- vidual needs of clients. Clients constantly seek help with vocational, social, and per- sonal problems, and consequently the counselor is often thrust into a role which requires him to assist other persons with decisions that may, in effect, ripple through a lifetime. In order for the counselor to manage the ubiqui- tous task facing him, it is essential for him to (a) examine his own developmental profile, (b) acquire the basic knowledge in the field of counseling, (c) understand the process of matching individuals with compatible environ- ments, (d) decide upon a growth or stabiliza- tion plan for clients, (e) develop prescrip- tive counseling skills, and (f) implement ap- propriate counseling strategies for each life style.

Profile of a Counselor

An extensive list of characteristics which are desirable for counselors to possess

35

would be extremely long and undocumented in
the empirical literature. However, awareness,
acceptance, sensitivity, flexibility, and resourcefulness have been selected as the characteristics which appear germane to delivering
counseling services via Graves' theory.

Awareness involves the ability to recognize the different existence levels of both
clients and resource personnel. This recognition of individual life styles entails using
such observational cues as dress, nature of
questions, nature of problems, nonverbal behavior, and language in order to determine the
psychological existence level of persons with
whom the counselor works.

Acceptance refers to the ability to respect or appreciate the values of others regardless of their dissimilarity to the counselor's personal values. Many counselors confuse acceptance with approval and thus limit
the range of people they can work with on a
mature level. Judgment does not need to be
incorporated in the acceptance process. Personal values which necessitate the judgment
of others may lead a counselor to impose values on clients which are not needed for the
client's growth and development. It is likely
that a helping relationship between the counselor and client will not ensue unless both
counselor and client agree on the objectives
that the relationship was formulated to accomplish. A counselor with intolerance for values not like his severely limits the range of
objectives he can work toward and restricts
the variety of means available to him for accomplishing given objectives. For example, if
a counselor is unable to tolerate long hair,
it is unlikely that he can develop the relationship with a long haired client that is
needed to accomplish counseling goals.

Sensitivity incorporates a motivation on
the part of the counselor to advance the dig-

nity of man. This sensitivity involves a self-directed responsiveness by the counselor to human problems which stifle growth and promote mediocrity. A mentally retarded client who seeks a job, a paraplegic who seeks vocational training, and an emotionally disturbed youngster who seeks to answer the question, "Who am I?" are examples of problems which should awaken the counselor's desire to respond enthusiastically. In essence, a counselor should enjoy delivering education and rehabilitation services to the majority of clients whom he is charged with serving.

Flexibility consists of two main components: (a) the possession of a broad range of behaviors, and (b) the ability to shift psychological gears as the needs of clients vary. To illustrate, let us consider two clients, one mentally retarded and one an intelligent paraplegic. The mentally retarded client wants help with the problem of getting transportation to work. It is highly probable the counselor will respond in a very directive manner and do most of the talking. On the other hand, for an intelligent paraplegic client who is seeking help with a career choice, the counselor is likely to respond in a non-directive manner in hopes of promoting self-inquiry. Moreover, counselors may rely on the learning principles and techniques of behavior modification to evoke behavior change in some clients but draw from humanistic strategies to promote growth in other clients.

It is likely that resourcefulness is the interface between effective and mediocre counselors. It entails the ability to locate, develop, organize, and coordinate services which facilitate the counseling process. It usually takes numerous services to complete the rehabilitation process. For example, physicians, visiting teachers, psychologists, employers, and many others often contribute to the rehabilitation plan of a client. Often the coun-

selor's effectiveness is directly related to
his ability to obtain and arrange the delivery
of timely services. Extensive, well organized
files, affiliation with appropriate professional groups, and daily contact concerning
employment situations are a few of the factors
which enable a counselor to develop and maintain his resources.

Knowledge Acquisition

The accumulation of knowledge embraced
by the field of counseling represents the second major dimension along which the training
of counselors may be viewed. This knowledge
is usually obtained in academic settings and
is organized under such headings as: the nature of counseling, occupational information,
abnormal psychology, small group dynamics, and
counseling techniques. In their training it
is essential that counselors accrue information and develop skills which enable them to
draw from a repertoire of counseling strategies (nondirective, directive, behavioral, and
psychoanalytic) which may be employed to assist clients. These strategies provide counselors with both a theoretical rationale and
a variety of approaches for accomplishing
their job. The parameters of awareness, sensitivity, acceptance, flexibility, resourcefulness, and knowledge acquisition are by no
means exhaustive, but they do represent the
essential elements that the counselor must
possess for accomplishing the task of matching
environmental situations to psychological
characteristics for the purpose of enhancing
human growth.

Matching Individuals with Therapeutic Environ- ments

A crucial feature of the education and
rehabilitation processes involves the placing
of individuals in environments which enhance
their growth. For most clients this process

usually entails placing the clients in environments where the prevailing values are congruent with their own values. Although a paucity
of investigations exists concerning the matching of individuals to environments on the
basis of selected factors, a review of several
studies serves to elucidate and tentatively
justify a type of matching process.

Perry (1970) examined the development of
Harvard and Radcliffe students over a four
year period and developed a theory which advocates that intellectual and ethical development occurs in an orderly manner. This orderly manner provided the framework for a nine
position theory of human development somewhat
analogous to Graves' (1970) theory. Perry
claimed that the nine position theory enables
teachers to effect "a differential address to
individual students 'where they are' (p. 210)."
He acknowledged two studies (Hunt, 1966; Wispé,
1951) which demonstrated that the differential
grouping of students according to developmental
stages produced the expected results. Students
who received incongruent instructional procedures were less satisfied than students who
received instructional procedures congruent
with their values.

Graves (1972) reported on an application
of his theory in a large manufacturing organization. The intervention involved the placing
of employees in positions where the modus operandi was congruent with their own values, and
it resulted in a 17 percent increase in production and an 87 percent drop in grievances.
Also, plant turnover dropped in a year from
21 percent to 7 percent.

Myers and Myers (1973) have examined
Graves' theory in a large industrial setting
for several years, and recently they suggested
that supervisors and managers need to operate
from a source of influence that does not produce conflict over values. In discussing this

desired change, Myers and Myers claimed that
in order for today's manager to succeed, "he
will be skilled in organizing manpower and
material in such a way that human talent can
find expression in solving problems and setting
goals. He will know he is succeeding when the
people stop fighting him, and show commitment
in achieving job goals (in press)." In essence, Myers and Myers suggested that management should eliminate the conflicts existing
between employees and employers by developing
managers to a level which enables them to respect and appreciate the value systems of subordinates.

A review of two studies which have insti-
tuted the matching of children with an intervention strategy on the basis of affective
factors serves to expand our perspective of
the process of placing people in environments
which compliment their life styles. Yando
and Kagan (1968) used the Matching Familiar
Figures Test to classify children and teachers
as either impulsive or reflective. They reported that the children changed in the direction of the tempo of the teacher assigned to
them. Since impulsivity is highly correlated
to learning problems, a salutary match was
determined to be the placement of impulsive
children with reflective teachers. Yando and
Kagan indicated that the most dramatic results
were obtained when impulsive boys were assigned
to a classroom with experienced reflective
teachers.

After three years of teaching hospital-
ized emotionally handicapped youth with learning problems at the Neuropsychiatric Institute
School at the University of California, Los
Angeles, Hewett (1964) developed a hierarchy
of educational tasks. The hierarchy consisted
of seven levels which reflected the integration of psychological principles into a pragmatic organizational framework for educators.
In addition to outlining the characteristics

of each level, Hewett described in affective
terms the instructional milieu appropriate for
each level.

Counseling for Growth or Stabilization

Early in the counseling relationship the
counselor must decide whether he is going to
employ strategies which promote intersystemic
growth or intrasystemic growth. Intersystemic
growth refers to growth from one psychological
level of existence to the next level, e.g., a
move from the conformist level to the materialistic level. Intrasystemic growth represents stabilization within a system, e.g., a
conformist may become a more mature person
within the framework of the conformist values.

Blood, sweat, and tears frequently parallel the arduous growth process from level
to level. This type of growth involves dramatic change and usually generates psychological conflict which may continue for long time
spans. An examination of the conditions for
intersystemic growth reveals the intense psychological processes which accompany man's
developmental trek.

Graves (1970) discussed four essential
conditions which characterize intersystemic
growth. These conditions are:
1. Man's needs at any one level must be satisfied to the extent that energy is released
for exploration.
2. Dissonance or challenge must enter his
life at a time when his needs at his present
level are satisfied and surplus energy is
available.
3. He has an insight and becomes aware of
man's problems at another level.
4. Barriers (old values) to growth must be
removed.

Solving the problems that exist in the
person's present level allows an excess of

energy to emerge that can be used to think
about the problems and ideas related to other
life styles. For example, at the tribalistic
level, the individual who has achieved a sub-
stantial degree of assurance and safety and
possesses few problems of adjustment to the
traditionalism of the tribe will discover
that he has an excess of time and energy on
his hands because things are going smoothly.
This excess of time and energy provides him
with the opportunity to question other things
and expand his experiential existence. As
Delamar (1972) pointed out, "he begins to
think about what is going on around him; he
begins to question tradition; but at this
point, he is not dissatisfied with his lot
(p. 17)."

Dissonance usually springs from a series
of traumatic circumstances or disturbances
which originate from both external and internal domains. This conflict will generally
serve to expose the shortcomings of the individual's present system. The realization of
the present system's inadequacies coupled with
the excess of energy created by the first condition heighten the possibility that change
will occur (Graves, 1970).

The emergence of essential insights involves the recognition of values at the next
level of existence. The person's awareness
and adoption of the next level values enable
him to resolve his dissonance and take a giant
step upward.

A fourth condition that is usually necessary for intersystemic growth entails the
weakening or removal of barriers (old values)
which interfere with growth. These barriers
masquerade in the forms of confrontations with
peers, family, and others who expect a continuation of the lower level psychological existence. For example, as a tribalistic level
person moves into the egocentric level, his

behaviors become unacceptable to the people
with whom he has traditionally worked and
lived. Barriers and confrontations result
and the perpetuation of the newly emerging
life style is determined by the person's dependency upon the tribe and its traditions.

The conditions for intersystemic growth
indicate that a counselor takes on a rather
formidable task when he decides to promote
it within a client. For the most part, rehabilitation clients seek assistance with
maintenance related needs, i.e., a job, medical services, vocational training, etc. Generally, the fulfillment of these needs does
not require a long-term relationship with the
counselor and usually entails the improvement
of a client's status within a particular level
of psychological existence. Due to (a) the
nature of the problems that most counselors
confront, (b) the short-term duration of the
client-counselor relationship, and (c) the
intense counselor-client relationship required
for intersystemic growth, it is feasible for
the rehabilitation counselor to focus the majority of his efforts toward intrasystemic
client growth.

Intrasystemic growth involves a quasi-
self-actualization process within a particular
level. It entails living a life characterized
by minimal conflict, and the expenditure of
excess energy is usually accounted for in avocational pursuits such as hobbies and socialization activities with peers having similar
values. Minimal conflict is frequently obtained by regimenting one's life to ritualistic routines and living patterns, i.e., work
every weekday from 9:00 a.m. to 5:00 p.m.,
bowl every Tuesday night with the boys, play
bridge every other Friday night with the girls,
watch selected television programs, etc. This
example of intrasystemic growth may lead a
person to assume that it is a life of drudgery
and repetition, but it is important to remember

that most of the individuals who have obtained a high level of intrasystemic growth
are productive and very happy within their
life styles. Intrasystemic growth enables
a person to stabilize and function within a
restricted set of values. When viewed within
a proper perspective, intrasystemic growth is
a challenging and noble objective for counselors to adopt in most rehabilitation cases.
Notable exceptions to the counseling goal of
intrasystemic growth occur when a client's
present life style unjustly imposes on the
rights of others or reduces the dignity of
others. At this point it is worthwhile to
note that these debilitating conditions may
occur within the first six levels, always
occur with reactive level individuals, and
may frequently exist with tribalistic and
egocentric level individuals. Finally, a
high level of intrasystemic growth results
ultimately from a person being surrounded with
value systems congruent with his to the extent
that conflict is minimized and stabilization
is secured.

Prescriptive Counseling

Due to the impact of environmental factors on the healthy development of individuals and the differential nature of therapeutic milieus for respective individuals, it is
essential that counselors recognize their existence as contributing environmental forces
in the client's world. Not only should the
counselor avoid the tendency to consider himself as separate from the client's world, but
he should attune himself to the relationship
in a manner which enables him to provide prescriptive counseling. Prescriptive counseling
is a process that enables a counselor to provide counseling services which are tailored
to the individual needs of clients. Simply
stated, it involves diagnostic processes, the
ability to plan and implement a strategy, and
constant evaluation of both the accuracy of

the diagnostic hypotheses and the effectiveness of the ongoing counseling services. Diagnostic goals usually include the assessment
of three things: (a) the problem with which
the client seeks help, (b) the level of psychological existence of the client, and (c) the
design of a feasible counseling strategy. The
implementation of the counseling strategy consists of coordinating the services of other
resources and effecting a counseling approach,
i.e., nondirective, directive, behavioral,
self-control, etc. Finally, evaluation is a
continuous process and serves to monitor each
stage of prescriptive counseling. Evaluation
reveals to the counselor the effectiveness or
failure of the rehabilitation plan and provides the counselor with a rationale for changing or continuing a counseling scheme. A discussion of the strategies appropriate for promoting growth at each existence level serves
to vitalize the counseling framework presented
thus far in this chapter.

Counseling Strategies for Each Level of Psy-chological Existence

   Reactive Level. The reactive level person is not likely to appear on the caseload
of most rehabilitation counselors, but, if he
does, counselors should be able to develop an
appropriate rehabilitation plan. The reactive
level person, with his nonproductive existence,
has a parasitic type of influence on the resources of a modern society. Not only does
he sap the society of its vital resources but
he fails to provide energy for its advancement.
Due to the debilitating effects that a reactive
level person has on a society it is imperative
for a counselor to design a plan which focuses
on growing the individual to the tribalistic
level of existence.

   Intersystemic growth for the reactive
level person is achieved via a nurturant counseling process (Graves, 1972). As Graves

(1970) pointed out, this type of nurturant
counseling involves caring for the client in
a mothering fashion. The nurturing process
enables the individual to accrue a stable set
of conditioned reflexes which provide auto-
matically and dependably for the continuance
of his existence. When the conditioned reflexes are established, the reactive person
has gained entry into the tribalistic level
(Graves, 1970). For many counselors it is
not feasible for them personally to provide
the mothering required by the reactive individual. However, the providing of nurturance
does not require professional personnel but
may be administered effectively by nurses'
aides, volunteer workers, and ward attendants
under professional supervision and guidance.

Tribalistic Level. Although the tribalistic level person tends to come from preindustrialized civilizations, it is not uncommon for rehabilitation counselors to encounter them in ghettos or in disadvantaged
neighborhoods. The tribalistic level person
is capable of productive work but only within
a highly restricted environment. The work
environment must be acceptable to the traditionalistic and magical thinking that the
tribalistic person employs. If he thinks a
condition in the work environment is incon-
sistent with his values, he will at best refuse to perform. An important factor to consider with a tribalistic level person is his
severe reactions to values or situations that
are not in accordance with his beliefs. His
reaction emanates from fear and is frequently
manifested in violent activities. Thus, a
counselor should strive to promote intrasystemic growth in this level client only as
long as the individual remains in a milieu
that fosters an existence which is similar or
congruent with the client's manifested life
style. If the client is likely to be thrust
into situations which are not complimentary
or supportive to his tribalistic way of exis-

tence (e.g., a migrant worker who is forced
to settle near an industrial setting), it is
feasible to implement a strategy designed to
facilitate intersystemic growth. A saturation of the tribalistic level person's physiological and assurance needs would be the first
objective of an intersystemic growth plan. A
second phase of action would entail gradually
exposing the person to brief encounters with
egocentric level values. This step would have
to be executed slowly, carefully, and gradually in order to avoid severe reactions. The
third phase of the plan would involve meshing
the person into the egocentric level society
at a pace regulated by the client's adjust-
ments. Also, the removal of barriers to growth
would parallel the third phase of the plan.
This would involve removing the client from
environments which purport the tribalistic way
of life, i.e., find him a job away from old
friends, parents, etc.

   The tribalistic level person achieves
intrasystemic growth by being successful in
fulfilling his physiological and assurance
needs. The means for achieving this success
must be congruent with tribalistic values.
The means issue is crucial to the counseling
strategy employed for this level person. The
counseling strategy employed with tribalistic
level clients has three components: (a) modeling for evaluation of values, (b) modeling for
skill acquisition, and (c) maintaining task
performance via conditioning. In order to
determine if the client is amenable to participating in growth related tasks i.e., do
a job, receive a physical examination, etc.,
it is necessary for him to watch a model perform the task and then be asked to emulate
the model. If he attempts to copy the model,
the task does not conflict with his value
system. Once he is amenable to performing
the task, the second component can begin and
consists of learning the task by continuing
to copy a model's behavior. The third com-

ponent involves regulating the performance
of the client through conditioning processes.
For example, in a job situation the counselor
would determine if the job were acceptable by
demonstrating the job tasks and seeing if the
client copied them upon request. If the job
is emulated by the client he then can proceed
to learn it by imitating a model over and over.
Once the job is mastered, the boss maintains
the client's performance via simple force,
punishment, or with primary reinforcers. The
same three step process would apply to learning self-help skills, academic skills, social
skills, etc.

It is apparent that the counseling strategies discussed for the tribalistic level person preclude much verbal interaction and are
very directive. However, the effectiveness
of these directive strategies depends on how
well the counselor understands the client and
his way of life. Most of this understanding
must be extracted from keen observation of
nonverbal cues. An accurate assessment of the
client's values and way of life enables the
counselor to determine (a) the characteristics
of the model to be used (female, male, bear,
etc.), (b) the appropriate time for client
exposure to the model, and (c) the types of
behavior to be modeled. Also, it is important
for the counselor to remember that the tribalistic person is essentially a nonverbal individual who is highly influenced by models
he values. This requires that the counselor
be highly cognizant of himself as a model and
function in a manner which enables him to enhance the growth of his "eyeballing" client.

Egocentric Level. The egocentric level
client, like the tribalistic level individual,
is usually encountered in disadvantaged societies and is capable of living a productive
life when handled properly. However, if he
is dealt with improperly, he is apt to use
ruthless force to exploit the situation for

his own egocentric survival needs. Thus it
is imperative for a counselor to employ counseling strategies which require the egocentric
level person to function in a desirable manner,
i.e., contribute to man's advancement and not
molest the society in which he lives.

Since the egocentric level person spawns
the power ethic and is prone to value the
ruthless use of power, he is capable of creat-
ing a society encapsulated with fear and in-
security. His destructive passions are controlled only by forces more powerful than his
own. Thus, intrasystemic growth is justified
only when it is likely that the egocentric
level client will exist in an environment domi-
nated by a powerful force which, in turn, supports the healthy advancement of society. Due
to the problems with securing and maintaining
the power contingency that enables the third
level client to function for the betterment of
mankind, it is often feasible for the counselor
to adopt intersystemic growth goals for this
level client.

An intersystemic plan for growth with the
egocentric level client would entail: (a) sat-
urating his survival and power needs, (b) in-
troducing the dissonance by presenting the
problems of the saintly level, (c) stimulating
insight concerning the reality of fourth level
problems, and (d) removing barriers to the development of insight and growth.

The saturation of survival and power needs
could be obtained by placing the client under
a powerful force (employer, probation officer,
counselor in residence, etc.) who constantly
monitors his behavior while simultaneously
guaranteeing him survival, i.e., job, food,
protection, etc. After the intensity of the
power and survival needs is lowered, the client
has energy available to confront some problems
of the saintly level person's existence. The
presentation of these problems is usually

spearheaded by discussions concerning death.
When it is pointed out to the egocentric level
person that all people no matter how powerful
or weak confront death with equivocal consequences, he recognizes the fallacies of the
egocentric power ethic. Then via insight and
reduced growth barriers (e.g., removing him
from the influences of an egocentric level
family and colleagues by placing him on a
highly supervised night job), he begins to
question the reason for his existential problems, i.e., Why was I born? Why can't I find
some success in life? Questions of this type
as well as questions concerning the reason
for the "haves" (affluent) and the "have nots"
(poor) impel him toward a quest of that ordered form of existence which assures a panacea. A quest of this nature places the egocentric level person at the gate of the saintly
level of existence.

    If the counselor had reason to believe
that the egocentric level client would continue to live in an environment where the
client's hostile aggression would be held in
check without debilitating effects on the
client's existence, he could justify an intrasystemic growth plan. This plan would
focus on providing for the client's survival
and power needs both on and off the job. The
job would usually be physical (construction
work) and highly structured and supervised by
a powerful force, i.e., ex-Marine sergeant,
professional athlete, etc. Avocational activities would be designed to encourage the
sublimation of aggression. Organized sports
such as boxing, wrestling, football, and bas-
ketball would be healthy outlets for his aggressive energy. Also, the possession of powerful motorcycles, leather jackets, customized
cars and power insignias (tatoos) facilitate
the release of the egocentric person's aggressive urges. The counselor of an egocentric
level person should realize that he must operate from a power position in order to be

effective. It is essential for him to approach the client as hard-nosed, calloused,
and extremely smart because the egocentric
level client will exploit situations characterized by the sociocentric ethic. Finally,
this hard-nosed power approach moderated by
reasonable compassion and sensitivity must be
exercised in order to bring many of these individuals to life styles which contribute
to the survival of their respective societies.

Conformist Level. The rehabilitation
counselor encounters many conformist level
clients on his caseload. Although the conformist level individuals are referred from
all social class levels, they tend to aggregate at the middle and lower classes. As mentioned in Chapter 2, these clients value structure, rules, authority, hard work, and sacrificial pursuits. Much of the credit for the
accelerated rise of the United States is due
to the contributions of hard working persons
at the conformist level. In our society many
conformist level persons achieve a high degree
of intrasystemic growth because our democratic
ideals enable them to worship as they desire
and the capitalistic aspects of our society
enable them to work as hard as they please.
Thus, intrasystemic growth is usually a feasible goal for the rehabilitation counselor
to embrace with this level individual.

In order to be effective or promote intrasystemic growth with the conformist level
client the rehabilitation counselor must assume a counseling approach which is directive,
structured, and highly organized. Also, for
the counselor to be effective he should be
sensitive to the client's religious or philosophical values and not argue or confront him
with the irrationality of his espoused values.
In seeking a vocational placement for the conformist level client, the counselor should
look for an authoritative employer whose employees have well-designed roles and constant
supervision.

Within the behavior modification domain, the conformist level individual may be viewed as a person who primarily performs to avoid guilt. This level person has an internalized punisher (superego) which generates a guilt that usually springs from religious values in order to shape the person's behavior. These self-inflicted punitive measures are often triggered by expressions of displeasure on the part of an authority figure whom he reveres. Positive reinforcement from his revered authorities (counselors, employers, ministers, government officials, parents, etc.) motivates him because he usually feels guilt for not deserving the reinforcement in the first place. In other words, he strives to think and act in accordance with the expectations inferred by authority figures whom he respects and admires.

Materialistic Level. The caseload of a rehabilitation counselor consists of many clients who function at the materialistic level of existence. This level represents the mode of existence for most middle-class Americans. The materialistic person's competitive nature and desire to perform in a manner which brings him possessions and prestige have traditionally coupled to operate in a manner that has advanced the general welfare of society. The freedom and capitalistic structure that exists in our society enables the materialistic level person to achieve intrasystemic growth. In essence he has the freedom to choose and change jobs or start his own business as a means to materialistic ends.

To be effective with a materialistic level client the counselor must be perceived by the client as a highly skilled professional. The materialistic level individual responds to a directive style of counseling as long as it is administered in both a firm and fair fashion. The client responds to rules, role de-

scriptions, and policies that are formulated
by an authority figure he respects and en-
forced in an objective fashion. In essence,
this level client responds to reason (hard
bargaining) and respects mastery and power.

Within a behavior modification framework,
the materialistic level client may be regarded
as the first level person in the hierarchy who
primarily responds to the positive aspects of
reinforcement. Whereas the tribalistic, egocentric, and conformist level individuals perform primarily to avoid negative consequences,
the materialistic level person performs primarily to gain positive consequences, i.e.,
money, prestige, power, etc. Thus, a prime
rationale for the counselor to use with a materialistic level client is to explain the
rehabilitation plan in terms of materialistic
values, i.e., "If you receive this type of
vocational training, you will be able to pursue a career which allows a person to advance
quickly while making a good salary."

Sociocentric Level. The sociocentric
level individual usually emerges from a mid-
dle- to upper-class environment and is found
frequently on the caseloads of rehabilitation
counselors. These individuals are characterized by their humanistic concerns, i.e., ecology, population growth, ill effects of capi-
talism, human feelings, self-actualization,
poverty, etc. Sociocentric level individuals
have certainly contributed to the general
welfare of society by spearheading movements
designed to reduce human suffering and increase man's sensitivity to man. The sociocentric level individual is highly motivated
to participate in intrasystemic growth plans.
Moreover, the sociocentric person frequently
stabilizes at this level because growth from
the sociocentric to the cognitive level is
extremely difficult. The move from sociocentric to cognitive is the most difficult transition to accomplish as compared to the other
level transitions.

A sociocentric level client, unlike the previous levels, responds to nondirective counseling techniques. He seeks to understand his feelings, explore his alternatives, and share experiences with the counselor. Because the sociocentric level client resists directive counseling, authoritarian bosses, and highly structured task-oriented environments, the counselor-client relationship needs to be very client-centered. This level client seeks a job which enhances his personal growth and taps his emerging resources. His motivation on the job originates from the interaction of his valued peer group. As long as his peer group has objectives that are compatible with the organization's objectives, the sociocentric level person will perform adequately. The meshing of six-level objectives with organizational objectives is accomplished by: (a) working in a helping profession, i.e., nursing, mental health, education; (b) working with people, i.e., receptionist, counselor, operator, etc.; and (c) working with fellow employees where a high degree of esprit de corps exists. Also, the composition of the valued peer group does not need to be exclusively a group of sociocentric level individuals. The sociocentric ethic itself enables this level person to suppress his own needs for group purposes, thus enabling him to mesh with a group whose values reflect a different level. However, it is true that sociocentric persons will aggregate when enough are present.

Within a behavior modification perspective, the sociocentric person represents an enigma. He does not respond well to threat or traditional rewards, i.e., money, prestige, etc. He is only concerned about the consequences of his behavior as it relates to the welfare of mankind and his valued peer group. However, it is possible to consider the sociocentric person within the behavioral paradigm by realizing that he performs for opportunities

to engage in social interaction and activities
which foster human development.

Cognitive Level. Due to his sophisti-
cated survival skills and scarcity, the cognitive level man is not likely to be found
on the caseloads of rehabilitation counselors.
Nevertheless, a counseling strategy with a
cognitive level person would consist of the
counselor explaining the services he can provide and then allowing the client to select
which services enhance his goals. This level
person resists demanding relationships and
insists on handling his own growth or rehabilitation plans. In essence, the counselor
offers his services and delivers them on request. Although this counseling strategy
appears to thrust the counselor at the mercy
of the client, it would not operate in that
manner. The cognitive level person is a very
mature individual who respects the counselor
and his function. He would not jeopardize
the counselor's position unless he thought
the counselor was unfit for the job and dam-
aging to the dignity of man. Finally, if the
counselor were at the cognitive level, it is
possible that a close relationship would develop and be characterized by insightful discussions concerning the existential problems
of man.

Experientialistic Level. Due to the experientialistic level person's lack of concern
with earthly problems and his extreme scarcity,
he would not appear on a rehabilitation counselor's caseload. It is possible he would be
referred by persons concerned with his intact-
ness, but he would never agree to participate
in a rehabilitation plan.

At the conclusion of this brief presentation of Graves' theory as applied to a rehabilitation counselor's job, it is important to
reflect for a moment. As noted in Table 1, it
is readily apparent that a counselor must op-

Table 1

Counseling Strategies for Each Level of Existence in Graves' Theory

Graves' Levels	Counseling Strategy	Motivation
Reactive	Nuturant Treatment	External
Tribalistic	Modeling	External
	Force	
	Negative Reinforcement	
	Primary Reinforcers	
	Directive	
Egocentric	Power	External
	Negative Reinforcement	
	Directive	
Conformist	Structure	External
	Negative Reinforcement	
	Directive	
Materialistic	Reasoning--Bargaining	External
	Positive Reinforcement	
	Directive	
Sociocentric	Nondirective	External
	Democratic	
	Group Counseling	
Cognitive	Facilitative	Internal
	Nondirective	
Experientialistic	Support	Internal
	Nondirective	

erate from a very sensitive and flexible posture. At one moment he is directing and telling; yet, at the swing of his door, he is re-
flecting, supporting, and sharing, and who
knows, the next entry might stimulate meditation and self-inquiry. Graves' theory impels
us not to label people but to respond to them
in a prescriptive manner. The theory eluci-
dates the fact that in order for people to
grow it is necessary to operate within their
value system. Myers and Myers (1973) recognized this in their concluding remarks concerning managers:

> Value conflicts ... can be ameliorated
> only by learning to operate from a new
> source of influence. The level 4 or
> 5 manager tends to operate from influ-
> ence derived from official authority
> and tradition. To succeed with the
> new work ethic, he must operate from
> a base of influence stemming from the
> competence of people at all levels of
> the organization (in press).

In addition, it is helpful to consider a
point Graves (1972) made during a recent seminar. He implied that effective counseling
does not necessarily depend on a theory of man
but on resourcefulness and sensitivity to feedback. Resourcefulness entails the mastery of
an array of counseling strategies, and sensitivity to feedback involves the capacity to
evaluate the appropriateness of the strategy
and change it when it is not working.

Conclusion

Included in this chapter was a discussion
of six major areas which were organized under
the following topics: (a) profile of a counselor; (b) knowledge acquisition; (c) studies
about matching individuals with therapeutic
environments; (d) counseling for growth or
stabilization; (e) prescriptive counseling;
and (f) counseling via Graves' theory.

In a discussion on the profile of a counselor, awareness, sensitivity, acceptance,
flexibility, and resourcefulness were featured
as the essential characteristics of an effective counselor. Knowledge acquisition was
presented as a factor which enables the counselor to develop an extensive repertoire of
strategies. Selected studies concerning the
matching of individuals to therapeutic environments were reviewed from two perspectives:
(a) adults in working environments, and (b) children in school environments. Counseling for
growth or stabilization was discussed in terms
of intersystemic growth (changing levels) and
intrasystemic growth (within a level). Although it was concluded that intrasystemic
growth was a feasible objective for most rehabilitation clients, it was pointed out that
intersystemic growth is required for clients
who do not promote the healthy advancement of
society. Prescriptive counseling was presented
as a process which involves: (a) a diagnostic
phase; (b) the ability to plan and implement
a strategy; and (c) the constant evaluation of
the accuracy of both the diagnostic and intervention phases. Counseling via Graves' theory
was presented to provide the counselor with a
framework for effecting prescriptive counseling. In conclusion, the reader was encouraged
to recognize the application of Graves' theory
as a means to stimulate and maintain the growth
and adjustment of individuals with vocational
and social adjustment problems.

REFERENCES

Delamar, W.   Graves and behavior in the work
    system.   Unpublished manuscript, May,
    1972.

Graves, C. W.   Levels of existence: An open
    system theory of values.   Journal of
    Humanistic Psychology, 1970, 10, 131-155.

Graves, C. W.   Levels of human existence and
    their relations to management problems.
    (Brochure).   Management Center, Institute
    for Business and Community Development,
    University of Richmond, 1972.

Hewett, F. M.   A hierarchy of educational tasks
    for children with learning disorders.   Ex-
    ceptional Children, 1964, 31, 207-214.

Hunt, D. E.   A conceptual systems change model
    and its application to education.   In
    O. J. Harvey (Ed.), Experience, structure
    and adaptability.   New York: Springer,
    1966.

Myers, M. S., & Myers, S. S.   Adapting to the
    new work ethic.   Business Quarterly, 1973,
    38(4), in press.

Perry, W. G., Jr.   Forms of intellectual and
    ethical development in the college years.
    New York: Holt, Rinehart, & Winston,
    1970.

Wispé, L. G.   Evaluating section teaching meth-
    ods in the introductory course.   Journal
    of Educational Research, 1951, 45, 161-
    186.

Yando, R. M., & Kagan, J.   The effect of teach-
    er tempo on the child.   Child Development,
    1968, 39, 27-34.

4. THE MANAGING OF PEOPLE

Persons interested in assisting handicapped individuals in rehabilitation and/or
education need to be familiar with employer
and business thinking. Life styles of people
and how to influence these life styles have
been discussed in the previous chapters. Here
we will discuss traditional administrative
theories through a historical perspective and
dovetail people's life styles with types of
administrative structures. Most conversa-
tions about administrative theory concern how
to get the job done. This chapter will describe two traditional administrative theories,
their relationship to Graves' theory, the administrative theories' assumptions, implications, and how they purport to get people to
do a job and like it.

Theory

In essence, a theory about man has three
functions: (a) to make sense out of chaos,
(b) to assist in predicting behavior, and
(c) to facilitate behavioral change. A theory
about man takes the complex inner workings of
human actions and makes some sense out of them,
e.g., he did that because his ego was deflated,
he did that because he was not getting reinforced enough, etc. As the theory begins to
clarify why people behave in a certain manner,

it begins to predict, i.e., if that continues, he will quit, get mad, withdraw, etc. A viable theory not only helps to explain and predict behavior but also suggests ways to change behavior--ways to get people to behave differently, i.e., if we do this, he will do that.

Most administrative theories make some assumptions about man, life, and work. Based on these assumptions, a system of management is developed to get employees to work toward job objectives. If the individual employee does not fit into the system, he is usually fired.

The strength of a theory about man rests on its ability to explain, predict, and control human behavior. The strength of an administrative theory rests on its ability to get people to do the job.

One of the most effective ways to get people to do their job is to directly tell them what to do and then pay them to do it or punish them when they do not do it. This type of management is referred to as directive or authoritative management. This predominant management system is described by McGregor (1960) as Theory X. Theory X is based on the following assumptions:
1. The average man dislikes and will avoid work.
2. He therefore has to be forced, controlled, and directed to work.
3. He prefers to be directed and has little ambition.
4. He seeks only security.

Based on these assumptions, a Theory X work environment exemplifies structure and control. Managers are authoritarian and they constantly stress the directive and control functions of management. Rigid working hours, evaluation forms, punitive corrective measures,

absolute authority, and explicit role definitions provide the nucleus of tools for a
Theory X mode of operation. A Theory X manager must often exhibit that he is knowledge-
able about the jobs of his subordinates. It
is desirable that his subordinates feel that
without their supervisor's guidance and knowledge their performance would drop to unacceptable standards. This dependency relationship
with the manager enables the manager to gain
the control that is so important in a Theory
X work environment. The dependent subordinate
strives to please his boss and diligently
avoids his wrath. To these employees "hell
hath no fury like a boss's wrath."

Many well-known organizations stress
Theory X or some modification of it as their
managerial style. The United States Army is
an excellent example of Theory X management.
The army thrives on punctuality, policy, rules,
structure, control, punishment, and the rank-
ing system. All these tools characterize a
Theory X management scheme. Public education
is another well-known institution that has,
for the most part, functioned on Theory X
assumptions. The teacher is an authority
figure and students are the subordinates.
Tests, punishment, rigid time schedules, highly structured activities, and control devices
are used today in most schools.

Although Theory X administrative thinking
has been with us for centuries, its popularity
in this country was accentuated by Frederick
Winslow Taylor. Taylor became a pillar in
industrialized management around the turn of
the century and his impact on management is
prevalent today. He worked with Bethlehem
Steel Company in Philadelphia and is considered to be the father of "scientific management." Knezevich (1962) explained,

The ear known as that of "scientific management" did much to improve

production and profit, but man was
looked upon more as a producing
machine than a personality. Through
scientific study it was hoped that
it could be discovered what positions, which hand, and what order
of movement were to be followed by
the "imperfect robot" called man,
so that he might be a more efficient
producer. It was not out of consideration to human qualities that
better lighting, better heating,
and ventilation were introduced in
industry or business, but because
the "imperfect robot" could produce
better under certain conditions
than others. The results of scientific management were less wasted
effort and more efficient production in industry and government
than ever before (p. 105).

The reason for Taylor's impact on management was because he got the job done better,
quicker, and for less money, and his popularity was enhanced through his writing style.
Taylor's graphic descriptions of work situations are so real it almost hurts. Here is
an example of his writing style explaining
"systematic soldiering."[1]

There is no question that the
tendency of the average man (in all
walks of life) is toward working at
a slow, easy gait, and that it is
only after a good deal of thought
and observation on his part or as a
result of example, conscience, or

----

1. Taylor, F. W. The principles of
scientific management. New York: Harper &
Brothers, 1913, pp. 19-20, 42-47. Reprinted
in part by permission.

external pressure that he takes a
more rapid pace ....

This common tendency to "take
it easy" is greatly increased by
bringing a number of men together
on similar work and at a uniform
standard rate of pay by the day.

Under this plan the better
men gradually but surely slow down
their gait to that of the poorest
and least efficient. When a nat-
urally energetic man works for a
few days beside a lazy one, the
logic of the situation is unanswer-
able.

"Why should I work hard when
that lazy fellow gets the same pay
that I do and does only half as
much work?"

A careful time study of men
working under these conditions will
disclose facts which are ludicrous
as well as pitiable (Taylor, 1913,
pp. 19-20).

There is not a manager or working person
alive who does not recognize the painful elements of truth projected here. Taylor was
clever and he was explicit about the management of people. Here he talks about how he
got Schmidt to increase his loading of 12½
tons of pig iron to 47 tons of pig iron per
day.

Once we were sure, however, that
47 tons was a proper day's work for
a first-class pig-iron handler, the
task which faced us as managers under the modern scientific plan was
clearly before us. It was our duty
to see that the 80,000 tons of pig
iron were loaded on the cars at the
rate of 47 tons per man per day, in
place of 12½ tons, at which rate the
work was then being done. And it was

further our duty to see that this
work was done without bringing on
a strike among the men, without any
quarrel with the men, and to see
that the men were happier and better
contented when loading at the new
rate of 47 tons than they were when
loading at the old rate of 12½ tons.

Our first step was the scientific selection of the workman. In
dealing with workmen under this type
of management, it is an inflexible
rule to talk to and deal with only
one man at a time, since each workman has his own special abilities
and limitations, and since we are
not dealing with men in masses, but
are trying to develop each individual
man to his highest state of efficiency and prosperity. Our first step
was to find the proper workman to
begin with .... Finally we selected
one from among the four as the most
likely man to start with. He was
a little Pennsylvania Dutchman who
had been observed to trot back home
for a mile or so after his work in
the evening, about as fresh as he was
when he came trotting down to work in
the morning. We found that upon
wages of $1.15 a day he had succeeded
in buying a small plot of ground,
and that he was engaged in putting
up the walls of a little house for
himself in the morning before starting to work and at night after leaving. He also had the reputation of
being exceedingly "close," that is,
of placing a very high value on a
dollar. As one man whom we talked to
about him said, "A penny looks about
the size of a cart-wheel to him."
This man we will call Schmidt.

The task before us, then, nar-
rowed itself down to getting Schmidt

to handle 47 tons of pig iron per
day and making him glad to do it.
This was done as follows. Schmidt
was called out from among the gang
of pig-iron handlers and talked to
somewhat in this way:

"Schmidt, are you a high-priced
man?"

"Vell, I don't know vat you mean."

"Oh, come now, you answer my
questions. What I want to find out
is whether you are a high-priced
man or one of these cheap fellows
here. What I want to find out is
whether you want to earn $1.85 a day
or whether you are satisfied with
$1.15, just the same as all those
cheap fellows are getting."

"Did I vant $1.85 a day? Vas
dot a high-priced man? Vell, yes,
I vas a high-priced man."

"Oh, you're aggravating me. Of
course you want $1.85 a day--every-
one wants it! You know perfectly
well that that has very little to do
with your being a high-priced man.
For goodness sake answer my questions,
and don't waste any more of my time.
Now come over here. You see that
pile of pig iron?"

"Yes."

"You see that car?"

"Yes."

"Well, if you are a high-priced
man, you will load pig iron on that
car tomorrow for $1.85. Now do wake
up and answer my question. Tell me
whether you are a high-priced man or
not."

"Vell--did I got $1.85 for load-
ing dot pig iron on dot car tomorrow?"

"Yes, of course you do, and you
get $1.85 for loading a pile like
that every day right through the
year. That is what a high-priced

man does, and you know it just as
well as I do."

"Vell, dot's all right. I could
load dot pig iron on the car tomorrow
for $1.85, and I get it every day,
don't I?"

"Certainly you do--certainly you
do."

"Vell, den, I vas a high-priced
man."

"Now hold on, hold on. You know
just as well as I do that a high-
priced man has to do exactly as he's
told from morning till night. You
have seen this man here before, haven't
you?"

"No, I never saw him."

"Well, if you are a high-priced
man, you will do exactly as this man
tells you tomorrow, from morning till
night. When he tells you to pick up
a pig and walk, you pick it up and
walk, and when he tells you to sit
down and rest, you sit down. You do
that right straight through the day.
And what's more, no back talk. Now
a high-priced man does just what he's
told to do, and no back talk. Do you
understand that? When this man tells
you to walk, you walk; when he tells
you to sit down, you sit down, and
you don't talk back at him. Now you
come on to work here tomorrow morning
and I'll know before night whether
you are really a high-priced man or
not."

This seems to be rather tough
talk. And indeed it would be if
applied to an educated mechanic, or
even an intelligent laborer. With
a man of the mentally sluggish type
of Schmidt it is appropriate and not
unkind, since it is effective in fix-
ing his attention on the high wages
which he wants and away from what, if

it were called to his attention, he
probably would consider impossibly
hard work.

What would Schmidt's answer be
if he were talked to in a manner which
is usual under the management of "initiative and incentive?" say, as follows:

"Now, Schmidt, you are a first-
class pig iron handler and know your
business well. You have been handling
at the rate of 12½ tons per day. I
have given considerable study to handling pig iron, and feel sure that
you could do a much larger day's work
than you have been doing. Now don't
you think that if you really tried
you could handle 47 tons of pig iron
per day, instead of 12½ tons?"

What do you think Schmidt's answer would be to this?

Schmidt started to work, and all
day long, and at regular intervals,
was told by the man who stood over
him with a watch, "Now pick up a pig
and walk. Now sit down and rest. Now
walk--now rest, etc. He worked when
he was told to work, and rested when
he was told to rest, and at half-past
five in the afternoon had his 47 tons
loaded on the car. And he practically
never failed to work at this pace and
do the task that was set before him
during the three years that the writer
was at Bethlehem. And throughout this
time he averaged a little more than
$1.85 per day, whereas before he had
never received over $1.15 per day,
which was the ruling rate of wages at
that time in Bethlehem. That is, he
received 60 percent higher wages than
were paid to other men who were not
working on task work. One man after
another was picked out and trained to
handle pig iron at the rate of 47 tons

per day until all of the pig iron
was handled at this rate, and the
men were receiving 60 percent more
wages than other workmen around
them (Taylor, 1913, pp. 42-47).

As can be seen in this illustration, Taylor knew his business. It is especially impressive that on two separate occasions he
remarked that he not only wanted the job done,
he wanted the employees to like it. Taylor
was an expert at analyzing the task to be
done, he knew the value of individualized instruction, and he used good reinforcement
principles.

It is apparent that Theory X management
is ingrained in our democratic society and in
many instances deserves credit for advancing
the country to its current status as a world
power. Although many outstanding accomplish-
ments have been achieved under Theory X, many
problems have arisen as a result of it. These
problems have culminated in the development of
powerful unions, featherbedding, and open re-
bellion. Currently many employees are resist-
ing restricting structure and tight controls.
Townsend's (1970) statement, "And God created
the Organization and gave It dominion over
man (p. 7)," satirically epitomizes the current rebellious spirit toward the organization.

The antithesis of Theory X is Theory Y,
sometimes referred to as humanistic management. According to McGregor (1960), Theory Y
assumptions about man and work are:

1. The expenditure of physical and
   mental effort in work is as natural as play or rest.
2. External control and the threat
   of punishment are not the only
   means for bringing about effort
   toward organizational objectives.

Man will exercise self-direction
and self-control in the service
of objectives to which he is
committed.
3. Commitment to objectives is a
function of the rewards associated with their achievement.
4. The average human being learns,
under proper conditions, not
only to accept but to seek responsibility.
5. The capacity to exercise a relatively high degree of imagination, ingenuity, and creativity
in the solution or organizational
problems is widely, not narrowly,
distributed in the population.
6. Under the conditions of modern
industrial life, the intellectual
potentialities of the average
human being are only partially
utilized (pp. 47-48).

Theory Y focuses on the inherent goodness of man. It adovcates that an employee
will function efficiently in a free environment, providing certain conditions exist.
These conditions are contingent upon the employee's need level and his understanding of
the organization's objectives. McGregor (1960)
refered to Theory Y management as integrative
management. That is, the employee's needs
and the organization's objectives are integrated in a way in which organizational objectives become meshed with personal objectives. The reasoning is that if employees
are instrumental in formulating organizational
objectives, they literally interject their
own ego needs into the objectives. Thus, involvement becomes the springboard for motivation. This integrative process presupposes
that the psychological existence level of the
employee is predominantly characterized by
ego and actualization needs.

Theory Y operates through the following practices:
1. Employees participate in developing organizational objectives.
2. Employees and employers interact in problem solving.
3. There are a minimum number of policies and rules.
4. There is a lack of employee fear of management.
5. Employees are free to pursue organizational objectives.
6. Managers are not considered all-knowing.
7. Open communication exists laterally and vertically.

The basis of Theory Y thinking stems from a series of studies conducted at the Hawthorne Plant at the Western Electric Company in Chicago. The most comprehensive account of the Hawthorne Studies is reported by Roethlisberger and Dickson (1939) in <u>Management</u> <u>and</u> <u>the</u> <u>Worker</u>. This volume is lengthy, filled with details, and considered by management people to be a classic. At the college and university level the Hawthorne Studies are often reported inaccurately. Many times a series of illumination studies are referred to as a part or in their entirety as the Hawthorne Studies. Actually the illumination experiments were conducted during 1922 to 1927 prior to the Hawthorne Studies. The illumination studies, although not an actual part of the Hawthorne Studies, provided a necessary stimulus for the Hawthorne Studies and they are reported in the original Hawthorne report.

The illumination studies were composed of three separate experiments all of which attempted to determine what effect the manipulation of light intensity had on production. The first study was conducted in three departments and illumination was progressively increased. Production increased but was erratic and seemed to be independent of illumination.

In the second experiment, only one department was used and control and experimental groups were assigned. The results indicated production increased in both the control and experimental groups. The third experiment resembled the second except only artificial illumination was used and the light intensity was decreased rather than increased. Once again production increased in both groups. Since there did not seem to be any relationship between illumination and productivity, no interpretation was made of the three studies. An informal experiment was mentioned by Roethlisberger and Dickson (1939) about two workers involved in coil winding. These workers were placed in a locker room that could be made completely dark. At one point illumination was reduced to .06 of a foot candle, "an amount of light approximately equal to that on an ordinary moonlight night. Even with this very low intensity of light, the girls maintained their efficiency. They said that they suffered no eyestrain and that they became less tired than when working under bright lights (p. 17)."

The illumination experiments led the way to the Hawthorne Studies. The first of the Hawthorne Studies was conducted in the relay assembly room. The purpose of the study was to determine what effect rest pauses and length of the working day had on production. The task was putting a small relay assembly together. Six female employees were involved. The specific working conditions altered were length of workday, length and number of rest pauses, lunch program, and group rate pay. Over a three year period 13 separate conditions took place and production tended to increase. These increases in production were not attributed to any one experimental variable. It was noted, however, that the girls grew more friendly toward each other and they reported they liked the freedom of not being told what to do.

A second relay assembly group was developed to assess the importance of varying the wage incentive as a function of production. After approximately 16 weeks it was concluded that not all increases in production could be explained by the incentive wage factor. Concurrently with the second relay assembly group a study was conducted in the mica splitting test room. In the mica splitting test room there was great variability in the girls' production, there was lower group spirit, and the girls never regarded themselves as special.

It was concluded from the three studies that neither the wage incentive system, improved working methods and materials, rest pauses, nor length of working day could be attributed to the rate of production. It was felt that there was a need to study employees' attitudes. Employees' attitudes were examined through the use of interviews and counseling sessions. The employee-counselor discussions started out in a structured fashion and later were nondirective. The techniques used throughout the study were structured and unstructured interviews, observation, content analysis, and documentary records. Although Roethlisberger and Dickson (1939) were not explicitly clear about the findings[2] of the original Hawthorne Studies, it seems clear to others in the field of management that workers bring with them many motives, needs, and expectations which influence the quality and quantity of their work as well as affect their relationship to the organization (Schein, 1970). An oversim-

---

2. For an accurate yet concise description and analysis of the Hawthorne Studies the reader is directed to: Landsberger, H. A., Hawthorne Revisited, 1968. Order from: Distribution Center, N. Y. S. School of Industrial & Labor Relations, Cornell University, Ithaca, N. Y. 14850 (Price $1.75).

plification of a commonly accepted explanation
of the Hawthorne Studies is that if an employee
feels important, feels cared about, or feels
he is a part of the organization, he will work
harder and do a better job.

The term "Hawthorne effect" which is often
referred to in educational literature was first
reported in Research Methods in the Behavioral
Sciences (Festinger & Katz, 1953). An accepted
definition of the Hawthorne effect is, "a phenomenon characterized by an awareness on the
part of the subjects of special treatment
created by artificial experimental conditions.
This awareness becomes confounded with the
independent variable under study, with a subsequent facilitating effect on the dependent
variable, thus leading to ambiguous results
(Cook, 1962, p. 118)." In other words, people
in experiments who know they are in an experiment do unpredictable things.

The whole idea about the Hawthorne Studies,
whether in business, management, or education,
is that man has feelings and the individual
and social treatments of man are very important variables.

Although organizations tend to adopt one
theory or the other, it is apparent that both
Theory X and Theory Y are very prevalent in
management thinking. However, each theory in
itself is not sufficient to explain the broad
range of work behavior. Both theories account for a large segment of employee behavior,
yet they are based on opposing assumptions
about man and work. One claims that man is
basically lazy, while the other insists that
he is quite responsible. Since management
style is basic to establishing functional programs, it is essential that a management model
be adopted. Flipping a coin provides an easy
alternative but leaves us victims of the chosen
theory's inconsistencies.

Instead of choosing one theory it is
possible to "have the cake and eat it too"
by using both theories. Accepting both
theories is feasible if people are viewed
as different and changeable. In other words,
some people are lazy while others are very
responsible and energetic. Thus the assumptions that people are different, and that
these different people are not static but
changing, allows the acceptance of Theory X
and Theory Y depending on the basic nature of
the individual employee.

The combination theory appears simple,
but it must be remembered that occasionally
individuals who are lazy break out of their
pattern and emerge as basically responsible
employees, while responsible individuals may
regress to a state of basic laziness. When
a boss decides to function on the basis of
a Theory X-Y combination, flexibility in management style becomes essential. Some people
need Theory X while others need Theory Y, and
occasionally the same person will require a
change in styles. The problem was described
by McGregor (1960) when he noted that people
with prevalent ego and actualization needs
function best under Theory Y and rebel under
Theory X. On the other hand, he mentioned
that people with prevalent dependency needs
function best under Theory X and become nonproductive under Theory Y.

Graves' Theory of Man

In this combination Theory X-Y approach,
the manager must constantly shift from one
style to the other. It is self-evident that
this constant shifting can be overwhelming
without a basic operational model or strategy.
The previous two chapters described and explained Graves' theory of man as a workable
model. Graves' theory presents management
strategies which stress both organizational
production and employee growth and it consid-

ers man as a changing nonstatic individual.
The remaining portion of this chapter focuses
on a brief description of each level and how
a manager might handle employees at each level.
Theory X assumptions and applications seem
feasible for levels 1-5 and Theory Y is applicable to level 6.

First Level of Existence: Reactive. Man
at the first level is not aware of self or
others. He is only concerned with the fulfillment of basic physiological needs. Graves
(1966) elaborated on this level of existence
by incorporating an individual's comments of
his experience at this level:

> My mind froze, grew numb, empty and
> dead, one is so tired, so utterly
> weary. Thoughts crawl. To think is
> such a labor and even the smallest
> voluntary act becomes painful to per-
> form. Even talking, having to reply,
> get one's thoughts together, jars
> on the nerves, and it is felt as sheer
> relief to doze, to not have to think
> of anything or do anything. The
> numbness may indeed grow into a
> dream-like state. Time and space
> disappear, reality seems infinitely
> far (p. 121).

The suggested managerial style is a form
of nurturant management. Nurturant management involves caring for the individual as
a mother cares for an infant in hopes that he
will grow to another level.

Employers are not likely to deal with a
first-level person as an employee. Persons
functioning at this level exist in infancy or
hard core welfare cases and institutional
cases.

Second Level of Existence: Tribalistic.
Man at the second level lives in a world of

magic and superstition. He responds to tradition and the power of authority figures. The
following description by Graves (1970) enhances
our understanding of second-level man:

> Causality is not yet perceived be-
> cause man perceives the forces at
> work to be inherent, thus linking
> human consciousness at the deepest
> level. Here a form of existence
> based on myth and tradition arises,
> and being is a mystical phenomenon
> full of spirits, magic and supersti-
> tion. Here the task of existence is
> simply to continue what it seems has
> enabled "my tribe to be" (p. 137).

Occasionally, a person at this level is
encountered as an employee in an unskilled or
semiskilled job. If he is not managed properly, he can present management with insur-
mountable problems.

The appropriate managerial style to use
with the second-level person is very restrictive and Theory X based. It is a style of
management that is often referred to as a
traditionalistic one. A manager must know
the life style of these people, understand
their thinking, and be accepted in order to
get them geared for work. Once they are amenable to working, their jobs are learned
through imitating models that are presented
many times by their boss. Thus, an appropriate managerial style would involve simple
task demonstration coupled with the use of
force to maintain production. However, Graves
(1966) cautioned managers about the use of
force since it only works when it does not
conflict with a strong second-level taboo.
If this conflict arises, the second-level employee is likely to respond with a force of
his own. At this stage Graves stated that
cautious use of force works with second-level
persons, but "it will not work with first-

level people (p. 122)." Hence, the need for
different managerial styles becomes apparent.

Third Level of Existence: Egocentric.
The third-level person is a rugged individu-
alist. He respects, admires, and responds to
raw power. Graves (1970) discussed man at
this level by examining his values and some
conditions of his world:

> It is a world driven by man's lusts
> and is seemingly noteworthy for its
> lack of a "moral sense." But this
> is an error for at this level, where
> man is led to value the ruthless use
> of power, unconscionably daring deeds,
> impulsive action, volatile emotion,
> the greatest of risk, morality is ruth-
> less .... This is not an attractive
> value system from other frames of ref-
> erence, but for all negative aspects,
> it is a giant step forward for man.
> Some men, in their pursuit of power,
> do tame the mighty river, do provide
> the leisure for beginning intellectual
> effort, do build cities ... (p. 146).

It is possible that a large number of
people in unskilled jobs and a few in semiskilled jobs exist at this level. They are
potentially productive when managed correctly.
If third-level persons are handled improperly,
they will use ruthless force to exploit the
business and fellow employees for their own
egocentric survival needs.

Third-level man must be managed in an
authoritarian manner. A manager must "out-
power" this person in order to relegate him
to a job role which involves taking directions
and guidance. This style of management is
called exploitative authoritarian (Likert,
1967) and is unquestionably based on Theory X
assumptions about man. Exploitative management, moderated by reasonable compassion and

sensitivity, must be exercised in order to
bring many of these persons to productive
effort. Possibly, the more power needs the
job role allows, the less power a manager
would need to use. If one considers using
an alternative management style, it is worthwhile to note that a Theory Y management scheme
with third-level employees would be as disastrous as hiring a vampire to operate a blood
bank. Under Theory Y the program would be
exploited and stripped of its humanistic function. Also, it has been pointed out by the
Staff at the Management Center, University of
Richmond (1971), that a supervisor would have
great difficulty managing more than three egocentric-level employees at any one time.

Fourth Level of Existence: Saintly and/or
Conformist. Fourth-level man has a low tolerance for ambiguity and values rigid roles,
rules, and policies. A person at the saintly
level is typically motivated by a religion,
philosophy, or cause. Graves (1970) clari-
fies our view of fourth-level man in the following comment:

> He believes the task of living is
> to strive for perfection in his as-
> signed role .... He believes that
> salvation will come ultimately, re-
> gardless of his original position,
> to he who lives best by the rules
> of life prescribed for him .... He
> who sacrifices best his wants in the
> way authority prescribes is most
> revered (p. 148).

Fourth-level persons are very predominant
in industry. They are found at all levels
of employment from unskilled to professional.
For example, they are prominent in the professions of education, ministry, law, and medicine.

The fourth-level person is most productive in a work environment that is highly or-

dered, structured, and organized. Managers
of fourth-level employees must rigidly pre-
scribe and rigidly enforce rules. This style
of management is paternalistic in nature and
is based on Theory X assumptions. Also, it
is based on the assumption that some persons
(managers) have invested responsibility to
supervise the conduct of the managed through
fatherly concern. Likert (1967) referred to
management at this level as benevolently authoritative. This manager is directive, firm,
and authoritative, yet at the same time warm,
sensitive, fair, and philanthropic.

Fifth Level of Existence: Manipulator
and/or Materialistic. Fifth-level man values
"cause and effect," objectivity, prestige,
and material gain. According to Myers and
Myers (1973), "They tend to perceive people
as expense items rather than assets, to be
manipulated as supplies and equipment (in
press)."

Fifth-level persons are found in all walks
of life. These persons try to stay away from
the more affective positions and professions
such as ministry, social work, job corps, etc.

Fifth-level man performs best under an
autocratic style of management which is firmly
but fairly administered. This individual
likes for matters to be handled in an objective fashion. It pleases him if job descriptions, job qualifications, performance evaluation, and job policies are clearly defined
and objectively followed. He respects mastery
and power and responds well to hard bargaining
such as the "take name and kick tail" variety.
This person is motivated by a system that affords him equal opportunity to share in the
organization's gains.

This style of management is called bureaucratic by Likert (1967) and resembles a
very mechanical approach. Administration is

accomplished via a hierarchical authority
structure which functions according to a system of well-defined rules, policies, and
standard procedures. As with the appropriate
managerial style for persons at levels 2, 3,
and 4, it is based on Theory X assumptions
about man and work.

Sixth Level of Existence: Sociocentric.
The sociocentric person dislikes violence,
tradition, and materialistic motives. He
places a high value on the dignity and worth
of man. His group behavior resembles that of
water being poured into a container. The water always takes the shape of the container,
and the level six person's behavior always
reflects the behavior of the group of which
he is a part. From this analogy it is easy
to perceive that level six man is very flexible and his behavior is predictable when
viewed in conjunction with peer influence.

The following excerpt from Graves (1970)
assists our understanding of existence at this
level:

> He values interpersonal penetration,
> communication, committeeism, majority
> rule, the tender, the subjective,
> manipulative persuasion, softness
> over cold rationality, sensitivity
> in preference to objectivity, taste
> over wealth, respectability over
> power, and personality more than
> things (p. 151).

Sixth-level individuals are gravitating
to universities and are interested in careers
which are service oriented, e.g., social work,
counseling, etc. They are interested in such
programs as job corps, Head Start, Zero Population Growth, Humane Society, Weight Watchers,
Rescue Squad, etc. These people are truly
concerned about helping fellowman.

Since the sixth-level person is democrat-
ically oriented and primarily concerned with
his social needs, the appropriate management
style emphasizes group effort and employee
participation in decision making. The management style for sixth-level employees is the
first one based on Theory Y assumptions about
man and work. The strength of this participa-
tive management depends on group standards
and values. If a sixth-level man falls under
authoritarian style of management, the ensu-
ing results are often disastrous. In this
situation he will exhibit a classic display
of passive resistance, and work performance
will quickly tumble. Hence, to maintain an
acceptable work performance, group management
must prevail.

Level six individuals are many times
looked upon by third, fourth, and fifth level
people as being nice but soft and weak. Therefore, level six persons are unable to manage
lower level persons adequately except for
level one. Persons at levels 3, 4, and 5
would manipulate and dominate a level six
manager for selfish purposes. This domination results in level three people ruthlessly
gaining more power, level four people being
exploited and sacrificed, and level five people achieving small degrees of material gain
through theft and devious ways. Meanwhile,
the level six people continue their meetings
and begin mumbling, "I don't understand why
people can't get along because these people
are basically good." Level six management
will usually allow itself to be run out of
business. Level six management can succeed
with level six and level four employees providing there is no competition in their particular type of business. Although sixth-
level persons do not possess the qualities
and characteristics necessary for managing a
business or program, they are invaluable in
the area of service. They make good counselors, social workers, and teachers of intel-

lectually normal clients, patients, and children.

Seventh Level of Existence: Cognitive.
Seventh-level man not only has a high tolerance but, more importantly, has an appreciation for people of differing values. Some have referred to man at this level as a self-actualized person. Graves (1966) discussed some problems concerning seventh-level man in the following passage:

> he will not follow standard operating procedure. He will produce well-- but only when the manager-producer role is reversed. ... he rebels against the idea that it is management's prerogative to plan and organize work methods without consulting him, ... management insists that he conform ... he refuses (p. 124).

Only a few seventh-level men are found in business and industry. If a manager or administrator were fortunate enough to have a seventh-level person, it would be wise to consider an efficient and effective management approach with him.

Since this man has much to contribute but refuses to be told how to do things, the appropriate management style is to achieve agreement on objectives with him and then support him. This facilitative style of management would unleash his productivity, thus enhancing the organization's objectives and man's existence. This person could be a dangerous administrator. His intense desire to enjoy living and becoming might encourage him to view chaotic and hellish actions as intriguing and extremely enjoyable as long as they were purposeful. It would be similar to a director standing off and observing the employees in an experimental box; and when things began to run smoothly he would shake the box a little to stir things up.

Eighth Level of Existence: Experientialistic. Eighth-level man communicates with an
external force via meditation. His relationship with the outside force resembles a part-
nership rather than a superior-subordinate
relationship. Man at this level operates on
a seemingly universal theory about the destiny
of man and subsequently reflects intuitive
genius. Graves (1970) stated:

> Since eighth level man need not at-
> tend to the problems of his existence
> (for him they have been solved) he
> values those newer, deeper things in
> life which are there to be experi-
> enced. He values escaping "from the
> barbed wire entanglement of his own
> ideas and his own mechanical de-
> vices." He values the "marvelous
> rich world of context and sheer fluid
> beauty and face-to-face awareness of
> now-naked-life" (p. 155).

Eighth-level man is very rare, and it is
unlikely that he exists in the typical business or industry. However, if he should, an
acceptance style of management would be essential.

Conclusion

Most employers will be very familiar with
Theory X and Theory Y types of administration.
Few employers know the history of Theories X
and Y and even fewer have ever heard of Graves.
At the very least this chapter has provided
some content that can give a vocational rehabilitation person something to relate to and
talk about with an employer. We hope that
this chapter will do more than supply vocational rehabilitation personnel with topics
for discussion. We would like for rehabilitation counselors to apply Graves' theory to
clients and employers by determining levels
of psychological existence and subsequently

matching compatible relationships. Take level
3, 4, or 5 clients and place them with level
five employers. Take level six clients and
place them in a six organization with hopefully level seven management or a benevolent
level five management. Never place a level
four or five client under a six manager or a
level three client in a six organization.
Graves' theory can be of assistance to educators and vocational rehabilitation personnel
in training clients as well as recommending
specific vocational treatments.

We feel that any individual who is psychologically perceptive and sensitive to the
needs or existence states of others has the
potential to facilitate human growth. Rehabilitation counselors are interested in assisting handicapped individuals with suitable
vocational placement. However, securing and
holding a job is only one side of the rehabilitation coin. The other deals with the
client's feelings of contentment and happiness
about himself not only as a worker but as a
person. A warning must go to the counselor
who is predominantly functioning in the level
six area. Level six counselors have a difficult time understanding lower level clients
and employers. Level six counselors must remember that they are in the minority and, for
the majority of people, growth is best accomplished through authoritative management practices. We hope someday (soon) the majority
of people will develop to the sixth level and
above so Theory Y management, with its assumptions about man, will be a viable, feasible,
and beneficial system of management for the
masses.

REFERENCES

Cook, D. L. The Hawthorne effect in educational research. Phi Delta Kappan, 1962, 44, 116-122.

Festinger, L., & Katz, D. (Eds.) Research methods in the behavioral sciences. New York: Dryden Press, 1953.

Graves, C. W. The deterioration of work standards. Harvard Business Review, 1966, 44, 117-126.

Graves, C. W. Levels of existence: An open system theory of values. Journal of Humanistic Psychology, 1970, 10, 131-155.

Knezevich, S. J. Administration of public education. New York: Harper & Brothers, 1962.

Likert, R. The human organization: Its management and value. New York: McGraw-Hill, 1967.

Management Center Staff. Clare W. Graves' theory of levels of human existence and suggested managerial systems for each level. Unpublished manuscript, Institute for Business and Community Development, University of Richmond, 1971.

McGregor, D. The human side of enterprise. New York: McGraw-Hill, 1960.

Myers, M. S., & Myers, S. S. Adapting to the new work ethic. Business Quarterly, 1973, 38(4), in press.

Roethlisberger, F. J., & Dickson, W. J. Management and the worker. Cambridge, Mass.: Harvard University Press, 1939.

Schein, E. H. Organizational psychology.
    (2nd ed.) Englewood Cliffs, New Jersey:
    Prentice-Hall, 1970.

Taylor, F. W. The principles of scientific
    management. New York: Harper & Brothers,
    1913.

Townsend, R. Up the organization. New York:
    Alfred A. Knopf, 1970.

Section II

VOCATIONAL ADJUSTMENT
OF THE HANDICAPPED

5. MEETING EMPLOYERS FACE TO FACE[1]

Placing handicapped individuals on jobs
in the community is the ultimate goal of a
vocational training program. Community employers provide a variety of services which
include: (a) general dissemination of vocational information, (b) specific skill training and client evaluation, and/or (c) terminal
employment. However, regardless of the services rendered by an employer, the techniques
used to develop good relationships with employers are essentially the same.

Although it is universally agreed that
good relationships with community employers
are essential to the operation of any vocational training program, there are only a few
references which recommend specific techniques
for establishing, developing, and maintaining
these relationships. Chaffin, Haring, and
Smith (1967) reported on their concerted efforts to utilize community employers which
resulted in productive employment of 95 percent

---

1. Adapted in part from: Payne, J. S.,
& Chaffin, J. D. Developing employer relations in a work study program for the educable
mentally retarded. Education and Training of
the Mentally Retarded, 1968, 3, 127-133. Reprinted by permission.

91

of the graduates in their Kansas Work Study
Program. They attributed much of their success to the elicitation of employer cooperation and commitment. Within a three year
period 164 employers participated in the project with only one dropping out (Payne & Chaffin, 1968).

Before considering specific procedures
for developing and maintaining good employer
relationships, Payne and Chaffin (1968) felt
two interrelated problems needed to be resolved before employers could be effectively
solicited. Their project dealt specifically
with mentally retarded clients but the issues,
problems, and procedures are germane to all
disability groupings. The first problem explored the nature of honesty in interpreting
the concept of mental retardation to the employer, and the second considered whether the
emphasis of the employer-counselor relationship should be directed to the program or the
product of the work study program.

Honest Interpretation

An honest interpretation of the retarded
client is paramount to long lasting employer
relationships. Of importance in developing
successful employer relationships is the determination of what constitutes an honest description for the employer. Does this require
using and defining the term mental retardation
or is it more meaningful to describe the client
in terms of his specific social, academic, and
vocational characteristics?

Fraenkel (1961) discussed employer contact and reported that it is "necessary to
tell the employer the nature of the disability, mental retardation (p. 73)." However,
the recognition that employers do not always
fully understand mental retardation is evident
in Fraenkel's later statement that "experienced counselors ... usually present the qual-

ifications of the worker first and leave the explanation of the disabling condition toward the end of the discussion (p. 73)."

Dubrow (1960) did not suggest that the term mental retardation be avoided but stressed that "placement personnel should share with the prospective employer information bearing on the limitations of the retarded job applicant. This is done in the context of an objective yet persuasive presentation of the individual's capabilities and assets (p. 53)." Dubrow indicated that this explanation to the employer "may range from descriptions of the applicant as having been slow in school, requiring a somewhat longer period of breaking in initially, to an explicit caution against promoting the individual to positions requiring more responsibility or judgment than can be exercised (p. 53)."

A third point of view is presented in the final report of the Oklahoma Project (Oklahoma Rehabilitation Service, 1964). It is emphasized in this report that the personnel on the project are completely honest with the prospective employer. Their interpretation of honesty involved presenting "an accurate description of a student client's potential for the job under consideration (p. 20)." It was pointed out in this report that "the staff discovered that the term educable mentally retarded should be used with discretion as the general public had insufficient understanding of its true meaning (p. 20)."

When the initial employer contacts were made in the Kansas project, the term mentally retarded was used in describing the students. Apparently, many employers had confused the term mentally retarded with mental illness, emotional disturbance, juvenile delinquency, etc. Consequently, the term mentally retarded was frequently eliminated from the _initial_ interview, and terms such as slow learner,

nonmotivated, low reading level, potential
dropout, and nonacademic students were substituted. In subsequent sessions with the
employer, the term mentally retarded was gradually incorporated. This procedure resulted
in significantly more employers agreeing to
participate in the project.

The previous discussion suggests that an
honest interpretation of mental retardation
will be guided by the employer's understanding
of professional terminology. An employer may
accept an individual with retarded behaviors,
but, because of public misconception, he may
not be as accepting of a person who is labeled
mentally retarded.

Therefore, here are two lessons: (a) honesty is relative, for the placement counselor
must use descriptive terms which accurately
communicate, and (b) as the employer-counselor
relationship matures, the counselor will begin
to share and in some cases actually teach the
employer technical terms and jargon to dimin-
ish the many misconceptions about handicapped
individuals and/or handicapping conditions.

Program Versus Product

The second consideration in establishing
employer cooperation concerns the merits of
emphasizing the employer as an integral part
or member of a training program for the retarded instead of merely providing him with a
product of the program. Through the efforts
of parent associations for retarded children
and other public and private organizations,
considerable emphasis has been placed on retarded individuals as employable products.
Through these organizations, pressures are
being brought to bear on business people throughout the country to employ the mentally retarded.
Newspaper and magazine articles, radio and
television messages, a variety of pamphlets
and brochures, and catchy slogans on billboards

along the highways make it popular to hire
the retarded. Invariably the public relations
expert describes the product by characterizing
him as a stable employer or a competent worker
who takes pride in his job. The employer is
also led to believe that retarded workers are
loyal, enthusiastic, and dependable.

Some educable mentally retarded young
adults are as they are advertised to be. However, for most it is necessary to provide
varying degrees of training, education, and
supportive follow-up to achieve even a mediocre product. Most mentally retarded individuals are vocationally handicapped and despite
intensive training efforts may never be "as
advertised."

The present national focus on employment
of the mentally retarded has certain advantages, for it has created a remarkable number
of job opportunities for retarded individuals.
However, it is important to remember that the
purpose of work study programs for the retarded
is to provide appropriate training experience
which will lead to productive employment. Because of the need to develop and maintain realistic training opportunities in a work study
setting, it is important to exercise caution
in making claims about the product when enlisting employer support.

Experience in the Kansas project has
shown that employers can be sold a program of
training without emphasizing the merits of
the product. The advantages of this approach
are obvious. The employer becomes a part of
the training team. He expects and enjoys success but will tolerate failure and setbacks.
Once he considers himself a member of the team
rather than just an employer of the retarded,
he can evaluate clients, develop specific vocational skills, or assist in modifying behaviors incompatible with work. Employers
apparently derived some satisfaction from as-

sisting in training, for none of the employers
who participated in the Kansas project were
reimbursed for their training role.

One disadvantage may arise when an employer becomes too deeply involved in the
training role. Some employers may begin to
understand the retarded so well that they
fail to provide realistic work experiences.
The advantage of using real employers and
work situations for training purposes lies
in the opportunity for students to learn the
natural consequences, either good or bad, which
are associated with the work world. When the
natural consequences are altered by the employer because the student is retarded, the
student may actually learn unsuitable work
habits. This disadvantage, while serious,
does not present a formidable problem if the
placement counselor is alert to its possible
development.

In the Kansas project the emphasis in
employer contacts invariably has been directed
toward the training program. This approach
assumes that if the product has been suffi-
ciently trained, he can sell himself.

The preceding sections have pointed out
that teachers or counselors while recruiting
employers for a work study program should consider: (a) what constitutes an honest relationship, and (b) whether they should sell a
program or a product. With these considerations in mind, more specific procedures for
establishing good employer relations can be
explored.

The heterogeneity of communities in which
vocational training programs will be developed
makes recommending specific procedures for establishing these programs somewhat precarious.
However, some general guidelines are suggested
which may be helpful in persuading employers
to join the rehabilitation efforts. The elic-

itation of employer cooperation and support
entails contacting employers in an effort to
acquire commitment from them. This initial
contact and subsequent commitment is referred
to as "Acquisition of Employer Participation."

Acquisition of Employer Participation

As a counselor begins to solicit for
business cooperation, it may be beneficial
to determine a ratio of successful to unsuccessful contacts after several businesses
have been approached. Once a success ratio
has been established, there are two major
methods for increasing business commitment:
(a) increase the number of businesses contacted and, if the ratio remains approximately
constant, this will increase the number of
cooperating businesses as a function of the
number of contacts made, or (b) perfect the
techniques for approaching businesses in an
attempt to increase the success ratio. Since
counselors do not have an abundance of time
to contact businesses, it seems logical that
increasing the success ratio is the more appropriate alternative. When the success ratio
is high, not only is time saved but business
contacts are less discouraging. Most counselors are not trained salesmen and it is natural for enthusiasm to lessen when the success
ratio is low. On the other hand, if success
comes often, the probability of continued solicitation is increased. With this in mind
the following information concerning organization and business contact techniques is presented for the explicit purpose of increasing
the success ratio of business support and cooperation.

The first step in organizing the approach
is to consider the variety as well as the
quantity of possible business contacts. This
can be done by studying a telephone directory,
reading newspaper ads, consulting The Dictionary of Occupational Titles, and talking with

friends and community leaders. Probably the
most effective way is to drive through the
business community in order to visually determine possible contacts.

After obtaining a general idea of the
potential supporters, standardized forms and
a system of filing should be carefully developed. Business contact forms should contain
the following information: (a) date of business contact, (b) name and type of business,
(c) address, (d) telephone number, (e) name
of informant, (f) business hours, (g) type of
participation, (h) type of work (skills included), and (i) comments. Table 1 is an example of a business contact form.

Thought should be given to a system of
cross-filing the business information obtained
since it is often desirable to retrieve the
information on the basis of: (a) nature of
business, (b) type of participation, and/or
(c) name of contact person. There are numerous ways of filing this information, but the
following will suffice for most vocational
training programs: (a) by name of business,
(b) by name of employer, and (c) by type of
participation. This may appear to be unneces-
sary duplication, but it will be a valuable
time-saver as the program develops and a large
number of businesses are accumulated.

Before proceeding to specific techniques
for actual employer contacts, it is advisable
to define clearly what is meant by employer
participation. There are three types of employer participation: (a) general dissemination of vocational information, (b) specific
training and/or evaluation, and (c) actual
job placement.

Dissemination of Vocational Information.
The first level of employer participation is
general dissemination of vocational information. While this level of participation is

Table 1
Business Contact Form

Date of Contact _____

Business Information
    Name of Business:_____
    Type of Business:_____
    Address:_____
    Phone Number:_____

Informant
    Name:_____
          (last)   (first)
    Position:_____
    Business Hours:_____
    Days Off:_____
    Convenient time to talk:_____

Type of Participation
    I. Interested in general dissemination
        of vocational information portion
        of the program:
   II. Interested in specific training
        and/or evaluation portion of the
        program:
  III. Interested in the placement portion
        of the program:

Number of Persons Needed:
Male:
Female:
Days per week:
Hours per day:
Pay or Non-pay:
Type of Work:
Skills Desired:
Comments:

important, it is the lowest level of participation and involves the least amount of effort on the part of the employer. At this
level the employer agrees to come to the vocational training institution and present
some aspect of his business to the clients.
Also included at this level is the agreement
to allow the clients to visit the employer's
place of business for a field trip. This
level of participation is important for vocationally naive clients and is of value in
exposing clients to types of jobs and working
conditions, but for the counselor this level
of participation should be viewed as enticing
the employer into the training program. Many
employers who initially will not participate
in training clients are more receptive after
seeing the program via their own presentation.
This low level of participation is of vital
importance to the placement counselor because
it keeps him from being completely turned
down by many employers. The skillful use of
this level of participation will be explained
later in detail.

   Training and/or Evaluation. Specific
training and/or evaluation refers to the employer who is willing to try the client to
see if he can do the job or to train the client
on the job. This is referred to as OJT (on
job training) and can be handled in numerous
ways: (a) employer pays client full salary
while in training; (b) employer pays client
partial salary and training institution pays
remaining portion; (c) training institution
actually pays employer to train the client,
i.e., the institution purchases a training
service; or (d) the employer trains the client
for "free," i.e., neither the employer gets
paid for training nor the client gets paid
while in training. In this latter case the
training is viewed as if the client were going
to shop class or a vocational training class.
Pay versus non-pay for work while in training
refers to the client being paid or not paid

while in OJT. In vocational rehabilitation circles there is a great deal of discussion about whether clients work better and more effectively for pay or for no pay. In actuality, no one really knows if pay is the ultimate factor in training clients. The discussion is similar to the situation in which the philosophers were discussing the number of teeth in a horse's mouth--it was more fun to talk about it than to go out and actually count the number of teeth in a horse's mouth.

Placement. Job placement is the ultimate level of participation, for it refers to the hiring of the handicapped client. This type of placement is appropriate for clients who are ready to assume the responsibilities of full-time employment and for the employer who has a vacancy and/or is willing to hire the client.

Once a counselor has determined a potential business to be contacted, studied program participation options, and given thought to organizational details, he may begin to contact business personnel. After reviewing the literature related to contacting community work situations, we have compiled the following list of suggestions:
1. Use outside organizations as much as possible. Talks made to service clubs such as Lions and Kiwanis generally make the employer aware of the program (Cohen, 1962).
2. Use business cards and other printed material whenever possible. The counselor should leave descriptive background material about the program and a business card at each place of employment (Cohen, 1962).
3. Leads can be found many times through the want ad section in the local newspaper and through staff acquaintances. Many work opportunities may be developed by: (a) contacting individuals in the community who are aware of the program, (b) addressing civic organizations, (c) using want ads, and (d) inquiring

at various places of business (Cohen & Williams, 1961).

4. An attempt must be made to know the community. The contact person is always a public relations agent. Visits with employers serve two useful purposes: (a) to acquaint them with the employment oriented program, and (b) to enlist their cooperation in calling this program to the attention of others with the end result being suitable placements for handicapped workers (Kruger, 1963).

5. Do not overlook government placement possibilities. Growth industries in the nation which need exploring for the handicapped are state, federal, and local government jobs (Kruger, 1963).

6. The contact person must have the desire to make the placement and this desire must be backed up with action. The success of the employment preparation program depends to a large measure on the placement counselors themselves. There is need for a commitment-- an affective will to action. Counselors must want to do something which will facilitate the employment of clients--action (Kruger, 1963).

7. Businessmen like the idea of working with public schools in general. Businessmen like the connection with the educational community. They feel that they are doing something for some youngsters who have received a "bad break" from society (Cohen, 1963).

8. Once the program has been sold, use testimonials and successful employer references. In developing subsequent jobs, counselors can use the experience of people who have participated in the program for some time as a means of selling new employers on the idea (Cohen, 1963).

9. As the program grows, become more selective and secure those jobs which best meet the objectives of the program. Although the initial concern of a rehabilitation staff is to find enough jobs for the trainees, it becomes increasingly possible when the program develops

to select jobs on the basis of their suitabil-
ity rather than availability (Cohen, 1963).
10. To date, there are no known ways to predict employability. Therefore, do not guar-
antee anything. A placement counselor knows
that he cannot predict to a reliable degree
whether a client can succeed in a community
vocational position if his only means of evaluating the student before placement is based
on information obtained from an academic setting (Kokaska, 1964).
11. Do not get depressed if things start off
slowly. If at first you don't succeed, try,
try again. Contrary to frequent comments expressed about difficulties in securing suitable employment, today there is a waiting
list. When an individual fails, another employer is found but only after the reasons
for the failure are studied. Second placements usually meet with success. The key
factor is the employer's sincere interest in
the individual's rehabilitation (Boyd, 1964).
12. In any way possible, promote community
acceptance. In the Kansas program a Citizens
Advisory Committee was organized which was
made up of 23 members who held personnel jobs
in leading industries. Persons asked to be
members of this committee were selected to
provide the greatest representation from business and industry. The objective was to help
assure acceptance of the program by business
and industry. Even though these members were
representatives from the larger business and
manufacturing concerns, they were not expected
to provide the actual work training situations.
Their public, personal, and organizational en-
dorsement served to develop the desired community acceptance and this was their major contribution to the project (Chaffin, Haring, &
Hudson, 1965).
13. Placement is a two-way proposition. The
importance of salesmanship cannot be overem-
phasized. The key to involving businessmen
from the community is to recognize that, by
asking them to give, the counselor will also

be required to give. The counselor must provide a source of inspiration and sell the
clients in his program (Chaffin, Haring, &
Hudson, 1965).

14. _Placement is time-consuming hard work._
Placing handicapped clients is time-consuming
and often results in trial and error procedures (Oklahoma Project, 1964).

15. _At all times keep in mind the program's
goals and objectives, and continuously inform
the employer of these._ The employer must be
considered a part of the program, but he is
not in charge or running it. Rehabilitation
staff need to communicate the goals and objectives of the program, both prior to its
start and also as a continuing effort. For
example, Dick (1965) reported that businessmen frequently relate to him personally that
they are quite happy the school is attempting
to provide for all types of boys and girls.

16. _Civic responsibility is the businessman's
Achilles' heel._ It is not always possible to
convince an employer that he should participate in a rehabilitation program. However,
in many communities employers have responded
in the spirit of civic responsibility when
acquainted with the problems (Heber, 1963).

17. _Employers must be used time and time
again. Therefore, be sure to back up any
statements made. Do not make statements which
cannot be backed up._ Careful placements result in satisfied employers who "come back
for more." In small, nonindustrial communities, a saturation of the job market may become a problem which does not usually emerge
in larger industrialized communities. In
either case, however, it is important to have
"repeat" employers available for work placements (Miller & Danielson, 1965).

The following six statements represent
what seemed to contribute most to initiating
employer cooperation in the Kansas Work Study
Program:

1.   An enthusiastic approach, using techniques
of good salesmanship, seemed beneficial. No
discussion was initiated or attempted if the
employer seemed to be busy. The interview was
usually kept under four minutes unless the employer wished to discuss the project more fully.
2.   Mentioning the local high school elicited
immediate interest from the employers, for
many of them had either graduated from the
school or had children attending it. (The
program was jointly sponsored by the local
school district and vocational rehabilitation).
3.   Interest in helping problem clients was
expressed by nearly all employers.
4.   More descriptive and meaningful terms were
substituted for the term mental retardation.
5.   A program instead of a product was sold.
6.   The employers were told of their importance to the program and what would be expected of them.

Counselors who have approached businessmen on a large scale mention the importance
of being physically fit, for the majority of
this work requires standing, walking, and, on
occasion, some running. Appropriate dress is
important for initial business contact success, but caution should be exercised not to
overly dress the part. Also, a packet of appropriate forms, a booklet of matches for of-
fering lights, a roll of nickels for meters,
breath mints, extra pencils, and calling cards
represent items which enhance the counselor's
effectiveness as well as his efficiency.

The decision to "walk in" on a businessman without an appointment should be considered
carefully. The general rule of thumb is that,
if the proprietor or manager is readily available, then by all means "walk in." If two or
three unexpected "drop in" contacts fail to
produce results, use the phone to arrange an
appointment. Appointments are appropriate for
large businesses and corporations, but smaller,

local businesses prefer for the counselor just
to drop by during slow hours. In a phone conversation the counselor should state his name,
organization, who referred him to the business (if applicable), and that he would like
to explain the vocational program. The counselor should tell the employer that it will
take less than 10 minutes and ask when it
would be convenient to meet. He should <u>not</u>
ask if the employer is interested or if he
<u>can</u> meet with him. At <u>no</u> time should the
counselor ask any question which can be answered "Yes" or "No" because the employer
might say "No." The key question to ask is,
"When would be a good time for r ə to meet
with you?" This question cannot be answered
with a simple "Yes" or "No." If the employer
does not want to meet with the counselor, he
must at least tell him so in sentence form.
Surveys indicate that if the individual under
question has to respond in sentence form it
is more likely that he will respond positively
than negatively.

Many beginning counselors are apprehen-
sive about asking employers for help. Do not
be concerned about that, for employers are
asked by many different people for donations
and support of some kind or another almost
every month. The worst thing they can say is
"No" and the counselor should make them do
that in sentence form. Approach solicitation
with a positive, enthusiastic attitude.

Every employer contact should be considered a part of good public relations. Employers need to know about vocational training
programs, and most employers want to be kept
abreast of local programs. Therefore, initial
contacts are twofold: (a) to share information
about the project, and (b) to elicit some type
of employer participation.

After getting a foot in the door, the
counselor needs something to say. It may help

for the counselor to bring a couple of pictures of program activities or clients engaged
in work so that the businessman has something
to look at while the counselor talks. Another
introductory device is the business card, but,
if a counselor does not wish to go to the expense of printing up business cards, a mimeo-
graphed sheet with his name, organization,
telephone number, and a description of what
he wants to do and why he needs help will
suffice.

It is difficult to tell exactly what to
do since communities differ, businesses differ, and times change. However, after making
about 10 to 15 contacts, it is helpful for
the counselor to sit down and see if he can
list what he feels he is doing right and what
he is doing wrong. Also, he should try to
categorize his "turn downs." Was he turned
down because: (a) the business man was not
at work, (b) the businessman was too busy,
(c) the "buck was passed," (d) he met passive
resistance, or (e) the businessman did not
have anything to offer? After determining
his strengths, weaknesses, and reasons for
being turned down, the counselor should think
of alternatives for approaching various types
of businessmen who have refused to talk to
him. For instance, if the counselor is having trouble catching the man in charge, he
can try a surprise visit by dropping in and
stating, "I was in the area and thought I'd
drop by and pay a visit ...." If he meets
passive resistance, the counselor can become
more direct and suggest specific ways the
businessman can be of help.

It is unlikely that the counselor will
convince every businessman to participate.
However, within a short period of time, he
at least should be getting his foot in the
door and be having an opportunity to give his
presentation to 75 percent of the employers
he contacts. If he is falling short of this

percentage, he should begin to concentrate on his entry skills because without improving this stage of the business contact he is certain to fail and get discouraged. Remember the counselor has two goals: (a) to share information about his program, and (b) to elicit some type of employer participation. Some counselors have enjoyed talking with businessmen about their vocational programs even though their acquisition of successful employer participation is low, but no counselor will continue to attempt business contacts if he fails to get his foot in the door. The majority of counselors receive the most satisfaction when participation is procured at levels two and three, i.e., specific training and/or evaluation and actual placement.

Fortunately many employers are quite receptive to counselors and most counselors are able to get their foot in the door. However, if the counselor is being turned away more than 25 percent of the time, he may be running into more than his share of resistant employers. Resistant employers can be grouped into four categories: (a) passive resistance, (b) lack of competence, (c) illness, and (d) too busy.

Passive Resistance. Passive resistance is manifested when the employer consistently breaks appointments with the counselor. The counselor sets up an appointment but at the last minute the employer has to leave unexpectedly. These employers do not want to meet the counselor face to face and thus avoid any confrontation. With this type of resistance a surprise visit by the counselor is necessary. The counselor could unexpectedly arrive and explain that he was in the area on another matter and, since he was close by, thought he would stop. The element of surprise has won many battles, and often the employer is caught with his guard down and will consent at least to talk. Usually this type of employer will apologize for the broken appointments and will invite the counselor to talk. However, it is not unusual for this type of employer to be cooperative until the time comes for him to make any kind of commitment. In other words, he "drags his feet." When the employer makes a statement such as, "I don't know. I'm not sure ...," the counselor must respond with, "Look, just give it a try. You have nothing to lose. If the client does not work out, we will take him back." Then the counselor must take the initiative to suggest a specific plan.

Lack of Competence. The "lack of competence" employer is usually very humble and tries to pass the buck. He does not want to listen, for he does not want to be sold anything. He says, "Look, I don't have much education. Why don't you see Joe across the street. He would be interested in your project." The alert counselor will turn the employer's disability into an asset by saying, "We are looking for employers just like yourself. We want people who are practical and have learned by the school of hard knocks--sort of pulled themselves up by their own boot straps."

Illness. This employer says he cannot get involved because he has been sick or has a bad heart. Once again the alert counselor reverses the disability and says, "Listen, this is just what the doctor ordered (HA, HA). We can send someone to help you." With this type of employer the counselor should briefly explain the program and quickly try to get a commitment for training and/or evaluating a client.

Too Busy. The "too busy" statement is the oldest but most difficult to crack. Sometimes the counselor can appeal to the employer's sympathy with, "Look, I'm busy too. I've put in a hard day and I'm getting nowhere.

Just listen for a couple of minutes as a favor
to me. I'm desperate. If you listen, I'll
personally appreciate it."

One of the most effective means of getting the "too busy" employer at least to listen to the counselor is to quickly jump into
his hurried excuse of being too busy to talk
by saying, "What I have to say is important
and it will take less than five minutes. To
prove it to you I have here a 10 dollar bill."
Now the counselor quickly pulls a crisp 10
dollar bill from his pocket and dangles it in
front of the employer. The counselor will
notice at this point that he has the employer's
attention. Next, the counselor pulls a stop-
watch from another pocket and says, "To assure
you I am going to take less than five minutes
of your time, I am starting this watch and,
if I take more than five minutes, I'll take
my watch and go home and the 10 dollars is
yours. If I finish before five minutes, I
will take the watch and my 10 dollars and
leave you alone." Now the counselor starts
the watch, shows it to the employer, and says,
"See, the watch is moving. Is it a deal?"
This approach has been used many times and
it practically never fails to get five minutes
of time from any employer. However, when the
employer consents to listen, the counselor
needs to be organized, quick, and good. Before using this approach it is advisable to
rehearse a presentation and condense it to
about 3½ minutes. Then if the employer inter-
rupts, the counselor still has time to complete
his presentation. In this type of presentation
the use of small visuals, such as pictures and
key phrases typed on cards, is helpful in getting the message across clearly and concisely.

If the counselor perfects his entry techniques to the extent that he at least can talk
to resistant employers, it is probable that he
will be able to get in the door of 90 to 95
percent of all employers (receptive plus resistant).

Some counselors get discouraged and say, "If an employer doesn't want to listen, it won't do me any good to force the issue." Effective counselors have found that often the most resistive employers are the most cooperative. Frequently, if employers have trouble saying "No," they set up all kinds of barriers and defenses to keep from having to say it. When an employer is extremely resistant to talking with a counselor, the counselor should persist in his efforts to meet the employer face to face because the employer might be a person who will be easily persuaded to participate.

Once the counselor has mastered the skills necessary for getting his foot in the door of at least 75 percent of the businesses he contacts, partial success is assured because no businessman will throw out a counselor for explaining a project (providing the counselor does not take more than four or five minutes to tell the employer about it). In essence, the counselor is accomplishing his first goal, i.e., explaining the vocational program to every businessman who lets him in the door. However, the second objective, i.e., getting the employer to participate, is the crucial goal.

Getting the employer to participate in a program seems more difficult than getting in the door but it really is not. When a counselor learns to "read" employers and gains confidence, he will be highly successful in obtaining employer participation at one of the three levels of participation, i.e., (a) general dissemination of vocational information, (b) specific training and/or evaluation, and (c) placement.

Once the counselor explains his program, he must concentrate on getting a commitment. For beginning counselors it is best to start with the participation option of specific

training and/or evaluation. By starting with
this option the counselor can shift to other
options depending on the reaction of the employer. If the counselor starts with the
first option (dissemination of vocational information) and meets resistance, he has no
other choice but to leave. On the other hand,
if he starts with the placement option, he
might overwhelm an employer.

Once the counselor has decided to solicit
specific training and/or evaluation, it is important for him to learn to "read" the employer. Most employers fit into one of three distinct personality types, and they give cues
about the type of person they are. The three
types of employers are: (a) conformist, (b) materialistic, and (c) sociocentric. These three
levels correspond to Graves' levels of human
existence which are discussed in Chapters 2,
3, and 4.

The conformist employer usually wears
old clothes, clean and pressed, and does not
look comfortable in a suit. He frequently
wears traditional work shoes and white socks.
He believes in hard work, runs a straight
ship, and likes rules and regulations. This
person will often have a picture of his family
on his desk. This type of employer will want
the counselor to be organized and have some
written material to hand out with objectives
of the program clearly listed. It is important for the placement counselor to project
his dedication and sincereness and, if the
occasion arises, get the employer to talk
about his family. Likewise, the counselor
should talk about his own family and, if possible, show the employer a billfold snapshot
of them.

Many conformist employers view a handicapping condition as a result of some outside
force inflicting the person. The disabling
condition is viewed as a means by which the

outside force is trying to teach someone a
lesson. For this reason many employers at
this level will not be sympathetic even though
they may verbalize sympathy. However, since
the conformist employer likes structure, rules,
and policies, the counselor will tend to be
successful in getting him to participate if
the presentation is clear, concise, and matter-
of-fact, e.g., "Here is the problem. Here is
our program. Here is what we need from you.
Could you give us a hand? Just give it a try.
I know it will work out for the best." This
straightforward approach will work. If the
counselor cannot persuade the employer to
take on a trainee, he should try a lower option and invite him to share his business expertise with the clients. Conformist employers especially enjoy telling about their experiences.

The materialistic employer will dress
the part, drive an expensive car, have a ring
or rings on his finger, and look comfortable
in a suit. He usually wears expensive, shined
wing-tip shoes. He believes in cause and effect and merit through work. He likes a bargain, and the placement counselor must approach
this employer on the basis that hiring the
handicapped is good business. Materialistic
employers will allow the counselor to purchase
training services, for they are very receptive
to training funds. If training funds are not
available, then the assets of the vocational
program must be sold to convince the employer
he is going with a winner. If the trainee
does not do well, the counselor should send
him another. Unlike conformist employers, the
materialistic employers like money and will
accept funds. Conformist employers like money
if it is earned and worked hard for, and since
training funds are viewed as easy money they
do not want it. The materialistic employer
considers the vocational program as just another facet of business.

The sociocentric employer wants to make friends. He seldom wears a coat and if he wears a tie it will be loose. He usually wears causal shoes (hush puppies are common). This employer is warm, receptive to ideas, and wants to be liked, but he is the most difficult to pin down because he does not like to make decisions. He will say, "Let me think about it." This type of employer fools most counselors because he is so nice yet so evasive when it comes time for making a commitment. The counselor almost always has to solicit the lowest level of employer participation so he can have time to discuss the program with the employer. When the counselor is with a sociocentric employer, he should ask permission to loosen his tie or to take off his coat. He should talk about clean air, trees, etc. Sociocentric employers often have a terrarium or an ecology poster in their office. An employer at this level wants to help but needs time to know the counselor. The counselor should not use hard sell techniques nor offer to use training funds, for this will insult the sociocentric employer. Also, the counselor should not negotiate or drive a hard bargain. He needs to sit back, take it easy, and have the employer come and talk to his clients.

Graves' seventh level person, the cognitive employer, will not be discussed for two reasons: (a) there are not many of these individuals, and (b) they will only participate if they want to or if the counselor is extremely skillful, and then the cognitive employer will participate only out of respect for the skills the counselor has acquired.

Conclusion

We have discussed the purposes for which community employers may be used, the interpretation of honesty, and whether a program or a product should be emphasized. We described

how to organize a counselor's approach to the
community and suggested a business contact
form and ways to file the information. When
meeting employers face to face, we suggested
how the counselor could get his "foot in the
door." Once entry skills are mastered, the
counselor has two objectives: (a) to share
information about the project, and (b) to enlist employer participation. Three types of
participation were suggested: (a) general
dissemination of vocational instruction,
(b) specific training and/or evaluation, and
(c) job placement. Techniques were discussed
for persuading various types of employers to
participate in the vocational training program. Once an employer participates at the
training and/or evaluation level or higher,
the next set of skills for the counselor to
acquire is how to develop and maintain employer support. Developing and maintaining employer support are discussed in the next
chapter.

REFERENCES

Boyd, W. N. Vocational rehabilitation of the mentally retarded. Canada's Mental Health, 1964, 12, 17.

Chaffin, J. D., Haring, N. G., & Smith, J. O. A selected demonstration for the vocational training of mentally retarded youth. Kansas City, Kansas: University of Kansas Medical Center, 1967.

Chaffin, J. D., Haring, N. G., & Hudson, F. I've just found a job. Kansas Teacher, 1965, 74, 30-35.

Cohen, J. S. Community day work in an institutional vocational training program. American Journal of Mental Deficiency, 1962, 66, 514-579.

Cohen, J. S. Employer attitudes toward hiring mentally retarded individuals. American Journal of Mental Deficiency, 1963, 67, 705-713.

Cohen, J. S., & Williams, C. F. A five phase vocational training program in a residential school. American Journal of Mental Deficiency, 1961, 66, 230-237.

Dick, F. The Sylvania work-study program. In D. Y. Miller & R. H. Danielson (Eds.), Work-study for slow learners in Ohio. Columbus, Ohio: Columbus Blank Book Co., 1965.

Dubrow, M. On the job assistance. In The Woods Schools, Outlook for the adult retarded. Langhorne, Pennsylvania: The Woods Schools, 1960.

Fraenkel, W. A. The mentally retarded and
    their vocational rehabilitation: A re-
    source handbook. New York: National
    Association for Retarded Children, 1961.

Heber, R. (Ed.) Special problems in voca-
    tional rehabilitation of the mentally
    retarded. U. S. Department of Health,
    Education, & Welfare, Vocational Reha-
    bilitation Administration, Rehabilita-
    tion Service Series No. 65-16, 1963.

Kokaska, C. A tool for community adjustment.
    Mental Retardation, 1964, 2, 365-369.

Kruger, D. H. Trends in service employment:
    Implications for the educable mentally
    retarded. Exceptional Children, 1963,
    30, 167-172.

Miller, D. Y., & Danielson, R. H. Summary.
    In D. Y. Miller & R. H. Danielson (Eds.),
    Work-study for slow learners in Ohio.
    Columbus, Ohio: Columbus Blank Book
    Co., 1965.

Oklahoma Rehabilitation Service, Division of
    the State Board for Vocational Education.
    Bridging the gap between school and em-
    ployment. A cooperative program of spe-
    cial education-vocational rehabilitation,
    1964.

Payne, J. S., & Chaffin, J. D. Developing
    employer relations in a work study pro-
    gram for the educable mentally retarded.
    Education and Training of the Mentally
    Retarded, 1968, 3, 127-133.

6. DEVELOPING AND MAINTAINING
EMPLOYER SUPPORT

After "knock on the door" techniques have
been perfected and a sufficient number of employers are training, evaluating, and hiring
vocational rehabilitation clients, efforts
should be directed toward further developing
the employers' interest in working with handicapped individuals as well as increasing their
skills in training.

When a counselor's caseload includes a
handicapped client who, after completing some
type of training routine, is employable, everything is satisfactory, and the client, counselor, and employer are happy. Unfortunately,
most vocational training programs do not go
according to game plan, i.e., most handicapped
workers experience difficulty in securing and
holding a job. If handicapped workers had
little or no difficulty in employment endeavors, there would be little need for comprehensive vocational rehabilitation programs.

Articles printed in weekly and monthly
magazines, advertisements over radio and television, and billboard signs along the highways report the vocational rehabilitation
client as a nonhandicapped individual. Employers are told by the government and news
media that the handicapped:

1. want to make good.
2. will work particularly hard to make good.
3. are not anxious to change jobs frequently.
4. are happy to learn a job and remain with it.
5. have an attendance record which is usually better than average.
6. will stay with routine tasks.
7. come to work dependably and on time.
8. are quiet, well behaved, and inclined not to gossip or "goof off."
9. are well trained vocationally.
10. take pride in their work and try hard to please.
11. do not get restless.

In some cases guarantees are made to the employer. The prospective employer can be certain the client:
1. is not a misfit.
2. is a competent worker.
3. is stable and takes pride in his work.
4. has a high degree of loyalty, enthusiasm, dependability, and above all can perform his job well.

All of the above statements have been taken from various rehabilitation advertisements. Today's by-line is, "It pays to hire the handicapped." To put it mildly, the rehabilitation client is probably being slightly oversold. The nice, easygoing, well rounded, eager, punctual, trustworthy, loyal, helpful, friendly, courteous, kind, obedient, cheerful, thrifty, brave, and clean individual is a boy scout, not a vocational rehabilitation client.

Many handicapped clients make good workers, but few if any are "as advertised." In most cases even the good workers are developed after some type of training, and after the training (no matter how good and thorough it is) handicapped clients need a period of time to adjust to the job even if they have acquired the necessary job skills.

The ultimate success of job adjustment and rehabilitation rests with an interested employer. The successful placement of handicapped workers is not a job which can be done by well-wishers, do-gooders, or through the use of snappy slogans. It is a job which requires professional skills and knowledge and must be done on an individual basis. The capabilities and limitations of the individual client must be realized. Also, the employer's requirements must be accrued by visiting the place of employment and noting the job skill requirements, the kind of people, and the working climate (Pinner, 1960). Counselors must develop and perfect skills for enhancing employer interest in working with the handicapped.

Developing Employer Interest

An employer's interest may be enhanced in a number of ways. One technique is to "lead with a winner." Providing a fairly good worker as the employer's first trainee will reduce the anxiety which the employer may have developed about participating in the program. There is almost universal agreement that, in opening up work samples, work sites, or job placement situations, it is always best to begin with a client who is most likely to succeed. This appears feasible until a counselor realizes that his caseload no longer includes "good ones." In the Kansas Work Study Program it was demonstrated that it is possible to lead off with high risk clients and still maintain employer interest. For example, clients were placed in a local cafeteria on four occasions, and on all four times the clients did a miserable job. However, the clients were able to learn and profit from their experiences, and the cafeteria's personnel and facilities served valuable training purposes. In addition, on the average of once every two months the counselor received a call from the personnel manager asking if

anyone else could be placed there. It was
not known if they were trying to get prepared
for another client or if they actually wanted
some more clients (Payne, 1966). Nevertheless, the door was always open. The reason
it was possible to lead off with poor workers
and still keep the employers participating
was because the program and not the client
was sold via honest and accurate communication.

Another way to increase the employer's
interest in working with the handicapped is
to emphasize constantly the importance of his
role in the program. The best way for a client
to learn to work is actually to work. This
assumption makes the employer the central figure in the training program. Straightforward
and unsophisticated statements such as, "If
it weren't for your (the employer) assistance,
John might never have learned to work," can
be very meaningful and effective in developing
the employer's interest. The straightforward
yet sincere approach is invaluable to employers at the conformist level and the sociocentric level. Conformist employers want to be
told directly and specifically how important
they are. Sociocentric employers want to feel
they are important because others like them.
They do not want to be viewed as manipulators.
Therefore, a positive comment might be a statement such as, "If it weren't for your concern
and sincere interest in John, he might never
have come as far as he has." Materialistic
employers like to be told and shown how important they are as is illustrated next.

A third method for increasing the employer's interest is to reinforce his participation by reporting changes which have been observed in the handicapped employee during his
tenure with the employer. Changes in behavior
almost always occur when a client is placed
on a new job, and they should be communicated
to the employer, especially if the employer

is functioning within the materialistic level.
The alert counselor is aware of these changes
and reports them to the employer through the
use of such statements as, "You sure shaped
up John's appearance since he started with
you," or "John averaged five tardies a week
before he started on this job. Now he is
late only about twice a week." Showing the
employer specific changes in a client's work
behavior is most impressive and appreciated
by any employer but especially by the materialistic employer. The materialistic employer
likes to see cause and effect and believes
he can make things happen. Manipulation to
the materialistic employer is a way of life,
and he views it as a positive means of helping handicapped workers learn and adjust to
their job. A conformist employer likes to
see changes but does not necessarily need to
be shown he was the cause of the change. Sociocentric employers like to see change in
clients but only if the clients verbalize that
they like the work, their job, their employer,
etc. When showing the sociocentric employer
changes in the client, it always should be
accompanied with statements such as, "He's
smiling more. He doesn't have that chip on
his shoulder any more. He was telling me the
other day that he is the happiest he has ever
been in a long, long time."

All of these techniques may be used to
develop the interest of the employer in working with handicapped clients. A different
approach is required when the objective is to
assist the employer in improving his training
techniques when working with vocational rehabilitation clients.

Developing Employer Training Skills

An effective means of teaching employers
techniques for training handicapped clients
is behavioral management. Behavioral management skills do not have to be taught in a

classroom or laboratory setting but rather on a casual or informal basis. The first step in helping the employer to develop behavior management skills is to persuade him to describe the client's work behavior in precise, descriptive, behavioral terms rather than with intuitive or general impressions. This approach is based on the rationale that information such as knowing that a client is "not getting along well" or "seems unhappy" does not provide useful information for a corrective training program. If the employer is to report precise and descriptive information, it is necessary for him to observe behavior in an objective manner. If he feels that the youngster is "not doing well," he should attempt to specify the behaviors which give him that impression. It may be that the client "works slowly," "fumbles with materials," or "spends a lot of time in the rest room." This kind of information, while still somewhat imprecise, can provide some basis for a corrective program.

Employers should be encouraged to carry a small notebook and record specific behaviors for later reference. The skillful counselor often can prompt the employer to count and record the frequency of some behaviors which he feels are important. Knowledge of the frequency of occurrences, both before and after the application of corrective techniques, adds considerable precision to the training program and leads into the actual teaching of behavior management techniques.

In the teaching of behavioral management techniques to employers, the basics include: (a) identifying the problem behaviors in observable terms; (b) counting the frequency of problem behaviors; (c) doing something about it (treat, counsel, teach, train, etc.); and (d) determining if the treatment improved the situation by counting the frequency of problem behaviors during and after treatment.

If enough change has not been found, another treatment or treatments should be tried.

The following situation illustrates the behavioral management technique. An employer says that a client is doing poorly on the job because he is not motivated. Since motivation cannot be observed, it is necessary to determine what "not being motivated" is in observable and hopefully quantifiable terms. Through further questioning it is found that the client is projecting nonmotivation by arriving late to work. The employer reveals the client's time card and it is discovered he is late for work two or three days a week. The vocational treatment might be to talk with the client about the problem. The employer checks the time card the following week to determine the effectiveness of the treatment. If appropriate changes have been made, success has been experienced with this aspect of job motivation. However, if no success is experienced, other types of treatment will have to be tried. Typical vocational cases report tardiness due to a number of factors which include: (a) client not being able to tell time, (b) no alarm clock, (c) lack of knowledge about how to set the alarm clock, (d) transportation difficulties, (e) not understanding the importance of arriving at work on time, and (f) lack of enough sleep the previous night. Regardless of the numerous reasons for the client's tardiness, the use of the behavioral management schema at least determines the behavioral problems and facilitates the development of appropriate intervention strategies.

During the developmental phase it is extremely important for the counselor to visit the employer at regular intervals. Contacts should be made at least once a week. Also, the counselor should respond immediately if the employer requests help. A phrase often used is, "I'm as close as the telephone." Em-

ployer visits can consume a considerable amount
of staff time, but as employers become better
trainers they can work more independently.
Careful execution of the developmental phase
is essential to success in the final phase of
maintaining the employer's support.

Maintaining Employer Support

During the previous phase the counselor
served as a reinforcer for the employer by
saying statements concerning the client which
made the employer feel that what he was doing
was successful and worthwhile. The controlling
factor in the maintenance phase is the employer's ability to recognize changes in the client
without being told or prompted by the counselor. This can be brought about by having the
counselor phrase questions which will elicit
verbal responses from the employer concerning
changes in the client's behavior. Once elicited, these responses can be reinforced. The
initial stages of this phase will require contact by the counselor. However, visits can be
less frequent and less regular than during the
development phase.

The key to maintaining employer support
is to facilitate the development of interest
and skills in the employer so he develops
training skills to the extent that he himself can determine what the problem is, how
severe the problem is (record and quantify
the problem behaviors), and what to do about
it. Employer conferences represent a training
device used by counselors to assist employers
in the development and maintenance of training
skills.

Employer Conference

The employer conference is a monthly meeting attended by employers, supervisors, and
vocational personnel who are responsible for
the vocational adjustment of handicapped clients

It is best to limit the conferences to 10 employers and/or supervisors at a given time. These management representatives act as consultants, and the conferences are designed to provide opportunities to discuss specific problems related to the hiring of the handicapped. Employer conferences complement any vocational program and are important in the development and maintenance of interest and skills related to working with handicapped clients. The conference, however, should not be considered a replacement for individual contact and supervision by the vocational counselor. Employer conferences contribute to the success of a training program in many ways, e.g., improved client placement, more adequate supervision of clients, employer identification with the project, acquisition of new work sites, teaching and training implications, aids to employer understanding of workers in general, improved communication, and improved client evaluation.

Improved Client Placement. As a client's work experience is discussed, it is not unusual for an employer to suggest a particular job in his establishment which might be suitable for certain clients with specific limitations. For example, at one employer conference two former employers of a trainee concluded that the client could benefit from a routine job which would allow him to work side by side and in cooperation with another person. Another employer replied, "If that's the case, I'd like to try him on one of my folding machines with the job of folding sheets. All he would have to do is take out the sheets and fold them with the help of another person. I can regulate the machine to run as fast or slow as I want. This should be just the thing he needs."

The situation of how to train and where to place the more limited clients is a serious problem in most vocational programs. As pro-

grams get started, the number of work sites
is limited; therefore, the more restricted
clients are very difficult to place. During
employer conferences it is advisable to discuss specific clients and their limitations.
Usually an employer will volunteer to attempt
to work with a very limited client on a specific job. Some employers will adjust the
duties and tasks of a job to fit the client's
abilities. No one knows more about particular
jobs than employers, and it is interesting
to see how employers communicate among themselves and how they are able to adapt the
tasks to fit an individual client. One specific example of this occurred in a high volume restaurant in which the employer trained
an extremely limited youngster as a garnish
person. Usually a garnish person is required
to move very fast, possess much finger dexterity, and be able to think fast in order
to get the correct garnish on the right sandwiches. This employer divided the garnishing
job into small steps. First, as the sandwiches crossed in front of the handicapped
employee, he was required only to place two
pickles on each sandwich. After doing this
for approximately two weeks, the client was
instructed to place the two pickles on the
sandwich and then add mustard. Next he was
instructed to differentiate between sandwiches which needed pickles and mustard from
sandwiches which needed mayonnaise, lettuce,
and tomato. (Another employee had been garnishing the mayonnaise, lettuce, and tomato
sandwiches while the handicapped client was
learning the pickle and mustard operation.
Thus during the initial weeks of the training
program, the handicapped client only saw and
garnished those sandwiches which needed mustard and pickle.) Over a period of time the
client was able to function adequately in this
job. To give an idea of the number of sandwiches which were handled by the client, this
restaurant would use over 18 dozen buns within
less than an hour. This pace represented over

200 sandwiches per hour for a three hour period.
When the client worked on the work sample, he
handled over 650 sandwiches during the lunch
period.

   More Adequate Supervision of Clients.
Since the conference occurs at a convenient
time when the employers are not distracted
by daily routine, the vocational staff may
easily acquire and disseminate information
about a specific client as well as the project in general. Also, it cannot be overlooked
that some employers learn from fellow employers. An example of this occurred when one
employer mentioned how a client manipulated
the employer into doing some of the client's
work. She explained that, when the client
would slow down to an extremely low production
level on tasks which she disliked, the employer ended up helping or sending another employee to assist the client. On a couple of occasions the employer ended up doing the work
while the client stood and watched. Upon
hearing this, another employer smiled and in-
terrupted the conversation to explain how he
had been manipulated into transporting a client
home. During the winter months the employer
drove the client to the bus stop so that he
would not have to walk in the bad weather.
However, when the weather was pleasant, the
employer still found himself transporting the
client to the bus stop. When the employer
realized he was being manipulated, the client
began staying overtime which caused him to
miss his bus. Thus, the employer was placed
in the situation of transporting the client
all the way home. Needless to say, after the
employers' conference both of these situations
were solved by the respective employers.

   Employer Identification with the Project.
It is important for the employer initially to
feel that he is an intricate part of the rehabilitation team. The employer conference
is an excellent means by which this can be

projected. Also, thank you letters from staff
and clients help to express the importance of
the employer. Allowing employers an opportunity to share experiences informally promotes employer identification with the rehabilitation process.

Acquisition of New Work Sites. As an
active member of his community, the employer
has frequent associations with other employers
in both social and professional realms. It
is not uncommon for participating employers
to invite other employers to attend the employer conferences. As the vocational program
is discussed, the new employers frequently
offer work samples and placement sites. Most
employers are members of a variety of civic
organizations, and they often invite a vocational staff member to share information about
the vocational program. Presentations of this
type are excellent for enlisting the participation of new employers.

Teaching and Training Implications. Employer conferences are an excellent source for
obtaining ideas about teaching job related
activities and skills. On one occasion a
client was working at a high volume ice cream
parlor, and it was discovered that she was
experiencing difficulty in making correct
change. Previously the client had gone through
a comprehensive change making instructional
unit. Even though the client had successfully
completed the unit, she still made mistakes on
the job. As the problem was discussed among
the employers, one employer suggested that,
since the mistakes were always under five
cents, perhaps she could not read the tax
chart. Upon further investigation it was discovered that the client was confused on the
proper procedure for using the tax chart.
Many different types of tax charts were secured and a tax chart subunit was added to
the change making instructional unit.

Aids to Employer Understanding of Workers
in General. Employers frequently mention that
what they learn at the employer conferences is
directly applicable to other employees. Careful observation and simple methods of treatment, as exemplified in the behavior management approach, are essential to good training
and evaluation for all workers. In other words,
employers are discovering that the methods
which work for handicapped clients are excellent techniques to use with their regular employees.

Improved Communication. Improved communication between vocational staff and employers is probably the most important aspect
of the employer conference. Terminology used
by the professional rehabilitation staff is
not always understood by participating employers. An example of this is the manner in
which employers toss around the term "initiative" as if it were understood by all concerned. Actually, initiative means different
things in different businesses. To some employers, the term "self-starter" would coincide
with initiative and to others initiative means
starting to work on time and working without
being told. Initiative may also mean willing-
ness to work overtime. Through the employer
conference both the employer and the vocational rehabilitation staff find common ground for
communication.

Improved Client Evaluation. The evaluation and feedback concerning a client's job
performance is vital for program improvement.
As employers learn to observe and record specific behaviors which occur on the job, the
foundation for an accurate and beneficial
evaluation has been established. Evaluation
techniques are constantly under revision and
through employer conferences these techniques
are refined. Because of the importance of
developing effective evaluation and follow-up
procedures, the next chapter will be devoted
to the development of these necessary skills.

REFERENCES

Payne, J. S. Kansas vocation rehabilitation
and special education cooperative project. In J. D. Chaffin, L. Edwards, &
F. Hudson (Eds.), Workshop on cooperative
development of vocational rehabilitation
services to the handicapped in public
schools. Lawrence, Kansas: University
of Kansas, 1966.

Pinner, J. I. New York State employment service's experience in placing the mentally
retarded. In the Woods Schools, Outlook
for the adult retarded. Langhorne, Pennsylvania: The Woods Schools, 1960.

7. EVALUATION AND FOLLOW-UP

An important facet of any vocational program is obtaining information about the client
in a job situation. At the present time many
vocational programs use a check sheet which,
in some cases, is given to the employer or
direct supervisor to complete. This type of
evaluation sheet covers a number of general
areas which will be discussed later. However,
first it is of benefit to discuss the rationale
for work evaluations and their uses.

In the Minneapolis program (Project 681)
it is stated that 77 of 138 terminated clients
were released from their jobs because of inadequate attitudes and motivation patterns.
Thirty were dismissed because of their inability to handle their job duties and instructions. Other projects have described
similar reasons for job terminations, and thus
the evaluation and employer feedback are vital
if fewer failures are to be experienced.

In the field of rehabilitation, learning
is frequently by trial and error. However,
because of the communication barrier or break-
down between the placement person and the employer, it is extremely difficult to learn
from the client's mistakes. Many times the
employer is unable to interpret the mistakes
in specific terms which can be communicated

132

to the client. Feedback and interpretation
of problems are of paramount importance and
provide the rationale for evaluation sheets
and follow-up sessions. Also, it should be
mentioned that the knowledge gained from evaluation and follow-up sessions can be used in
formal training sessions prior to placement
on a community work sample. This information
is invaluable to the development of a vocational curriculum. It is realized that rehabilitation has progressed throughout the
years, and many excellent employer-counselor
relationships have been established; however,
even with these excellent relationships, it
is rare for counselors to receive meaningful
evaluations.

Employers usually know their jobs and
people better than anyone else, but their
ability to communicate specific problems and
reasons for client failure on the job is
usually limited. Sometimes an employer is
too busy to report either orally or in written
form a long detailed account concerning the
success or failure of a client. Many times,
if the client is a success, the employer is
happy and sees little reason for an evaluation. If the client is unsuccessful, the employer sometimes has a tendency to evaluate
him in general terms, such as, "He lacks motivation," "He is lazy," or "He just can't cut
the mustard." When a client is terminated for
nonspecific reasons, it is difficult to improve the client's working ability because
the specific reason for failure has not been
conveyed.

How does a counselor train or counsel a
client who lacks motivation or just cannot
cut the mustard? Even though the most conscientious employer knows the client is failing, he finds it difficult to express himself
and state specific objective reasons for the
client's failure.

The following example of a client working
in a grocery store serves to elucidate the
communication problem between counselor and
employer. After two weeks on the job, a follow-up session with the employer revealed
that the client was functioning below average.
The employer diligently tried to explain why
the client was failing. However, after one
hour the only reason actually discovered was
that the client was not working as fast as
other employees. The reason given by the employer for this slow pace was that the client
lacked motivation and was distractible. This
was difficult for the placement person to believe because, during a counseling session
with the client, the client frequently expressed a strong liking of the job, the employer, etc. It was suggested to the employer
that he carry a small piece of paper in his
shirt pocket and make note of the client's
inappropriate behavior. Two days later another follow-up session occurred, and the employer's list revealed that the client reported to work on time but did not start working until 15 minutes after the starting time.
Also, it mentioned that the client did not
properly rotate stock and many times he was
found reading magazines. Later in the conversation with the employer it was discovered
that the employer thought these were motivation factors because the client never looked
busy and was not producing. When the client
got off work that day, the counselor emphasized to him that people not only report to
work a little before starting time but also
start working on time. Also, reasons for
stock rotation were explained in detail and
examples were given. When the magazine problem was discussed, it was discovered that the
reading of magazines on the job had nothing
to do with motivation, boredom, or distracti-
bility. In actuality, the client did not
know what to do next and saw nothing wrong
with looking at magazines. The counselor then
explained that the client should talk to his

employer about this, and if the client could
not think of work to do he should consult his
immediate supervisor. Needless to say, improvement was observed and reported to the
counselor by the employer and much was gained
by all concerned.

Many times an employer will give only
one reason for a client's failure or lack of
success, but after probing into the situation
other reasons will be found to exist. In
fact, usually many reasons exist, especially
ones which seem small and insignificant when
considered by themselves. However, after
putting many of these small reasons together,
an accumulation occurs and each small reason
becomes quite valid.

If a handicapped client is to succeed,
he must perform satisfactorily. According
to Scott, Dawis, England, and Lofquist (1960),

> Satisfactoriness is indicated by be-
> havioral criteria; such as produc-
> tivity, efficiency, absenteeism, dis-
> ciplinary problems, etc. The litera-
> ture indicates that the measurements
> of these criteria now available tend
> to fluctuate over time. Reliance on
> such measures taken at one point in
> time may be misleading. Work adjust-
> ment patterns may differ for different
> occupations. The set of criteria
> that is relevant may differ from oc-
> cupation to occupation. Even if the
> set of relevant criteria were the
> same, the pattern of inter-relation-
> ships among the criteria may differ
> (pp. 57-58).

This is exemplified by a client who consistently reported and started to work 15 minutes
prior to his regular working time. However,
as a union worker, he was forced to begin work
at the regular starting time.

Because job related activities vary and
differ between and among jobs, it is difficult to teach specific tasks which will gen-
eralize to a job. Basically there are two
major problems involved in teaching work tasks
or work related activities: (a) if the tasks
and/or activities are taught in general terms
or at an abstract level, clients are seldom
able to apply them to actual work, and (b) if
a task and/or activity is specifically taught,
the skill may not be transferable to the job
on which the client is placed. For instance,
many clients may be taught how to mop a floor.
They all are taught how to mop in a specific
way and learn a specific method for mopping
a floor. However, when they go to work on a
job, the clients may have to learn a new method
because the particular place of business requires that it be done in a different way or
with different equipment. This is paradoxical
since job skills are learned best through
specific examples, but many times the specifics are not transferable to jobs. How can
this problem be solved?

Possibly the best advice is to recommend
that the client be taught job related tasks
and skills in a variety of situations with a
variety of equipment. With this approach he
learns that there is no one way to perform a
task but that for each place of business there
is one accepted way to do it. This has been
referred to as contextualistic teaching. It
is taught that in one context things are done
one way and in another context another way.
Rather than teaching mopping one way with one
set of equipment, the skill of mopping should
be taught in a variety of ways with many different kinds of equipment. By being taught
in a contextualistic fashion, the client learns
how to think, adapt, and problem solve.

When evaluating, it is necessary to consider the source of the evaluation. One might
ask, "Why does the evaluation have to come

from the employer or direct supervisor?" In
some projects the entire evaluation is done
by the client. In other words, the client is
asked how he is doing and this information is
used for the evaluation. This may be of value
but, "The client whose limitations often affect his perceptions of how well or poorly he
may be doing on the job also fails to enlist
the aid of the counselor until after he has
quit impulsively or has been dismissed (Dubrow,
1960, p. 54)." Often the client may think he
is doing very well but the employer reports a
different story.

For example, there was a client working
as a busboy in a restaurant. After two weeks
a follow-up session with the restaurant employer was initiated. This follow-up session
with the employer was initiated after a counseling session had been held with the client.
During the client's counseling session, the
client verbalized how well he liked the job
and how well he was doing. However, during
the employer follow-up session, the employer
reported that the client was doing a poor job
and had to be told to bus a table every time
somebody got up to leave the restaurant. When
the employer was asked if he had discussed
this directly with the client, he stated that
he had and that the client was told specifically that he was not doing the job. Later
in the conversation the employer revealed that
he personally had told the client repeatedly
to clean off certain tables. The employer
had assumed that after about the two hundredth
time he had told this to his employee that the
client would figure out that every time somebody got up from a table to leave the restaurant he was to bus that particular area. Needless to say, the client was unable to understand this. In fact, the client felt that he
was doing a good job because the employer was
paying so much attention to him.

Another similar example was that of a
client in a grocery store. One task was to

take a pile of potatoes and place them into
small sacks so they would weigh 10 pounds each.
During counseling sessions, the client expressed a strong like for the job and his employer, and he explained that he felt he was
doing a terrific job. However, during a follow-up session the employer stated that the
client was working at an extremely low rate
of speed. When the employer was asked if he
had discussed the situation with the client
directly, he assured the counselor that he
had. The employer stated that he definitely
had told the client in such a way that he was
sure the client understood. He went on to
give this example. It seems as though the
client was sacking potatoes in the storeroom
in a very slow fashion. When the employer
noticed how slowly the client was working, he
stepped over very close to him, placed his
hands on his hips, looked the client in the
eye, and said, "Boy, these potatoes are getting
expensive." Then he walked away. The employer could not see how this could be interpreted
any other way than that the client was doing
a poor job. The client, however, thought it
was good that the price of potatoes was increasing because the employer would make more
money.

If the placement person had not done some
probing and questioning, these important details would have not been discovered. These
examples illustrate that the evaluation must
come from sources other than the client. This
is not to say that client self-evaluations are
unimportant, but they cannot be used exclusive
of other evaluations. It is not practical nor
feasible for the vocational counselor to observe the client directly over lengthly periods of time and conduct the evaluation alone.
This leaves the employer as an informant, and
this may be the best plan because ultimately
employers are the people whom the clients have
to satisfy. It should be emphasized that many
times the employers have the needed information,

but it has been demonstrated that this information, for the most part, is difficult to
obtain mainly because of a communications
factor.

To enhance the communication process between the employer and the counselor, it is
often necessary to use evaluation sheets.
Evaluation sheets usually list a variety of
factors and the employer is asked to rate the
client on a variety of work dimensions. Most
check lists for evaluating handicapped clients
on jobs use the following factors: (a) ability
to follow directions or understand work,
(b) ability to get along with co-workers as
well as supervisors, (c) ability to work stead-
ily or to sustain routine, (d) interest or
motivation, (e) ability to meet production
schedule or complete work on time, (f) punctuality or attendance, (g) personal hygiene
or neatness and cleanliness, and (h) concept
of self or self-confidence (See Tables 1, 2,
and 3 for Check List Evaluation Forms). Other
factors which are mentioned less often but may
be of extreme importance are: (a) initiative,
(b) safety consciousness, (c) ability to mind
own business, (d) quality of work, (e) ability
to work unsupervised, (f) trustworthiness or
honesty, (g) correct use of tools, (h) ability
to communicate, (i) ability to perform simple
counting, and (j) ability to perform simple
reading. The main difficulty with the check
sheet type of evaluation seems to be that the
items are too general to get a true and accurate picture of the client's performance or
behavior. Also, the terms used may have an
entirely different meaning to the employer
than they do to vocational personnel. Another
major problem with the traditional evaluation
sheet is that some of the factors which must
be rated by the employer are factors which are
taken for granted by him. An example of this
would be the item of punctuality or reporting
to work on time. It is assumed that when the
employer hires the client he will arrive at

Table 1
Check List Evaluation

Client _____   Date _____

	EXCELLENT	GOOD	AVERAGE	NOT SATISFACTORY
Ability to follow directions				
Ability to take correction				
Ability to sustain routine				
Ability to get along with others				
Interest in work				
Work finished on time				
Attendance				
Punctuality				
Ability to work unsupervised				
Cooperation during rush periods and overtime				
Responsibility toward company property and equipment				
Personal appearance				
Willingness to work steadily				
Sees things to be done				
Overall progress				

_____
EMPLOYER

Table 2
Check List Evaluation

Trainee _____   Date _____

	ALWAYS	USUALLY	SOMETIMES	SELDOM	NEVER
Understands directions					
Sustains a routine					
Accepts pressure					
Accepts criticism					
Gets along with super- visors and co-workers					
Motivated					
Works without supervision					
Observes regulations					
Appropriate appearance					
Meets production schedule					
Is a steady worker					
Does satisfactory work					
Good attention span on job					
Able to reason on job					
Trustworthy					
Uses tools correctly					
Able to express himself					
Does simple counting					
Does simple reading					

Table 3

Check List Evaluation

Trainee's Name

Employer's Name

Address

Date Started

Job Title

Time on Job

Supervisor

	AVERAGE EMPLOYEE			
FACTORS	Less Than	Same As	More Than	Comments

GROUP I PERSONALITY AND SOCIAL ADJUSTMENT

- Self-confidence
- Cheerful
- Cooperates with supervisor
- Cooperates with other employees
- Respects supervisor
- Minds own business
- Accepts criticism
- Mixes socially with other employees
- Neat and clean
- Other

Table 3 (continued)
Check List Evaluation

FACTORS	AVERAGE EMPLOYEE			Comments
	Less Than	Same As	More Than	
GROUP II WORK HABITS & EFFICIENCY				
On time				
Safety conscious				
Careful with materials and property				
Completes work on time				
Quality of work				
Understands work				
Shows initiative				
Other				

Would you be as willing to hire this individual as you would your average applicant if a job were available?

YES _____   PROBABLY _____   PROBABLY NOT _____   NO _____

If above answer is "PROBABLY NOT" or "NO," please answer the following:
Would hire IF ..... (State conditions):

work on time, but there is a strong tendency
to consider punctuality as a plus or bonus
area. Actually, if the client arrives at
work on time means little to the employer because an employee is expected to be at work
on time. Therefore, the only time that this
factor is really valid or pertinent from an
evaluation standpoint is when the client fails
to comply.

Regardless of what evaluation form is
used it is important to reemphasize that when
the information is detailed and objective, it
will be of greater value to the employer, counselor, and client. Many times "follow-up sessions are considered as a passive data gather-
ing process; however, they need and must be
viewed as an active service oriented procedure
(Dubrow, 1960, p. 55)." In an enthusiastic
evaluation follow-up session, it might be of
value to resist the temptation of handing the
employer the evaluation sheet for it might
limit his responses. It is better for the
placement person to have a sheet of paper
divided into three columns. The headings
of the three columns could be: (a) positive
aspects, (b) negative aspects, and (c) solution processes. When the employer discusses
the client's job performance, the counselor
notes the employer's comments in the proper
columns. A form of this kind would be extremely simple and possibly very useful when
handled by a skillful placement person (See
Table 4 for Employer Evaluation and Training
Report).

An example of reporting to work on time
illustrates the use of the three column sheet.
If the person reported to work prior to his
original starting time on a union job, this
would be placed in the negative column, but,
if this were done on any other type of job,
it would probably be placed in the positive
column. Even though most check lists have
places for comments, these comment areas are

Table 4
Employer Evaluation and Training Report

Trainee's Name
Job Title
Date Started
Date Completed
Employer
Name of Business
Address
Phone Number
Informant
Position

POSITIVE ASPECTS	NEGATIVE ASPECTS	SOLUTION PROCESSES

seldom uséd.   There is a definite tendency to
place check marks in the appropriate places
and not write comments. With the three column
evaluation work sheet, comments must be written
since there is nothing to check. With this
type of evaluation form the counselor would
approach the employer with the sheet attached
to a clipboard and begin the evaluation with
any style of questioning which seems comfortable to the counselor-employer situation.
Often a simple question such as, "How is Mary
doing this week?" is enough to begin discussion. As the employer talks, the counselor
makes note of the salient points in the proper
columns. When the employer talks in general
terms such as, "She can't cut the mustard,"
the counselor must seek clarification for
specifics by questioning, "What exactly do
you mean?" or "Could you give me a specific
example of when and how she doesn't cut the
mustard?"

Getting information down on a form of
this type assists the counselor to determine
quickly the client's strengths and weaknesses
and provides information which can be used in
a one-to one counseling session with the client.
The counselor may want the counseling session
to begin with a few positive comments and end
on a positive note. This procedure is sim-
plified by selecting points of discussion
from the applicable column. The three column
evaluation sheet provides a great deal of
flexibility as well as an adequate amount of
structure to the counseling session. Sometimes,
when a client is given negative feedback, he
may become overly depressed or tend to drift
out of contact for awhile. By periodically
injecting positive comments into the discussion, the counselor is able to keep the client
involved. Positive topics for comment and
discussion are readily available from the
three column evaluation sheet.

For the inexperienced counselor it may
be necessary to provide more structure to the

evaluation session. The counselor may have
difficulty getting the employer to discuss the
client. When this happens, an outline of
possible evaluation factors may help the counselor to ask specific questions (See Table 5
for Possible Evaluation Factors). These evaluation factors are general and are ones often
used by employers. Thus, when the employer
responds to these items, the counselor may
want to explore the area in more detail. For
instance, the counselor might ask, "Do you
feel that the client is self-confident?" Regardless of the employer's response, the counselor must ask next if this factor is important
to the client's job performance. After determining its importance, the counselor may want
to ascertain the client's specific behavior
which reflects self-confidence. In essence,
the three key words in evaluation procedures
are adaptability, flexibility, and specificity.

It is important for the counselor to remember that when the client is experiencing
difficulty on the job the counselor has three
major alternatives: (a) change the client,
(b) change the job, or (c) change the employer. For example, an employer in a gasoline
station stated that the client was not motivated and lacked initiative. The client verbalized that he liked the job and wished to
continue. Later it was found that the "nonmotivation" and "lack of initiative" were projected by the client's not smiling and drag-
ging his feet when he walked to a car. In
fact, the soles of his shoes had holes in them
and the heels were worn down. It would be
possible to teach the client to maintain good
posture, not drag his feet, and smile more
while on the job. These would be ways to
change the client. The client's job could be
changed by requiring the client to pump gas
on a night shift when it is permissible to
walk slowly and look tired, or the client
could find another occupation which would be
more acceptable to his behaviors. Lastly,

Table 5
Possible Evaluation Factors

I.   Individual
     A.   Self-confidence (realistic)
     B.   Disposition
     C.   Appearance (clean, appropriate)

II. Relations with Co-Workers
     A.   Cooperation
     B.   Attitude
     C.   Interpersonal

III. Relations with Management and/or Cus-
     tomers
     A.   Cooperation
     B.   Attitude
     C.   Interpersonal
     D.   Criticism (effective)

IV. Vocational Expectations
     A.   Attitude
     B.   Distractible
     C.   Punctual
     D.   Careful with property

V.   Vocational Bonus Abilities
     A.   Initiative (specific examples)
     B.   Perseverance
     C.   Production
          1.   Rate
          2.   Quality
          3.   Comprehension
          4.   Efficiency

the employer could be changed. This refers
to changing the employer's attitude or perspective of the situation. It could be explained to the employer that the client actually enjoys his job but he comes from a home
in which all of the family members drag their
feet and do not smile. Some employers will
accept this and continue to employ the client.
Others will retain the client but alter his
duties so he has less customer contact. Finally, there are employers who would say, "I
don't care where he comes from. I just want
him to pick up his feet, walk straight, and
smile." With this type of employer, it may
be feasible to place the client on another
job under a different employer.

REFERENCES

Dubrow, M.   On-the-job assistance.   In The
     Woods Schools, Outlook for the adult
     retarded.   Langhorne, Pennsylvania: The
     Woods Schools, 1960.

Retarded youth: Their school rehabilitation
     needs.   Research and Demonstration Proj-
     ect 681 sponsored by Minneapolis Public
     Schools, Federal Vocational Rehabilita-
     tion Administration, March, 1965.

Scott, T. B., Dawis, R. V., England, G. W., &
     Lofquist, L. H.   A definition of work
     adjustment.   Minnesota Studies in Voca-
     tional Rehabilitation, 1960, 10(30).

8. VOCATIONAL ADJUSTMENT IN PERSPECTIVE

Throughout this section of the book an array of techniques and suggestions has been presented which focused on developing the skills of handicapped individuals to the extent that they are employable in a job which they enjoy. By now it is apparent that the helping professions (educators, rehabilitation personnel, social workers, psychologists, etc.) share the common goal of assisting in the attainment of vocational success for individuals in our society whose career development is restricted as a result of a disabling condition. This common concern is readily justified when the impact that a job has on a person's life style is considered. In order to evolve a functional perspective of vocational adjustment this chapter presents a discussion of (a) the importance of job choice, (b) the nature of jobs, and (c) the conditions of job adjustment.

Job Selection

The selection of an occupation often determines whether an individual will be employed or unemployed. If a client selects a job which has historically remained stable, he will increase the likelihood that he will be employed while others are unemployed. Striking differences in unemployment occur among the different

industries during periods of economic recession. For example, Hoppock (1967) reported
that in April, 1961, "18 percent of the workers in construction were unemployed, but only
6 percent of those in transportation and public utilities and only 2 percent of those in
government were out of work (p. 1)."

The choice of a job may determine whether
the client succeeds or fails. The abilities
required for successful job performance vary
from job to job. If a client chooses a job
which uses his strengths and minimizes his
weaknesses, he increases his probability of
success and advancement.

The choice of a job frequently determines
whether a client enjoys or detests work. Although work has historically been considered
the albatross that people must bear, it is
possible for people to select jobs which are
pleasurable and highly satisfying. Job satisfaction and pleasure are more easily understood when the emotional dimensions of a job
are considered. Frankwood F. Williams, medical director of the National Committee for
Mental Hygiene, discussed the emotional side
of work in the following passage:

> One's job must furnish an out-
> let suitable to one's particular,
> personal emotional needs. The great-
> est part of one's emotional life is
> lived in one's job, not elsewhere,
> as is commonly supposed. Different
> professions and vocations ... offer
> quite different emotional outlets;
> even specialties within a profession
> offer different outlets. One may
> be more than adequately equipped
> intellectually, and with special
> ability for a given profession, but
> if that profession does not offer
> the emotional outlet peculiar to
> one's own needs, unhappiness and

discontent follow (Hoppock, 1967,
p. 2).

The choice of an occupation greatly influences the life style of a person. For example, a job may determine: (a) where a person lives, (b) with whom he associates, (c) his
income, (d) where his children go to school,
(e) his mental and physical health, and (f) the
amount of time he has for family and avocational pursuits (Hoppock, 1967).

Finally, job choice is paramount to the
functioning of a democratic society. In a
democratic society each individual has the
opportunity to select his occupation. However,
this freedom of choice threatens the welfare
of the nation when too few people select an
occupation and create shortages in critical
jobs, e.g., physicians, mechanics, teachers,
and farmers. These types of problems are al-
leviated when people are provided with comprehensive and current occupational information. In the case of handicapped clients it
is imperative for them to be provided with extensive occupational information so they can
exercise a freedom of choice within the vocational arena open to them.

The Nature of Jobs

The Dictionary of Occupational Titles
alphabetically lists over 21,741 job titles.
These job titles are organized within nine
occupational categories which are delineated
as follows:
1. Professional, technical, and managerial
occupations.
2. Clerical and sales occupations.
3. Service occupations.
4. Farming, fishing, and forestry occupations.
5. Processing occupations.
6. Machine trades.
7. Bench work occupations.
8. Structural work occupations.
9. Miscellaneous occupations.

The complex nature of jobs in a modern
society is enough to stagger the beginning
counselor's imagination. However, this myriad
of job information becomes manageable when the
counselor considers that the handicapped client's job choices are restricted by: (a) what
is available, (b) what the client can do; and
(c) what the client will do. With these three
criteria in mind it is helpful for the counselor to view the nature of jobs in his community within a skill framework which includes
five job levels--unskilled, semiskilled, skilled, professional-technical, and managerial.
The nature of a client's handicap often restricts the types of jobs available to him.
For example, a mentally retarded client is
usually confined to unskilled and semiskilled
occupations. Thus a counselor would provide
job choices to a mentally retarded client by
determining the availability in the community
of unskilled and semiskilled jobs which the
client would consent to do.

In order for the counselor to afford clients the opportunity to choose from an array
of appropriate jobs, it is necessary for the
counselor to ascertain extensive occupational
information. On a local basis the counselor
may acquire occupational information from the
chamber of commerce, state employment office,
professional associations, labor unions, newspaper ads, telephone directory, plant surveys,
and personnel managers. Although the occupational information that the counselor obtains
within the community setting is very helpful,
it is frequently necessary for the counselor
to supplement it with other sources of occupational information. For example, a client
may need job information to help him explore
various careers and guide his decision concerning which vocational training program he
should choose. Some of these sources of occupational information are:
1. The Dictionary of Occupational Titles,
(3rd ed.), Vol. I. Definitions of Titles;

Vol. II. Occupational Classification and Industry Index. Washington, D. C.: Government Printing Office, 1965 (See new editions as issued).
2. Occupational Outlook Handbook. Washington, D. C.: Government Printing Office (See latest edition).
3. The Counselor's Guide to Occupational and Other Manpower Information. Washington, D. C.: Government Printing Office (See editions as issued).
4. Current and back issues of journals and periodicals in the fields of counseling and vocational education, e.g., Career Index, published periodically by Chronicle Guidance Publications, Inc., Moravia, New York.

As the counselor begins to tap the vast resources of occupational information, he encounters a problem in storing and retrieving it. The organization of the information is often crucial to a counselor's effectiveness. The classification system employed by The Dictionary of Occupational Titles offers a comprehensive format for organizing occupational information. However, many counselors choose to organize their occupational files according to a different format. Hoppock (1967) provided an extensive list of how jobs can be categorized to fit the counselor's preferences. Hoppock's list includes:

Jobs may be classified according to the activities involved, such as selling, teaching, typing.
Jobs may be classified according to their function, such as research, finance, manufacturing, distribution, education.
Jobs may be classified according to the product which they produce, such as automobiles, chemicals, steel.
Jobs may be classified according to the employer, for example

American Cyanamic, General Electric,
F. W. Woolworth.
Jobs may be classified according to the expressed interests of
students or clients.
Jobs may be classified according to measured interest patterns,
such as artistic, computational,
persuasive.
Jobs may be classified according to the school subjects which help
to prepare workers for them, such as
mathematical, musical, scientific.
Jobs may be classified in other
ways that may occur to the reader and
in still other ways that have not yet
been conceived (p. 58).

Job Adjustment

The counselor is constantly charged with
the responsibility of (a) predicting the job
performance of clients, and (b) assisting with
the evaluation of the client's performance
once he is on the job. This responsibility
makes it necessary for the counselor to acquire
an understanding of the parameters involved in
job adjustment. A perusal of the vocational
literature concerning factors which contribute
to job success provides a multitude of variables crucial to vocational adjustment. However, the long lists of variables that appear
germane to job adjustment tend to confuse
counselors. Thus it is imperative for the
counselor to acquire a gestalt of the job adjustment phenomena. In essence, the counselor
must develop a conceptual framework of job
adjustment which enables him to organize the
matrix of variables into a meaningful pattern.
The following job adjustment model features
work personality, general job skills, and
specific job skills. Within the boundaries
of these areas the model provides a comprehensive and pragmatic framework for examining
the conditions of job adjustment which are
applicable across job situations.

Work Personality

Many writers (Peck & Stephens, 1964; Peterson & Jones, 1964; Warren, 1961) have acknowledged the importance of personality variables in relation to job success. Although a preponderance of variables exists concerning the importance of personality variables to job success, it is possible to categorize them into three areas: (a) relating to others, (b) relating to things, and (c) relating to self.

Relating to others encompasses the client's ability to work effectively with peers, bosses, customers, and others. Specifically, variables which may be categorized under relating to others are:
1.   Reaction to supervision.
2.   Relations with co-workers.
3.   Consideration for others.
4.   Social acumen.
5.   Adaptation to different social groups.
6.   Relations with family.

Many workers fail in job situations because they have not developed the ability to relate effectively with things. Specific variables that may be grouped under relating to things are:
1.   Ability to respond to work pressure.
2.   Neatness of work.
3.   Care of property.
4.   Ability to work in a safe manner.
5.   Ability to judge time.
6.   Ability to value time.

Finally, many workers experience difficulty on jobs because they are unable to relate to themselves effectively. Specific variables which may be grouped under relating to self are:
1.   Using one's abilities.
2.   Opinion of self.
3.   Personal appearance.

4. Personal hygiene.
5. Self-control.
6. Realistic goals.
7. Ability to handle misfortune.
8. Honesty.
9. Motivation.

General Job Skills

As with personality factors a multitude
of lists exists which are related to general
job skills. However, the factors relating to
general job skills may be classified into
three areas: (a) education, (b) mental capacity, and (c) physical capacity.

Education refers to the development of
basic academic skills and the education level
specific to particular occupations. Basic
academic skills include:
1. Expressive communication skills, i.e.,
speaking and writing.
2. Receptive communication skills, i.e.,
listening and reading.
3. Arithmetic skills, i.e., computation and
reasoning.

Education level as it refers to occupational clusters includes:
1. College degree for professional and managerial careers.
2. Technical school for careers at the skilled
level.
3. High school diploma for most jobs at the
skilled and semiskilled levels.
4. Upper elementary level education for most
jobs at the unskilled level.

Many clients are unable to succeed in
certain jobs because of a limited mental capacity. Mental capacity refers to the ability
to problem solve, exercise discretion, etc.
Some specific variables which may be classified under mental capacity are:

1.   Memory.
2.   Following directions.
3.   Logic development.

Finally, physical capacity represents a variable which is highly related to job success. Professional sports best illustrate the profession which places a premium on physical capacity. Factors which may be classified under physical capacity are:
1.   Manual dexterity.
2.   Finger dexterity.
3.   Body coordination.
4.   Stamina.
5.   General health.

Specific Job Skills

Specific job skills represent the third major area in the work adjustment model which is illustrated in Table 1. Specific job skills refer to the development of skills which are specific to a particular job, i.e., auto mechanic training for auto mechanics. Many vocational programs mistakenly only consider this aspect of job adjustment, and they launch programs in comprehensive vocational facilities without portioning time for the development of work personality and general job skills.

An examination of the vocational adjustment model readily reveals that it provides the counselor with a simple but comprehensive framework for examining the adjustment of clients to jobs. In addition to presenting job adjustment criteria the model may serve as a foundation for organizing a comprehensive career education program.

Summary

This chapter presented a perspective of occupational adjustment couched within the headings of job selection, the nature of jobs, and job adjustment.

Table 1
Job Adjustment Model

Job Adjustment	=	Work Personality	+	General Job Skills	+	Specific Job Training
		Relating to Others		Education		e.g., auto-mechanic training for auto mechanics
		Relating to Things		Mental Capacity		
		Relating to Self		Physical Capacity		

The ramifications of job selection were discussed in terms of stable employment, job success or failure, job satisfaction, an individual's life style, and the democratic process. The nature of jobs was represented as they are categorized in The Dictionary of Occupational Titles as well as on the basis of job levels--unskilled, semiskilled, skilled, technical, and managerial-professional. Finally, a job adjustment model was presented which features three major categories: (a) work personality, (b) general job skills, and (c) specific job skills. As we move to the next section, the emphasis shifts to a concentration on educational strategies and rehabilitation services which are aimed at minimizing or preventing the debilitating effects of disabling conditions on individuals of all ages.

REFERENCES

Hoppock, R. Occupational information. (3rd ed.) New York: McGraw-Hill, 1967.

Peck, J. R., & Stephens, W. B. Success of young adult male retardates. Cooperative Research Project No. 1533. Austin: University of Texas, 1964.

Peterson, R. O., & Jones, E. M. Guides for jobs for the mentally retarded. Pittsburgh: American Institute for Research, 1964.

Warren, F. G. Ratings of employed and unemployed mentally handicapped males on personality and work factors. American Journal of Mental Deficiency, 1961, 65, 629-633.

Section III

OVERVIEW OF SERVICES

9. EARLY INTERVENTION

The first two sections of this book have
focused on the rehabilitation of persons entering the job market. Attention now is directed toward preventive rehabilitation methods. Preventive rehabilitation programs are
educational in nature and most vocational rehabilitation personnel refer to these efforts
as habilitation programs.

Though both rehabilitation and habilitation efforts are directed toward growth of
the individual, the timing of the intervention
strategy defines the particular process. Rehabilitation refers to restoring the handicapped individual to an optimum state of functioning for useful employment. The clients
in a rehabilitation program typically are in
their late teens or early adult years. Habilitation, on the other hand, refers to the
preventive aspects of education. Thus, habilitation programs usually focus on younger individuals.

Habilitation projects can be divided into
two broad categories: career education and
early intervention. Traditionally, career education programs have been confined to the junior and senior high school years. Today, however, the career education movement includes
within its target population children in the

early education grades. The main task of
these strategies is to expose children to the
number of alternative careers and vocational
programs. The relevance of career education
for younger children will be specifically discussed in the next chapter. This chapter discusses early intervention which focuses on
enhancing the cognitive development of children by attempting either to reverse loss or
halt declines in cognitive performance.

In order to conceptualize the immense
importance of early intervention, a comprehensive review of the effects an impoverished
environment has on young individuals in presented. Prior to a discussion of studies related to humans, an overview of selected research with animals which accentuates the role
of environmental stimulation is outlined. Although some educators and rehabilitation personnel may question the relevance of animal
research, the findings provide a sound rationale for the importance of early experiences
relative to early intervention.

Animal Deprivation and Enrichment Studies

The literature on animal research provides an opportunity for underscoring the importance of early experience. The types of
experimental situations in animal research
involve either the addition or restriction of
certain types of stimulation. At the human
level rarely does one find this type of experimental manipulation. Two barriers inhibit
conducting this type of research with humans.
First, in order to manipulate the necessary
variables, investigators must go into the
natural habitats of the homes, day care centers, nurseries, institutions, and orphanages.
The natural setting, while providing a unique
picture of life, creates the additional problem of lack of control over experimental variables. For this reason inferences drawn from
these studies must be tempered with restraint.

A second barrier involves moral and lawful considerations. Neither ethically nor legally would society (nor should society) condone extreme manipulation of the environment. For these reasons the literature on animal studies is directly relevant to a discussion of early experience.

The theorizing of Hebb, in his book, The Organization of Behavior (1949), which emphasizes early experience for neurological development, stimulated a research movement designed to question and determine the effects of restriction and enrichment on learning (Thompson & Grusec, 1970). His main proposition stated that adult learning depends on the kind of learning which occurred early in life. In testing the validity of his position Hebb compared the performance of two differently reared groups of rats. The experimental group included rats which were home reared as pets, whereas the control group were laboratory rats reared in cages. Comparisons on the Hebb-Williams maze task found the home reared rats, which had a more enriched environment, superior in performance on the problem solving task. Other researchers (Forgays & Forgays, 1952), associates of Hebb from McGill University, have confirmed Hebb's basic findings. Data showed that a richer environment, one with more space and a greater opportunity for sensory stimulation, increased problem solving ability on the Hebb-Williams maze task.

Experiments similar to Hebb's have been conducted with other animal species. Thompson and Heron (1954) investigated the effects of different rearing conditions involving various forms of restriction on Scottish Terriers. Three different deprivation conditions were used with 13 dogs: (a) two were raised in complete isolation without the benefit of seeing or hearing other dogs or humans for eight months; (b) eight were in cages where they could hear and smell but could not see other

dogs or humans; and (c) three were deprived
as any laboratory animal is typically restricted. The control group included 13 dogs reared
as pets. Four months after termination of the
deprivation condition, the animals were tested
and the Terriers in the control group performed
significantly better on all the problem solving
measures.

A second area of research related to early
experience involves imprinting. Konrad Lorenz,
a well-known European psychologist, has contributed to our knowledge of imprinting with
such animals as ducks, chickens, and geese
(Sluckin, 1964). In animal populations, imprinting describes how social attachment is
formed between the mother and her offspring.
With birds, the hatchling, after initial perception of an object in its environment, develops a permanent attachment to that object
which usually is the mother. Related to the
topic of imprinting is the concept of a critical or sensitive period which describes a
permanent effect of early experience. Based
on certain rules of maturation and growth,
specific responses and behaviors are irre-
versibly learned during a particular period.
Conversely, failure to acquire these behaviors
during this period implies that these responses
will not be learned.

In a review of social deprivation studies
with dogs, Scott and Fuller (1965) observed
the social attachment between mother and puppy
and found that social attachment was strongest
between six and eight weeks of age. From an
accumulation of other research, Scott and
Fuller defined the period between four and
14 weeks of age as a critical period in developing socialization behavior in dogs. Isolation from the mother or lack of contact with
any other living organism during this period
would predispose the animal to later maladap-
tive social behavior. Consistent with this
position, Freedman, King, and Elliot (1961)

reported that dogs isolated during this period never developed normal social behaviors.

Various social deprivation experiments have also been conducted with primates. In this area of social restriction the work of Harlow (1965) at the Wisconsin Primate Laboratory represents the greatest concentration of effort. In a series of investigations, Harlow observed the effect surrogate "parents" had on the social and learning performance of the monkey. Surrogate rearing severely crippled the capacity for successful breeding, and those females which did breed became poor mothers. The females did not adequately care for their offspring and behaved either in an apathetic or violent manner to their children. The repeated attempts at attachment behavior by the young led to continual rejection or physical abuse. In a second series of studies, Harlow investigated the influence of social isolation over time. Early social isolation resulted in a deficit in social behavior and temperament. These monkeys were more unstable and socially immature than normally raised monkeys. Those isolated for the longest period between six and 12 months showed the greatest deviations. Specifically, the potential for any lasting social interaction was absent. Typically the behavior of these monkeys was characterized by autistic actions and an aversion to physical contact with any peer.

As stated earlier, the study of early experience with animals provides a pathway into the study of early human experiences. From this discussion two essential points emerge.
1. Presented with a given genotype (genetic endowment), the environment acting in either an enriching or restrictive manner greatly influences the social and learning performance of the organism.
2. Learning in the present is greatly effected by experiences which occurred earlier in life.

The last point to be made in this section on animal studies concerns the importance of intervention in an organism's environment. In developing her own rationale, Caldwell (1970) draws inferential justification for early intervention from a review of animal literature. She stated, "The animal literature suggests that the critical time for manipulation of experiences is during the early infancy of the animals under study (p. 719)."

Human Deprivation Studies

Unlike the deprivation and enrichment studies with animals, the human literature does not come from laboratory research. As previously cited, ethical and moral considerations dictate against the use of children as experimental subjects. For this reason much of the early experience literature measures the effect that unusual child rearing practices have on later cognitive and social behavior. The main research, therefore, comes from children reared in institutions and in culturally deprived environments.

In one of the earliest studies, Spitz (1945) compared the developmental records of infants from two different institutions. In one case the youngsters were offspring of delinquent girls living in a penal institution and attending a special day nursery. Here an attempt was made to emulate the typical home environment. In the second institution the children were separated from their mothers and reared in a foundling home. The difference between the environments, other than the presence or absence of maternal life, was that the foundling home lacked adequate physical care and stimulation. In the foundling home few toys or sensory apparati were present and, thus, the children had little opportunity to interact with stimulating objects. Human contact was also limited to only scheduled feeding from the nurses, and this

exchange may best be characterized as mechanical. In addition, the infants spent a large
period of the day lying in their cribs without
the benefit of visual stimuli. Comparisons
between the two groups showed that the foundling group was lower on all developmental test
measures. Moreover, this group had a dramatic
decrease in scores between the first and third
years. During the second examination retardation was noted in their physical and social
development and in the basic skills of feeding,
dressing, and toilet training. In explaining
the vast difference between the groups, Spitz
attributed the retardation to a lack of mothering.

Another researcher, working independently
of Spitz, came to similar conclusions. Ribble
(1944), following the Freudian tenet that mothering during infancy is needed for the child's
psychological and biological growth, reported
the ill effects of lack of mothering in hun-
dreds of infants. She found that babies lacking in maternal care developed marasmus, a
condition characterized by severe physical
deterioration.

In each instance the causal factor presented for the development of retarded behavior
was lack of mothering. In neither case did
the experimenters consider the physical setting
and the lack of environmental stimulation. The
research came under severe questioning by Pinneau (1950, 1955). The flaws in the investigations were: (a) the statistical analysis and
methods of reporting were inadequate; (b) neither experimenter correctly reported the restricting environments; and (c) the conclusions
were directly influenced by each experimenter's
personal bias.

The viability of the lack of mothering
hypothesis purported by Spitz and Ribble may
be further investigated by examining whether
all institutions inhibit growth. Rheingold

(1956, 1961), in a series of investigations
in which institutionalized reared children
were compared with home reared children, found
no significant differences for either cognitive or social behavior. Dennis and Najarian
(1957), studying infants raised in three institutions, found that institutional life per
se is not directly related to retardation.
The determining factor in each case was the
degree of physical and social deprivation
found in each orphanage. In essence, a shift
in emphasis occurred away from the lack of
mothering hypothesis to the more empirically
documented position that deficits appear in
institutionalized children due to the restricted environment and lack of opportunities to
learn.

The lack of a stimulating environment by
no means is confined to institutional life.
Many of the negative features are descriptive
of inner-city inhabitants and the rural poor
and, in short, are characteristic of the life
style of many lower socioeconomic citizens of
our country. Thus, one factor consistently
related to poor cognitive functioning is a low
socioeconomic profile (Caldwell, 1970).

Coleman and Provence (1957) documented
the restrictive conditions found in lower-class
homes. They studied the life patterns of two
children and illustrated how the environment
reduced the opportunities to learn and led to
retarded growth in language, motor, social,
and cognitive functions. In the much publi-
cized Coleman Report (Coleman, 1966), it was
reported that early experiences in an impoverished environment hindered average school
performance. Minority group and lower socioeconomic status children upon entrance into
first grade scored below the national average
on school performance measures. Deutsch (1963)
reported that these differences seem to widen
with each successive grade, thus becoming a
cumulative deficit.

The negative living characteristics attached to the lower socioeconomic class are
not confined solely to inadequate physical
conditions. Many problems of an experiential
and social nature are typical of the life
style. Hess and Shipman (1965), in comparing
middle- and lower-class families, contended
that different types of parental control influence later cognitive and social behavior.
In general, the lower-class family uses a
manner of control which is less verbal, thus
reducing the child's alternatives for action
and thought. For example, the lower-class
mother is more likely to say, "Shut up!" rather than, "Would you please quiet down? I am
trying to talk to your brother." Over time
this interaction restricts the development of
the child's language and cognitive structures.
Hess and Shipman further reported that parental
actions are governed by different norms. Lower-class parents are motivated by immanent
rules of right and wrong while middle-class
parents attend more to the individual characteristics of the child and specific situations. The relevance of these findings for
the lower-class child is that he does not learn
the consequences of his behavior nor the relation between two continuous events. The child
thus becomes more impulsive and bound to immediate goals rather than developing a reflective anticipation for long range goals. The
inability to perceive cause and effect together with an impulsive tendency is not conducive
to educational performance.

Low socioeconomic homes are deprived in
other ways. In the typical overcrowded walk-
up tenements or single bedroom homes, the infant is apt to be bombarded with visual and
auditory stimuli. In the normal course of
development the child is able to discriminate
the essential aspects of the setting. Unfortunately, in these homes a stabilizing force
is absent and the child fails to organize his
world. When the infant approaches the toddler

age, characterized by unbounded curiosity
about the environment, he is either ignored
or isolated. The learning process is further
attenuated and the child still does not assim-
ilate the essential features of his world
(Hunt, 1961). The continued inability to
discriminate and orient stimuli has a pro-
found influence on the infant and his cognitive performance.

The work of Harvard psychologist Jerome
Kagan (1970) has identified other psychological
differences between the lower-class and more
privileged children. These differences which
emerge during the first three years of life
are stable over time. Kagan has identified
seven major variables: language, mental set,
attachment, inhibition, sense of effectiveness, motivation, and expectancy of failure.
All of these variables directly or indirectly
influence school performance. Deficits in
these areas limit the child in problem solving
situations, as the following example illustrates.

> If an adult presents a different
> puzzle to a 5-year-old middle class
> child, he will work at the task for
> a minute or two and, if he cannot
> solve it, push it toward the adult
> explaining, "I can't do it," "It's
> too hard," or "Let's do something
> else." Despite failure, he makes
> an active response. The poor child
> is less likely to take responsibility
> for terminating this painful experi-
> ence. An examiner might wait 3 or 4
> minutes of interminable silence be-
> fore asking, "Can you do it?" The
> child quietly shakes his head from
> side to side (Kagan, 1970, p. 15).

In conclusion, an environment lacking in
material stimulation and in healthy adult in-
teractions will be deficient in opportunities

to learn. Infants raised in such an environment generally will be retarded in motor, language, cognitive, and social skills. These
deficits will have a limiting effect on school
performance and later career development.

Classic Early Intervention Programs

Concern for the deleterious effects that
an impoverished environment has on child development paved the way for the initial interest in early intervention. The conclusions
drawn from the deprivation studies illustrated
that during the first years of life the environment has a maximum impact on the young
infant. This led to the belief that efforts
to habilitate and/or ameliorate disabilities
would be most effective during this period.
In recognition of the validity of this argu-
ment, the era of massive intervention programs
was crystalized in the mid-1960s with the
birth of the Head Start programs. However,
such a mobilization in resources was predated
by other intervention strategies.

Skeels and Dye (1939), in one of the earliest programs, reported on an effort to reverse the devastating effects of an impoverished environment. The program, which was
unusual in its inception and implementation,
was based on the observation of two infants.
In describing the children, Skeels (1966)
wrote:

> The youngsters were pitiful little
> creatures. They were tearful, had
> runny noses, and sparse, stringy,
> and colorless hair; they were ema-
> ciated, undersized, and lacked muscle
> tonus or responsiveness. Sad and
> inactive, the two spent their days
> rocking and whining (p. 5).

Though their chronological ages were 13 and
16 months, their developmental levels upon

psychological examination were six and seven
months respectively. Recognizing the imprac-
ticability of placing the children with either
foster parents or an adoptive agency, Skeels
and Dye transferred the children to an institution for the mentally retarded. Six months
after the transfer the children were described
as "alert, smiling, running about, responding
to the playful attention of adults and generally behaving and looking like any other tod-
dlers (Skeels, 1966, p. 6)." Repeated observation during follow-up examinations attested
to the reversibility of behavior and the per-
manence of change. Evaluation of the ward
life style provided the answer concerning why
the change occurred. Each girl was "adopted"
by an older re†arded patient who functioned
as a surrogate "mother." The children received the necessary parental care and attention prerequisite for normal development, and
also the appropriate levels of perceptual enrichment and physical stimulation were provided. In time both youngsters were returned
to the orphanage and successfully placed for
adoption.

Based on the knowledge gained from the
program, an enlarged strategy was designed
to empirically determine the significance of
the intervention. Skodak and Skeels (Skeels,
1966) selected 13 children under three years
of age for their study. This group of 13
subjects was composed of 10 girls and three
boys with an average IQ of 64. All but two
children in this group were classified as retarded and were judged by the state law as
unsuitable for adoption. A contrast group
of 12 children under three years of age was
selected for comparative purposes. The control group was composed of four girls and
eight boys with an average IQ of 86. All but
two of these children were classified as in-
tellectually normal.

The control group, for the most part, remained in an orphanage and received adequate

health and nutritional services. The environment was far from stimulating and was described
as meager and desolate. On the other hand,
the 13 experimental subjects were transferred
to Glenwood State School and received care on
a one-to-one basis from adolescent retarded
patients. Each young child was assigned to
an adolescent patient who had been classified
as mentally retarded. Each adolescent "mother"
was given instructions on how to care for her
child. The "mothers" were instructed and
trained on how to hold, feed, change, talk to,
and stimulate the young children. No other
educational experiences were provided for the
children.

Two years later when the groups were re-
tested, the 13 retarded children showed a mean
gain of 28 IQ points. Approximately four and
one-half years from the origin of the study,
11 of the 13 experimental children had IQs
high enough to be selected for adoption and
were thus placed into good homes. In 1965,
25½ years after the original study began, a
follow-up study reported that 11 of the 13
had married and only one of the 11 marriages
had ended in divorce. A total of nine children, all of normal intelligence, were produced
from these adults. Of the 12 contrast children,
one was deceased, two had married, and one of
the two marriages ended in divorce. These
control group adults produced five children,
one of which was diagnosed as mentally retarded
with an IQ of 66. An investigation of educational levels showed that the contrast group
had completed a median of less than three
grades, while the experimental group had completed a median of 12 grades. In the experimental group, four of the subjects had one
or more years of college work. One subject
received a B.A. degree and took some graduate
training. Difference in occupational levels
was also great. In the experimental group
all subjects were self-supporting or married
and functioning as housewives. The control

group's occupations ranged from professional
and business to domestic service for the two
girls who were never placed in adoptive homes.
Four of the subjects in the contrast group
were institutionalized and unemployed. Those
who were employed, with one exception, were
categorized as "hewers of wood and drawers
of water." Skeels (1966) concluded,

> It seems obvious that under present-
> day conditions there are still count-
> less infants with sound biological
> constitutions and potentialities for
> development well within the normal
> range who will become mentally re-
> tarded and noncontributing members
> of society unless appropriate inter-
> vention occurs. It is suggested by
> the findings of this study and others
> published in the past 20 years that
> sufficient knowledge is available to
> design programs of intervention to
> counteract the devastating effects
> of poverty, socio-cultural, and ma-
> ternal deprivation .... The unan-
> swered questions of this study could
> form the basis for many life long re-
> search projects. If the tragic fate
> of the 12 contrast group children pro-
> vokes even a single crucial study
> that will help prevent such a fate
> for others, their lives will not have
> been in vain (pp. 54-55).

A second major study predating the Head
Start movement was conducted by Kirk (1958),
who was interested in measuring the effects
that an enrichment program had on the social
and mental development of retarded preschoolers. Kirk identified 81 retarded subjects
between the ages of three and six with an IQ
range of 45 to 80 points. The children were
placed in four groups. The experimental groups
contained 28 children living at home and attending a special nursery school and 15 chil-

dren residing in an institution for the retarded who also attended a nursery school.
In the control, nonnursery groups were 26
children living at home and 12 children in
an institution. Cognitive measures were taken
periodically and significant differences were
reported between the groups. 'Those in the
enrichment nursery school programs reported
IQ gains ranging between 10 and 30 points,
while those without benefit of a stimulating
environment declined in performance. Over a
period of years the differences were lasting
for each group.

Early Intervention Programs

The success of the aforementioned classic
studies provided an impetus for a proliferation of programs in the early 1960s. In fact,
many of these programs were the precursors of
the later Head Start models. For this reason,
a selected review highlighting a variety of
the more fully documented programs is presented.
The diversity of the programs and the key characteristics common to the strategies which
bred success are discussed.

Bereiter and Engelmann (1966) determined
that the disadvantaged child typically ex-
hibits strength in two areas on mental tests:
immediate memory and rote learning. Noting
that the primary weakness of the population
is a lack of language development, they decided to use the child's strengths to overcome the debilitating characteristics. The
program used a highly structured sequence of
activities and drills to facilitate language
development. To capitalize on the assets
of rote learning and short-term memory, the
instruction was directive in nature with the
teacher positively reinforcing the appropriate
responses. Significant year-end intelligence
gains were reported. The feature essential
for academic gain was teaching in a direct
and forceful manner.

Karnes, Hodgins, and Teska (1968) evaluated the effects of two preschool programs on 55 disadvantaged children. The experimental group of 28 children had a highly structured cognitive and language development program. The control group of 27 children attended a traditional, nondirective preschool. After a seven month period the experimental group achieved significant gains in intellectual functioning and visual perception. Also, the experimental group attained greater scores on the Illinois Test of Psycholinguistic Abilities and the Metropolitan Readiness Test. Karnes et al. concluded that the highly structured program was more effective than a nondirective approach in developing intellectual functioning, language abilities, perceptual development, and school readiness.

Gray and Klaus' (1965) early training program was "an attempt to offset the progressive retardation commonly observed in the schooling of culturally deprived children (p. 887)." The intervention began three summers preceding school entrance and continued through the first years of school. The intent of the program by focusing on preschoolers was to be preventive rather than remedial. The experimental groups received summer enrichment activities, plus weekly home visits during the school year. The program was designed to increase the attitudes and aptitudes toward achievement for the disadvantaged subjects. The results, as of 1968, reflect intelligence score gains for the experimental group over a 39 month period (Gray & Klaus, 1968).

As the number of early intervention programs increased, there likewise was an increase in the number of critical reviews (Hawkridge, Chalupsky, & Roberts, 1968; Pines, 1966; Spicker, 1971). These critics stimulated empirical investigations to identify key features of successful programs. These features

led to the following factors which seem to
enhance development in children.
1.   Curriculum models which emphasize cognitive or academic skill development produce
the largest IQ score increases.
2.   Structured programs which are not cogni-
tively or academically oriented produce intellectual gains only when they incorporate
strong oral language development components.
3.   Unless the primary grade curriculum can
be modified, preschool programs must develop
the fine motor, memory, and general language
abilities of disadvantaged children. These
skills appear to be needed to succeed in the
primary grades.
4.   Home intervention appears most helpful
when it supplements a short-term preschool
program.
5.   The age of beginning intervention appears
critical only when the program is structured
in a manner which differentiates the program
according to a cognitive development theory.
6.   Most successful programs are highly structured and incorporate a deliberate plan of
sequences which lead children to specific
goals.
7.   In successful preschool programs time is
considered as critical and each activity is
selected for maximum contribution to learning.
8.   A characteristic of all successful intervention programs was a large proportion of
adults to children.
9.   Multiple year intervention has been justified since many studies have produced results
which indicate that children continue to develop in the second year.
10. Primary grades need to modify their curriculum to accommodate the disadvantaged child
who has received compensatory education.

    In recognition of the successful nature
of early intervention programs coupled with
the growing needs of the disadvantaged, an
intervention strategy on a larger scale was
designed. This large scale investigation became known as Head Start.

Head Start

The initial Head Start movement represented the nation's commitment to the disadvantaged and began with high aspirations, a
wealth of funding, and a galaxy of prestigious
supporters (Pines, 1966). The purpose of Head
Start included mobilizing the human resources
of a community (Payne & Mercer, 1974). The
initial program incorporated aspects beyond
the traditional educational realm and focused
on the delivery of medical and dental services,
social agencies, parental involvement, career
planning, and training of community parapro-
fessionals. As noted by Brazziel (1967), the
focus of Head Start represented "the country's
biggest peace time mobilization of human resources and efforts (p. 244)." Unfortunately,
the overnight need for service models led to
a pattern of helter-skelter program development. In education, the preschool programs
had few curriculum models from which to select
intervention programs. Consequently, the majority of Head Start centers adopted programs
similar to traditional nursery schools which
were inadequate in the job of educating culturally different children (Spicker, 1971).
The lack of readiness led the Head Start movement through three distinct stages of growth.

Halcyon Period (1965-1967). The developmental theories of Piaget, Hunt, and Bruner,
in tandem with the early intervention studies
by Skeels and Dye (1939) and Kirk (1958),
helped develop a euphoric atmosphere for those
involved in the planning stages. The period
was characterized by an abundance of funds and
statements resounding in optimistic prophecy.
Politicians praised the virtues, as typified
by Mrs. Lyndon Johnson's statement, "Head
Start will reach out ... in a gray world of
poverty and neglect, and lead them into the
human family (Payne, Mercer, Payne, Davison,
1973, p. 54)." Similar accolades from those
in the field reached Washington in the form

of anecdotical records and case reports. Reported incidents such as the following were
common during the initial period.

> (There was a) five-year old boy whose
> life was saved because a Head Start
> medical examination detected a seri-
> ous heart disease (Richmond, 1967,
> p. 6).
> One fifteen-year-old boy who was a
> potential school dropout worked as
> an aide and never missed a session
> (Levens, 1966, p. 482).

Rarely did professionals question the validity
of these statements (Wolff, 1967). By the end
of 1967 over one million children had come in
contact with Head Start.

Critical Period (1967-1969). As the descriptive reports of the halcyon days slowly
ebbed, a concern for greater empirical justification began to emerge. Already those in
powerful positions were raising the yellow
flag of caution. Shriver (1967), in anticipation of the possible erosion of gains, outlined what he felt should be done if Head
Start was not to become a "False Start."

During this period two other events of
importance dampened the original enthusiasm.
The first large scale investigation of Head
Start, commonly known as the Westinghouse Report (Cicirelli, 1969), evaluated 104 centers
across the country. Former Head Start children
in grades one through three were compared with
control groups in language development, learning readiness, and academic achievement. No
statistically significant differences for any
of the criteria measures were reported. As
summarized by Payne, Mercer, Payne, and Davison (1973), five main points emerged from the
study.

1. Summer Head Start programs did
not produce early cognitive and af-

fective gains that continue in the
first grade and beyond.
2. Full-year programs produced
marginal cognitive gains which continued through the first three
grades, but no affective gains were
made.
3. Programs worked best in Negro
centers, in some urban areas, and
in the Southeast region of the nation.
4. Project children were below national norms on the Illinois Test
of Psycholinguistic Abilities (ITPA)
and the Stanford Achievement Tests,
although Metropolitan Readiness Test
scores approached national norms.
5. Parents liked the program and
took active part in it (pp. 93-94).

The salience of the report appeared to dampen
enthusiasm as the news media reported the
failure and foretold the eventual doom of
Head Start.

The second blow to the program occurred
when plans were formulated to move Head Start
from the Office of Economic Opportunity to
Health, Education, and Welfare. Caught in
the bureaucratic gymnastics of the Washington
merry-go-round, the basic survival of Head
Start was threatened. A heated debate in the
press followed with advocates for both sides
espousing their point of view (Omwake, 1969;
Orton, 1969). Although Head Start survived,
both events marked the low depths of the program.

Consolidation and Refinement Period (1969-
1973). Emerging from the pathos of the critical years, the lessons of survival were well
learned. The rhetoric of the mid-1960s was
replaced with the awareness that only success
would neutralize the skeptics. Moreover, the
belief in early intervention was still alive

although the early naive beliefs were replaced
with a more pragmatic view. Efforts were made
to survey the existing centers and ascertain
from the effective programs those specific objectives and strategies characteristic of a
successful program (Bissell, 1972). From this
evolved specific models to function as alternatives to traditional practices (Payne & Mercer,
1974).

1. The behavior analysis model was designed
at the University of Kansas by Don Bushell.
Academic content and skill development are
the major concerns of the program. The methods reflect the behavioral principles of learning; therefore, token systems and programmed
instruction are used extensively.

2. The cognitive model based on Piaget's
theory was developed by David Weikart of the
High Scope Education Research Foundation.
The program emphasizes home instruction of the
parents and infants by public school teachers.
The content of the curriculum is directly related to each mother-child dyad.

3. The academically-oriented preschool model
was designed by Wesley Becker and Siegfried
Engelmann at the University of Oregon. The
academic areas of reading, arithmetic, and
language are the primary focus. Teaching
activities are tailored to small structured
group work using the Distar[1] materials as the
curriculum base. The teacher's task is to
elicit the correct response followed immediately by positive reinforcement.

4. The Tuscon early education model was designed by Marie Hughes and is currently sponsored by the University of Arizona. The development of the prerequisite skills in language, cognition, motivation, and social areas

---

1. Distar (Direct Instructional System
for Teaching Arithmetic and Reading) refers to
a commercial packaged program distributed by
Science Research Associates, Inc., 259 East
Erie Street, Chicago, Illinois 60611.

receives the primary emphasis. The environmental ingredients necessary to develop the
skills are characterized by: (a) freedom for
the child to choose among activities, (b) freedom among the children, and (c) systematic
reinforcement from teachers.
5. The pragmatic action-oriented model is a
spin off of the English Infant School and is
promoted by the Educational Development Center
in Newton, Massachusetts. The underlying assumption is that matching the individual characteristics of the child and classroom setting
will facilitate growth. Each classroom teacher is encouraged to experiment with new teaching techniques and receives support from an
educational consultant.
6. The Florida parent-educator model was developed by Ira Gordon from the University of
Florida. A parent educator is defined as a
mother from the community who functions as a
teacher aide in the home or classroom. The
primary goal is prevention via early intervention either in the home or preschool setting.
7. The responsive model was designed by Glen
Nimnicht of the Far West Laboratory for Educational Research and Development. The major
thrust of the program is to develop a healthy
self-concept. A responsive environment characterized by self-inquiry and self-pacing is
the cornerstone of the program.
8. The Bank Street College model was developed
at the Bank Street College in New York City.
Teachers are to attend to the individual characteristics and needs of each child and to
construct a warm supportive environment. The
primary goal is to foster a commitment on the
child's part to the learning process.

The move to develop workable prototypes
represents a concerted effort on the part of
educators to reverse the backlash from the
critical years of Head Start. The various
models can function as alternatives for other
Head Start centers. Though little theoretical

agreement exists concerning what constitutes
a good program, all models are designed with
one goal in mind--the facilitation of individual growth and development.

Emerging Direction

A review of current early intervention
programs leads one to forecast the emerging
direction as emphasizing infant education.
Head Start in its initial inception focused
on the five and six age range. As the evidence accumulated, the fact slowly emerged
that the most promising programs were those
which began in the earliest years. Caldwell
(1970) has commented that, "None of the known
studies that began enrichment programs as late
as age 6 produced gains as large as those of
either Skeels and Dye (1939) or Kirk (1958)
(p. 722)." Taking note of the success within
infant programs, those in charge of program
development shifted gears and redirected the
emphasis toward the first years of life. Il-
lustrative of this change are the aforementioned projects at the High Scope Educational
Research Foundation and the Florida parent-
educator model, which are representative of
the new Head Start era. To further explain
the change, two of the more popular programs
are described.

The Milwaukee Project (Garber & Heber,
1973; Strickland, 1971), which has received
attention in the professional journals as
well as from the lay media, exemplifies the
infant education movement. The project is
habilitative in nature, and Garber and Heber
(1973) refer to it as,

> an attempt to prevent intellectual
> deficits in "high-risk" children by
> early intervention. The intervention
> technique employs an intensive educa-
> tional program for the very young
> high-risk child, beginning before
> six months of age (p. 1).

After a survey of the inner-city community,
Garber and Heber concluded that deprived conditions produce a high risk potential for
mental retardation by virtue of the mothers'
intelligence, socioeconomic status, and community of residence. The program design was
a study to prevent a decline in intellectual
functioning and reduce the chances of mental
retardation.

The program is a longitudinal study in-
vestigating the effects of intervention six
months after birth. The experimental component is directed at two areas: maternal rehabilitation and infant stimulation. Forty
mothers with IQs of 70 or less and their infants were selected for inclusion in the study.
The maternal rehabilitation program reeducates
the mothers for later vocational positions as
well as trains them in child-rearing and home-
making skills. The infant stimulation component begins before the child reaches six
months. After entrance into the program, the
typical sequence of events provides the child
a one-to-one relationship with a teacher until the infant reaches 12 months of age, and
at that time the dyad is joined by a second
teacher-infant pair. At 15 months the two
children begin instruction with only one teacher. Then at 18 months small groups are formed
for teaching purposes. Structured teaching
groups are continued throughout the rest of
the program.

The curriculum is designed to attack the
major language and cognition deficiences which
are common to a disadvantaged population. The
theoretical rationale for intervention encompasses an eclectic approach which is grounded
on the bedrock of popularized developmental
theories, including those of Skinner, Piaget,
and Montessori.

A lengthy measurement schedule included
experimental and control comparisons on physi-

cal and developmental measures, intelligence
scores, learning tasks, language tests, and
various other scores. The interim report
(Strickland, 1971) showed that at 19-25 months
the experimental group began to acquire vocabulary rapidly, while the control group had no
vocabulary production until 28 months. At
30-32 months the experimental children were
using full sentences and the control children
were exhibiting unconnected words. Starting
at 36 months a grammar test was given every
three months. At every test interval the experimental group registered significantly
higher gains. When the children were reaching
42 months, the experimental children were on
the average 33 IQ points higher than the controls. In concluding the interim report, Garber and Heber (1973) noted,

> infant testing difficulties notwith-
> standing, the present standardized
> test data, when considered along with
> performance on learning tasks and
> language tests, indicate an unques-
> tionably superior present level of
> cognitive development on the part
> of the experimental group. Also,
> the first wave of our children are
> now in public schools. None have
> been assigned to classes for the re-
> tarded and we are collecting data
> on school performance generally
> (p. 10).

The results supported their position--that a
predicted decline in cognitive functioning
which is indicative of a low socioeconomic
population can be reversed via early infant
intervention. For this reason, many are prais-
ing the program as the "Miracle in Milwaukee."

The success, however, has received its
share of criticism from the research community.
Page (1972), in reacting to the avalanche of
acclaim in the lay press, has raised questions

which temper the early findings. The criticism, of a research nature, questions the possible sampling bias, contamination of criterion
tests, and failure to document fully the treatment. Although Page's reaction is viable, the
program remains to provide the impetus for a
replication of the study. For this reason,
the Milwaukee Project further propels energies
into habilitation programs for deprived children.

A second project, similar in nature to
the Milwaukee Project, is the Ypsilanti-Car-
neige infant education project (Lambie &
Weikart, 1970). Two theoretical assumptions
underlie the project: (a) preventive intervention must begin before the preschool years
because that is the time the environment ex-
erts its greatest influence, and (b) home
teaching for the infant and parent can be the
foundation of a successful program.

The basic strategy involves home teaching
by public school instructors. Each teacher is
assigned to a family and provides one-to-one
instruction with the parent and infant. The
teacher, over a period of time, develops a
strong relationship with the family. In this
fashion, the educator is keen to the child's
development and can provide the mother with
relevant information. The program essentially
is concerned with promoting parental effectiveness.

Without reviewing the procedures specific
to the program, the advantages of home instruction are briefly noted. Weikart and
Lambie (1970) have found that this type of
program with its distinctive features allows
for advantages foreign to other programs.
These include:
1. The convenience to the mother working in
her own home aids the success of the program.
2. The information documented by the teacher
and provided to the mother is directly related
to the mother-child dyad.

3. As the mother and teacher develop a trusting relationship, the teacher can give real
and genuine information.
4. Based on the working relationship between
teacher and family, the ability to establish
a link between family and school is greatly
enhanced.

Conclusion

The effects of a restricted environment
on the cognitive and social development of
children was discussed. Children reared in
such conditions do not blossom and mature as
their more privileged peers, nor do they ever
maximize their potential. Programs to ameliorate these debilitating conditions exist
today. In a nation wealthy in resources and
rich in energetic people, the negative consequences of an unstimulating environment must
be diminished by employing the most promising
intervention strategies. By facilitating the
cognitive, academic, social, and emotional
development of children, there is an increase
in the probability of assisting individuals
toward the attainment of becoming healthy,
self-sufficient, mature individuals. Basically,
this intervention strategy centers on the identification of high risk children (children who
are likely to experience difficulty throughout
life--especially in school) and subsequently
provides a program of educational treatment
designed to directly facilitate growth and behavioral change within the individual. Another
strategy designed to assist individuals in
becoming healthy, self-sufficient citizens is
career education. Career education at the
elementary level is designed for all children
including those identified as high risk.

REFERENCES

Bereiter, C., & Engelmann, S.   Teaching disadvantaged children in the preschool. Englewood Cliffs, N. J.:   Prentice-Hall, 1966.

Bissell, J. S.   Planned variation in Head Start and Follow Through.   Washington, D. C.:   Department of Health, Education, & Welfare, 1972.

Brazziel, W.   Two years of Head Start.   Phi Delta Kappan, 1967, 48, 344-348.

Caldwell, B.   The rationale for early intervention.   Exceptional Children, 1970, 36, 717-727.

Cicirelli, V. G.   The impact of Head Start: An evaluation of the effects of Head Start on children's cognitive and affective development.   Vol. 1.   Springfield, Va.:   Clearinghouse, 1969.

Coleman, J. S.   Equality of educational opportunity.   Washington, D. C.:   United States Government Printing Office, 1966.

Coleman, R. W., & Provence, S.   Environmental retardation (hospitalism) in infants living in families.   Pediatrics, 1957, 19, 285-292.

Dennis, W., & Najarian, P.   Infant development under environmental handicap.   Psychological Monographs, 1957, 71(7).

Deutsch, M.   The disadvantaged child and the learning process.   In A. H. Passow (Ed.), Education in depressed areas.   New York: Columbia University, 1963.

Forgays, D. G., & Forgays, J. W. The nature
    of the effect of free environmental ex-
    perience in the rat. Journal of Compara-
    tive Physiology and Psychology, 1952, 45,
    322-328.

Freedman, D. G., King, J. A., & Elliot, O.
    Critical period in the social develop-
    ment of dogs. Science, 1961, 133, 1016-
    1017.

Garber, H., & Heber, R. The Milwaukee Project:
    Early intervention as a technique to pre-
    vent mental retardation. Stoors, Conn.:
    The University of Connecticut Technical
    Paper, 1973.

Gray, S. W., & Klaus, R. A. An experimental
    preschool program for culturally deprived
    children. Child Development, 1965, 36,
    887-898.

Gray, S. W., & Klaus, R. A. The early train-
    ing project for disadvantaged children:
    A report after five years. Monographs
    for the Society for Research in Child
    Development, 1968, 33(4).

Harlow, H. Total social isolation: Effects
    on Macaque monkey behavior. Science,
    1965, 148, 666.

Hawkridge, D., Chalupsky, A., & Roberts, A.
    A study of selected exemplary programs
    for the education of disadvantaged chil-
    dren. Palo Alto, Calif.: American In-
    stitutes for Research in the Behavioral
    Sciences, 1968.

Hebb, D. O. The organization of behavior.
    New York: Wiley, 1949.

Hess, R. D., & Shipman, V. C. Early experience
    and the socialization of cognitive modes
    in children. Child Development, 1965, 36,
    869-886.

Hunt, J. McV. Intelligence and experience.
    New York: Ronald Press, 1961.

Kagan, J. On class differences and early de-
    velopment. In V. Denenberg (Ed.), Educa-
    tion of the infant and young child. New
    York: Academic Press, 1970.

Karnes, M. B., Hodgins, A., & Teska, J. A.
    An evaluation of two preschool programs
    for disadvantaged children: A traditional
    and a highly structured experimental
    school. Exceptional Children, 1968, 34,
    667-676.

Kirk, S. A. Early education of the mentally
    retarded: An experimental study. Ur-
    bana, Ill.: University of Illinois Press,
    1958.

Lambie, D. Z., & Weikart, D. P. Ypsilanti
    Carneige infant education project. In
    J. Hellmuth (Ed.), Disadvantaged child.
    Vol. 3. New York: Brunner/Mazel, 1970.

Levens, D. A look at project Head Start.
    Childhood Education, 1966, 42, 481-483.

Omwake, E. B. From the President. Young
    Children, 1969, 24, 130-131.

Orton, R. E. Comments on the President's
    January message. Young Children, 1969,
    24, 246-248.

Page, E. B. Miracle in Milwaukee: Raising
    the IQ. Educational Researcher, 1972,
    15, 8-16.

Payne, J. S., & Mercer, C. D. Head Start.
    In S. E. Goodman (Ed.), Handbook on con-
    temporary education. Princeton, N. J.:
    Xerox Corp. R. R. Bowker Co., 1974.

Payne, J. S., Mercer, C. D., Payne, R. A., &
    Davison, R. G. Head Start: A tragicom-

edy with epilogue. New York: Behavioral Publications, 1973.

Pines, M. Revolution in learning. New York: Harper & Row, 1966.

Pinneau, S. A. A critique on the articles by Margaret Ribble. Child Development, 1950, 21, 203-228.

Pinneau, S. A. The infantile disorders of hospitalism and anaclitic depression. Psychological Bulletin, 1955, 52, 429-452.

Rheingold, H. L. The modification of social responsiveness in institutional babies. Monograph of the Society for Research in Child Development, 1956, 21(2).

Rheingold, H. L. The effect of environmental stimulation upon social and exploratory behavior in the human infant. In B. M. Foss (Ed.), Determinants of infant behavior. New York: Wiley, 1961.

Ribble, M. A. Infantile experience in relation to personality development. In J. McV. Hunt (Ed.), Personality and the behavior disorders. New York: Ronald Press, 1944.

Richmond, J. B. Beliefs in action. Childhood Education, 1967, 44, 4-7.

Scott, J. P., & Fuller, J. L. Genetics and the social behavior of the dog. Chicago: University of Chicago Press, 1965.

Shriver, R. S. After Head Start--what? Childhood Education, 1967, 44, 2-3.

Skeels, H. M. Adult status of children with contrasting early life experiences. Monographs of the Society for Research in Child Development, 1966, 31(3).

Skeels, H. M., & Dye, H. B.   A study of the effects of differential stimulation on mentally retarded children. Convention Proceedings American Association on Mental Deficiency, 1939, 44, 114-136.

Sluckin, W.   Imprinting and early learning. London: Mcthuen, 1964.

Spicker, H. H.   Intellectual development through early childhood education. Exceptional Children, 1971, 37, 629-640.

Spitz, R. A.   Hospitalism: An inquiry into the genesis of psychiatric conditions in early childhood. Psychoanalytic Study of the Child, 1945, 1, 53-74.

Strickland, S. P.   Can slum children learn? American Education, 1971, 7(6), 3-7.

Thompson, W. R., & Grusec, J.   Studies of early experience. In P. H. Mussen (Ed.), Carmichael's manual of child psychology. New York: Wiley, 1970.

Thompson, W. R., & Heron, W.   The effects of restricting early experience on the problem-solving capacity of dogs. Canadian Journal of Psychology, 1954, 8, 17-31.

Weikart, D. P., & Lambie, D. Z.   Early enrichment in infants. In V. Denenberg (Ed.), Education of the infant and young child. New York: Academic Press, 1970.

Wolff, M.   Is the bridge completed? Childhood Education, 1967, 44, 12-15.

10. CAREER EDUCATION FOR THE YOUNG CHILD

The concept of career education is currently being projected into the pedagogical limelight. The United States Office of Education (USOE) is primarily responsible for the recent thrust of interest that the concept is receiving. Sidney P. Marland, Jr., U. S. Commissioner of Education, has spearheaded the career education emphasis. His interest and commitment to the concept of career education are demonstrated in the following passage.

> All education is career education--
> or should be. I propose that a
> universal goal of American educa-
> tion, starting now, be this--that
> every young person completing his
> school program at grade 12 be ready
> to enter either higher education
> or useful and rewarding employment
> (Marland, 1971, p. 22).

According to Marland (1971), all education--elementary and secondary--is career education or, more emphatically, a preparation for life. One direct inference is that career education should actively influence the curriculum in grades k-12. Vocational programs in secondary schools are discussed in Chapter 11, while the relevance of career education

within the elementary school is presented in
this chapter.

The essence of a career education curriculum in elementary school is one of exposure, i.e., to expose young children to the
full spectrum of potential occupations. To
the handicapped, the importance of early career experience is paramount. The school-
wide distribution of exceptional children, as
reported by Martin (1972), revealed that almost three-quarters of special education services are at the elementary school level.
Moreover, the trend toward early education
for exceptional children is expected to continue (Mackie, 1969). This increase in early
education of exceptional children allows educators to reverse the reported high unemployment statistics of exceptional children (Martin, 1972) via career education. At the elementary school level, then, exposure to various occupations through career education furnishes a needed vehicle to enhance the employability of exceptional children.

The Career Education Concept

Career education involves a comprehensive educational program which focuses on careers, begins in early childhood, and continues throughout adulthood. The USOE has delineated 15 occupational clusters appropriate
for career education content (Olympus Research
Corporation, 1972) which emphasizes a type of
work ethic instruction that is designed to
esteem the dignity and value of all work, regardless of its current social status.

Marland (1972) viewed career education
as a very humanistic approach because it enables an individual to explore the occupational world, to establish an identity with
it, and to assist himself in making vocational
decisions which facilitate a self-fulfilled
life. Wolfe (1973) reported that the USOE has

identified the following goals for career education.

1. To make all education subject matter more meaningful and relevant to the individual through restructuring and focusing it around a career development theme.
2. To provide all persons the guidance, counseling, and instruction needed to develop their self-awareness and self-direction; to expand their occupational awareness and aspirations; and to develop appropriate attitudes about the personal and social significance of work.
3. To assure the opportunity for all persons to gain an entry-level marketable skill prior to their leaving school.
4. To prepare all persons completing secondary school with the knowledge and skills necessary to pursue further education or to become employed.
5. To provide services for placing every person in the next step in his development whether it be employment or further education.
6. To build into the educational system greater utilization and coordination of all community resources.
7. To increase the educational and occupational options available to all persons through a flexible educational system which facilitates entrance and re-entry into the world of work or the education system (p. 195).

In essence, career education is designed to accommodate individual differences at all life span stations through a continuous experience-centered and evaluative process.

Uxer (1973) and Venn (1973) approached career education from a broad perspective.

This perspective is illustrated by Uxer's philosophical viewpoint and is reflected in the following passage.

> career education is a philosophy, one that includes the belief that every person, regardless of his assets or deficits, has the right to "become timely aware of occupational opportunities and competencies necessary for each" (p. 201).

From the perspective of special educators, the concept of career education is to enhance the exceptional child's outlook of vocational choice. A further message is that, regardless of career choice, each job affords its own merits and values to the individual. The choice of an occupation is a developmental process which begins early in life and is influenced by experience (Deiulio & Young, 1973). One method to facilitate the exceptional child's understanding of this message is via exposure to career opportunities.

Rationale

The raison d'être of career education is illustrated by an analysis of contemporary life. Society today is in a state of change with many social institutions in transition. The poor are not content with the conditions of poverty which result in inadequate housing, nutrition, and education. Moreover, middle-class youth are questioning the ethics and values inherent in the political and economic systems. In addition, recent criticism directed toward education depicts a mood permeated with dissatisfaction. Educators, parents, and students have protested the relevance of today's curriculum and the lack of adequate career preparation. In response to this voice, Hoyt, Evans, Mackin, and Mangum (1972) view career education as a viable alternative because,

(a) it has emerged at a moment when
dissatisfaction with educational
practices and outcomes are at a peak,
and (b) it promises to attack and
improve some of the apparent sources
of that dissatisfaction (p. 17).

In special education the protests have
reached the breaking point. Parents are no
longer content to have their children categorized with meaningless terms (Dunn, 1973).
The trend of placing children in special
classes, segregated from their peers, is being reversed. Recent court decisions have
declared unconstitutional the practice of
tracking students by ability which is harmful
to many children (Wright, 1968). From an objective view, a follow-up of handicapped
youngsters leaving school in the next four
years reveals an even more critical situation
than the one presented. Specifically, Martin
(1972) stated,

Only 21 percent of handicapped children leaving school in the next 4
years will be fully employed or go
on to college. Another 40 percent
will be underemployed, and 26 percent will require at least a partially sheltered setting and family,
and 3 percent will probably be almost
totally dependent (pp. 523-524).

Obstacles to Career Education

In order to enlighten one's perspective
of the career education concept, it is helpful
to examine some of the realities which may
restrict its impact. These restricting realities are reviewed under the topics of teamwork and dehumanization.

Teamwork. Teamwork appears to be the
interface between success and failure of the
career education movement. Marland (1972)

indicated that teamwork is the first step to
initiating career education. Harris and Grenda
called for the formation of an interdisciplinary task force to effect career education
(Lake, 1973). On the surface the teamwork
requirement does not appear to pose a critical
problem to the implementation of career education; however, the disciplines involved may
be steeped in traditions concerning commitment
and attitude which hinder the development of
effective teamwork. The various disciplines
responsible for delivering career education
to the handicapped must commit themselves to
the objectives which are best suited to the
needs of handicapped children. To accomplish
this all team members must resist the impulse
to allow peculiar disciplinary persuasions to
erode the team effort.

Dehumanization. Nash and Agne (1973)
have attacked the career education concept in
an unfettered manner. They claimed that the
current literature does not warn against the
possible misuses of career education and that
close scrutiny is justified. They inferred
that the literature accepts and supports the
notion of a continued existence of a corporate
social order. Nash and Agne cited critics who
said that formal education programs which are
shaped by business, production, and technology
systems tend to thwart individual expression
and mold students into workers motivated only
by the promise of external rewards and prestige. It was reported by Nash and Agne that
a commitment to career education is an acceptance and approval of the corporate influence
and the subsequent social order that it fosters, i.e., high productivity, automation,
systematic administration, and the technical
approach to human problems.

The criticisms by Nash and Agne (1973)
concerning the overwhelming responsiveness of
education to the corporate structure are epit-
omized in their writings.

> Many youths are resisting attempts
> to be siphoned off into careers, be-
> cause their educational experiences
> do not allow them to challenge the
> whole structure of corporate capital-
> ism. These youths believe that earn-
> ing a living is always secondary to
> living a life .... (p. 374).

Nash and Agne (1973) continued their criticism of the career education concept by con-
tending that it fosters the achievement drives
of youngsters by appealing to their acquisition needs. They reported that achievement
begets achievement, and personal satisfaction
and fulfillment are unobtainable due to the
insatiable achievement needs created by the
corporate value system. Nash and Agne discussed a study by Daniel Yankelovich which
demonstrated that many young people are highly
skeptical of achievement strivings as an exclusive formula for personal happiness.

Nash and Agne (1973) attacked what they
called the learning fallacies in career education. The first learning fallacy they discussed was specialism. They claimed that
specialization guided by occupational clusters
tends to fragment a person's view because it
stresses the outer reality, thus neglecting
the inner nature of man, i.e., that segment
of man characterized by intuition and emotion
and explored via the arts, humanities, and
religion. The second learning fallacy they
discusssd was sequentialism. The essence of
this criticism was based on the assumption
that occupational choice is a slow developmental process and consequently rigid sequenc-
ing of occupational education risks "swamping
the special tempo and style of each person's
unique rhythm for learning (p. 376)." The
third learning fallacy Nash and Agne discussed
was fundamentalism. They emphasized that to
stress any body of knowledge as fundamental
for all students is to ignore that (a) future

workers will need a diversity of skills and
attitudes, and (b) some of the skills and attitudes needed by future workers are still
unknown.

Finally, Nash and Agne (1973) suggested
that a likely failure of career education
would be to encourage or push young people
into the corporate sector of society while
simultaneously minimizing the value of careers
in the social services.

Facilitators of Career Education

In order to enhance one's perspective of
career education, it is feasible to examine
some of the thinking which has escaladed it
to its current high priority status. The advantages of the career education movement are
discussed under the headings of litigation
and scope.

Litigation. Gilhool (1973) reviewed
litigation which is relevant to the handicapped. He indicated that court cases involving exceptional persons securing their
rights are spiralling. Gilhool pointed out
that several cases revolve around the theme
of a right to treatment. The results of these
cases have established that handicapped citizens have the right to an individual program
tailored to their needs. Another group of
cases has resulted in the right of citizens
to question the standards used for assigning
students to special programs. A third group
of cases has established the right to public
education for all exceptional children. These
cases indicate that the courts represent a
viable tool to the handicapped for securing
their rights.

Career education is essential for many
handicapped persons not only to ensure success
but to obtain and maintain a more humane life
style. In conclusion Gilhool (1973) stated

"handicapped citizens no longer have what they have by grace ... but ... by right. It is now a question of justice (p. 609)." This brief review of litigation indicates that, when career education is deemed viable for the handicapped, they have a <u>right</u> to it.

Scope. Nash and Agne (1973) many aspects of career education as dehumanizing. They reported that it de-emphasizes the fine arts, religion, and philosophy and fosters a dependence on external rewards. In essence, Nash and Agne claimed that career education prepares people for the perpetuation of the corporate society while limiting individual expression and self-actualization processes.

The notion that career education could detract or impede a handicapped person's self-actualization experiences via a quest for esoteric renditions of truth and beauty within the fine arts domain is a deserving position. However, to restrict the avenues of self-fulfillment to spiralling abstractions and advanced cognitions ignores the position that there are individuals who ascertain beauty, truth, and self-fulfillment in things that appear to represent a much simpler phenomena, i.e., a successful day's work.

Marland (1973) responded to criticisms which claimed that career education is dehumanizing and anti-intellectual by acknowledging that the specific job clusters identified as the focal content of career education include the fine arts and the humanities. He presented career education as a humanistic program on the premise that employment is often germane to self-fulfillment processes. Klinkhamer (1973) discussed the role of work and its impact on the handicapped by stating, "Employment leads to personal growth, both social and intellectual. For the handicapped, employment is a brust of sunlight (p. 208)."

Finally, it is apparent that a meaningful perspective for many handicapped persons is anchored in the realistic notion of work and its relation to society and to mankind. Marland (1972) has proposed that all students be offered the opportunity to pursue and obtain a career commensurate with their unique abilities and needs. Implicit in this proposal is a diversity of programs--both academic and vocational. Hopefully, our educational leaders of the future will view the career education concept within the broad perspective of student needs that it encompasses and not within the perspective of the idiosyncratic persuasions of the disciplines involved.

Exemplary Programs

Concern for career education has created an expansion of vocational curricula at the elementary school level. The impetus for development of career education has come mainly from local school systems (Hoyt, Evans, Mackin, & Mangum, 1972). Programs are now in existence in every section of the country. In Dallas, Texas, over 21 million dollars has been spent to develop a career education program. Wyoming has implemented a program in one school district and intends to expand the program throughout the state. State governments are enacting legislation to furnish funds for career education. In 1970 five states had passed the legislation and 14 additional states had proposed career education programs. This increase in interest has ignited the federal government's attention, and massive financial support is now forthcoming to develop large scale demonstration models.

To further understand the development of career education at the elementary level, some of the exemplary programs are reviewed. The state of New Jersey has implemented the Technology for Children Program (T4CP) in Rahway,

New Jersey (Deiulio & Young, 1973). The purpose of the project is to allow students to
evaluate themselves in relation to specific
occupations. In class the students experience
many occupations (e.g., carpenter, electrician,
secretary) through the manipulation of job-
related tools and materials. Manipulation of
tools allows a child to assess his capabilities
and potential for employment in a specific job
area. This, in turn, aids the child in directing his energies to a chosen occupation. In
West Hartford, Connecticut, the World of Work
(WOW) program emphasizes exposure to occupations through field trips to work facilities
(Gysbers & Moore, 1972). During the trips,
the students and the workers engage in job-
related activities to expose the students to
the job's physical requirements. Frequently,
the students question the employees, and the
responses increase the students' perceptions
of work. The purpose of the program is to
promote students' awareness of their own vocational interests, attitudes, and aptitudes.
In Cobb County, Georgia, an elementary career
curriculum was developed to guide students to
engage in self-evaluation, explore various
occupations, understand the social and economic values of work, and introduce the psychological meaning of work (Gysbers & Moore,
1972). Career education specialists working
with classroom teachers have developed career
curriculum units. Each unit introduces an
occupation to the students through vocational
experience, field trips, visits from various
employers, and role-playing techniques. In
one unit the students explored the construction industry and role-played many occupations
in order to gain insight into the demands of
that profession. In brief, the Cobb County
program acquaints students to the world of
work.

These programs are representative of the
current career education movement. The purpose of the programs is to acquaint students

with various occupations and to have them
discover their interests or talents in relation to a career. Another program which in-
tegrates career education and the realities
of life is a currency based token economy.

A Currency Based System

One of the major problems in implementing
the career education concept and/or philosophy
in a public school classroom is that career
education becomes subject matter and is taught
as if it were a thing. Many times career
education becomes nothing more than a "show
and tell" of jobs. At the elementary level,
career information is directly taught to the
student and, after successfully completing a
specific career education unit, the student
may know some facts about a job or profession
but may lack a feeling for the whole process
of working, earning, spending, etc. At the
elementary level the goal of career education
must extend beyond the exposure of jobs and
the "show and tell" of professions and move
into cultivating a feeling for the world of
work. The purpose of this discussion is to
describe a method for teaching a feeling for
career education through the use of a currency
based token economy.

In a typical token economy the teacher
gives children points, poker chips, check
marks, and other tangible objects as rewards
or reinforcers for desirable behavior. The
points or objects are later used as a medium
of exchange with which the child can "buy" a
variety of goods (e.g., candy, toys, and games)
and services (e.g., recess, tutoring help, and
privileges). For example, a teacher may give
a child tokens for correctly completing a specified number of arithmetic problems or for
staying in his seat for a specified period of
time. The child may later exchange his tokens
for a desired object or activity.

Token economies have been used successfully to motivate children to learn presented factual information as well as to control disruptive children, but it appears that the use of token economies for teaching career education concepts has been overlooked. More importantly, by altering the traditional token economy to a currency based token economy where play money is used in the place of the typical poker chip, check mark, etc., a unique problem solving environment directly related to career education takes form.

Well developed currency based token economies are, essentially, miniature economic systems with characteristics of supply, demand, inflation, recession, and socioeconomic levels which are depictable in terms of economic theory. This is the basis for using a token economy to teach life to children rather than to teach children about life.

In regular classrooms children are taught about life in school. Supposedly this prepares them for adult life. The entire educational process often is viewed as preparation rather than participation. A currency based token economy allows the student an opportunity to do more than think about solutions on a cognitive level. It actually provides the student with a "cultural laboratory." Career education, as with most educational endeavors, is best learned through the use of, and involvement in, problem solving situations. The following passages describe a program where children are involved in life situations.

Three second grade teachers and a counselor established a currency based token economy in their 30 minute math classes. Initially students could earn token currency in a variety of ways. Currency was given for appropriate behavior such as entering the room quietly, taking a seat quickly, getting to work immediately, attending to the class presentations,

and raising their hands to ask questions.
Students also could earn currency for correct
verbal responses in class. When the students
were given seat work or work sheets, each
page was worth a certain amount of currency
upon completion. At this point it is important to mention that the currency was being
used for the purposes of motivation (currency
earned for completed seat work, answered questions, etc.) and control (currency earned by
keeping quiet, working on seat work independently, raising hand, etc.). The aspects of
career education entered into the picture as
the students began purchasing items from the
store.

Students were allowed to visit a school
store once a week to spend their earned currency. Merchandise appealing to second grade
children was displayed. Salable items included such things as balloons, candy, and
inexpensive toys such as cars, dolls, and animals. Also popular among second grade children were school items such as crayons, pencils, erasers, paste, and paper. As the children understood the earning and purchasing
program, representatives from each class were
taken on a field trip to visit with the managers and employers of local drug stores, grocery stores, and banks. Under the direction
of the counselor, the students were taken on
tours through the business community and were
encouraged to question the managers and employers about the various duties and responsibilities. The students began to organize
the information so it could be shared with
their classmates.

The students in the three classes discussed various ways and means they could assume
the operation of the school store. It was decided that applications for a store manager
and several store clerks would be taken. This
involved completing a simple application form,
an interview with the counselor, and a math

competency exam to assure that the employees
hired could make change correctly. As the
second grade students began to operate their
own store, the establishment of a bank seemed
appropriate. The purpose of the bank was to
exchange currency from small denominations to
larger denominations as well as to provide a
place to keep savings. Bank tellers, a store
keeper, and a bank manager were interviewed
and hired. When interest was paid on the
savings accounts once a week at the rate of
10% (this rate was chosen because of the ease
of computing for the students), additional
tellers were hired to handle the increase in
business. As the program progressed, other
career areas were explored. For example, an
employment agency was visited and a student
employment service was established where the
students interviewed other students for jobs.

In summary, a currency based system trans-
forms the regular classroom into a cultural
laboratory. An economic system which mirrors
adult society is developed in which the students can earn, spend, and save currency.
The necessary business enterprises (e.g., bank,
store) are constructed and staffed by students.
During the daily classroom routines the students come in contact with the currency based
system and indirectly learn many of the demands in the world of work. In essence, a
currency based system strikes at the heart
of the career education movement--the students
experience life.

Conclusion

In this chapter the idea of career education at the elementary school level was introduced as an alternative curriculum. The
concept of career education which is to broad-
en a child's perspective of vocational choice
was discussed. For handicapped youth the importance of career education is obvious when
one considers that the majority of exceptional

individuals enter the world of work unprepared to compete in the job market.   In order
to ameliorate this lack of preparation, exemplary programs were identified which serve
as prototypes.   To those involved in education
and rehabilitation these programs represent
the foundation from which to build viable career education programs for handicapped children.   In the next chapter the scope of career
education will be expanded to include educational efforts at the secondary school level.

REFERENCES

Deiulio, A. M., & Young, J. M. Career education in the elementary school. Phi Delta Kappan, 1973, 54, 378-380.

Dunn, L. M. An overview. In L. M. Dunn (Ed.), Exceptional children in the schools: Special education in transition. (2nd ed.) New York: Holt, Rinehart, & Winston, 1973.

Gilhool, T. K. Education: An inalienable right. Exceptional Children, 1973, 39, 597-609.

Gysbers, N., & Moore, E. Guiding career exploration: Any teacher can. Instructor, 1972, 81(6), 52-56.

Hoyt, K. B., Evans, R. N., Mackin, E. F., & Mangum, G. L. Career education: What it is and how to do it. Salt Lake City, Utah: Olympus, 1972.

Klinkhamer, G. E. The implications of career education for visually handicapped students. The New Outlook for the Blind, 1973, 67, 207-209, 215.

Lake, T. P., Career education and the handicapped child. Exceptional Children, 1973, 39, 657-667.

Mackie, R. P. Special education in the United States: Statistics, 1948-66. New York: Teachers College Press, Columbia University, 1969.

Marland, S. P., Jr. Career education. Today's Education, 1971, 60(7), 22-25.

Marland, S. P., Jr. Career education: Every
    student headed for a goal. American
    Vocational Journal, 1972, 47(3), 34-36,
    62.

Marland, S. P., Jr. Career education: A
    report. The Bulletin of the National
    Association of Secondary School Princi-
    pals, 1973, 57(371), 1-10.

Martin, E. W. Individualism and behaviorism
    as future trends in educating handicapped
    children. Exceptional Children, 1972,
    38, 517-525.

Nash, R. J., & Agne, R. M. Career education:
    Earning a living or living a life? Phi
    Delta Kappan, 1973, 54, 373-378.

Olympus Research Corporation. Career educa-
    tion: A handbook for implementation.
    Salt Lake City, Utah: Olympus Research
    Corporation; and Baltimore, Maryland:
    State Department of Education, 1972.

Uxer, J. E. Career education and visually
    handicapped persons: Some issues sur-
    rounding the state of the art. The New
    Outlook for the Blind, 1973, 67, 200-206.

Venn, G. Career education in perspective:
    Yesterday, today, and tomorrow. The
    Bulletin of the National Association of
    Secondary School Principals, 1973, 57(371),
    11-21.

Wolfe, H. E. Career education: A new dimen-
    sion in education for living. The New
    Outlook for the Blind, 1973, 67, 193-199.

Wright, J. S. The Washington D. C. school
    case. In M. Weinberg (Ed.), Integrated
    education: A reader. Beverly Hills,
    Calif.: Glencoe Press, 1968.

11. CAREER EDUCATION
IN THE SECONDARY SCHOOLS

In the preceding chapter career education was introduced as a viable curriculum
for elementary school children. Discussion
focused on the concept and rationale for early
career education as well as some of the negative and positive factors involved in the
career education movement. In this chapter
the emphasis is career education at the secondary school level. The shift in educational
levels (i.e., elementary to secondary) demands
a change in educational objectives. At the
elementary school level the primary objective
is exposure in order to heighten the student's
awareness of various occupations. The major
objective at the secondary school level is to
shape this new awareness into preparation for
a career. The change in career education objectives from career awareness to preparation
is graphically depicted in Figure 11-1.

Via reconstruction of current school programs and redirection of present resources,
career education enables school systems to
provide relevant, effective, career oriented
educational programs which increase later
student performance in the world of work.
Junior high school personnel facilitate career
orientation and exploration of various occupations through classroom experiences and

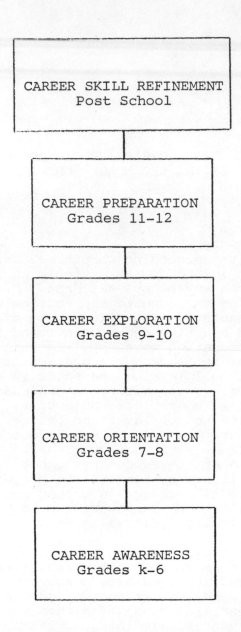

Fig. 11-1. Career education objectives by
grade level.

field trips into the world of work. Senior
high school teachers initiate career preparation through classroom instruction, simulated
work experiences, and on the job preparation.
In order to sharpen one's perspective of career education for the handicapped at the
secondary school level, the history of career
education is reviewed.

History

The comprehensiveness of the career education concept necessitates a broad historical
review in order to capture the various integral parts which have emerged from several
disciplines to contribute to the career education concept. The histories of vocational
education and special education reflect components of the career education movement which
have implications for the handicapped.

Some highlights of the vocational education movement which possess identifiable components to career education are exemplified
by the Ford Foundation Sponsored Projects
over the last decade, the Manpower Development Training Act of 1962, the Vocational Education Act of 1963, and the 1968 amendments
to the Vocational Education Act of 1963. The
recent (1969-1972) recommendations of the National Advisory Council on Vocational Education are congruent with the career education
concept being emphasized by the United States
Office of Education (Wolfe, 1973). The history of vocational education reflects several
events which have particular significance to
the handicapped. For instance, Olympus Research Corporation (1972) reported that the
"zero reject" concept employed in the San
Mateo, California Schools focuses on providing
salable skills to all students. The Manpower
Development and Training Act of 1962 emphasized remedial training and extended services
to disadvantaged people. The Job Corps was
established in 1964 to provide vocational

education for school dropouts without salable
skills. The 1968 amendments to the Vocational
Education Act of 1963 included a directive
which mandates that 10 percent of the federal
funds allocated for vocational education must
be used to provide vocational education to
the handicapped.

The history of special education reflects
a broadening scope of services directed toward
handicapped persons. In referring to the retarded, Goldstein (1964) acknowledged the expansion of services over the years by indicat-
ing how initial services were within state
operated institutions, then public schools,
and recently public and private habilitation
agencies and clinics. In terms of the career
education concept for the retarded, Dunn (1961)
credited Hungerford and his associates with
emphasizing the need for occupational information in public school classes. Although an
occupational core curriculum was suggested
by Hungerford in 1948, it was not until 1965
that legislation was passed which supported
a joint vocational rehabilitation-special
education effort toward preparing the retarded
for employment. Dunn (1973) claimed that even
today work study programs have been one of
the most innovative features of secondary
curricula to occur over the last decade. Although the importance of vocational training
for the retarded is universally acknowledged,
current trends reflect a dwindling interest
in cooperative work study programs (Dunn,
1973). The stage is set for vocational education (PL 90-576), vocational rehabilitation
(PL 333), and special education (PL 91-230)
to pool efforts to effect career education
and consequently achieve acceptance and integration for exceptional children. Although
it is apparent that the thinking of modern
times reflects an attitude of helpfulness and
responsibility (Younie & Rusalem, 1971), the
career education concept offers the philosophy,
if not the impetus, needed to achieve accep-

tance and integration for handicapped persons.
Complimenting this growth of the various disciplines toward occupational preparation of
the handicapped has been the USOE's very timely emphasis on career education. Career education depends on all the related disciplines
mutually planning and working together (Lake,
1973a).

Rationale

The raison d'être of career education is
illustrated by a brief review of some statistics. Marland (1972) reported that for every
10 students in high school, two receive vocational training and three go to college (although one drops out). These figures do not
include youngsters who drop out of school before reaching high school. This means that
over one-half of all students (1,500,000) need
more attractive options in occupational training (Marland, 1972). Marland continued by
acknowledging that in the 1970-1971 school
year a total of 2,450,000 pupils left school
unprepared for entering a job. He reported
that these 2,450,000 pupils cost about one-
third (28 billion dollars) of the entire educational expenditure for the nation. Finally,
Marland stated that an emphasis on career education is more realistic than a continuation
of overemphasis on academic programs since the
labor department indicates that for now and
the foreseeable future 80 percent of the nation's jobs will require less than a baccalaureate degree. Although many jobs now require
less than a baccalaureate degree, the number
of unskilled positions is diminishing (Wolfe,
1973; Dunn, 1973).

For exceptional children and young adults
this increasing demand for salable skills
comes as disheartening news. Their education
has unfortunately left many exceptional youths
as unemployable or underemployed due to a lack
of adequate vocational preparation. As Martin

(1972) noted, only 21 percent of handicapped children presently leaving school are fully employed or continue to higher education. This report underscores the need for handicapped children to receive vocational training in order to improve their position in the competitive job market. Career education at the secondary school level which affords to the exceptional student an opportunity to prepare for a career and job entry represents an effective vehicle for preparing handicapped students for the job market. In summary, the justification for increasing and improving career education programs for handicapped youth is fully documented. What remains to be done is the implementation of quality programs.

Obstacles to Career Education

Although the rationale of career education dictates the development of career programs at the secondary level, there are obstacles which represent barriers to implementing career education. These obstacles are reviewed under the topics of occupational stratification and pragmatic considerations.

Occupational Stratification. Occupations have become stratified according to a social order. Jobs which require extensive training or college and fall under professional or managerial classifications tend to be the most prestigious. Those which require little or no training and are classified as semiskilled or unskilled tend to infer positions low on the social hierarchy.

Wells (1973) depicted the stratification phenomena by noting that many parents have a bias against vocational education because success is equated with higher education. He mentioned that this same type of bias toward vocational education is reflected in the amount of energy and resources expended for college

guidance as compared with career guidance.
Johnson (1973), in a discussion concerning
preparing youngsters for the 21st century, indicated that people arbitrarily divide occupations between those requiring muscle power and
those requiring intellectual skills. He acknowledged that the United States culture currently values intellect and not muscles. He
stated that this type of attitude must not be
transferred to the next generation and suggested conteracting this attitude by teaching
every child in school at least one manipulative skill. Ebel (1972) exemplified a value
system capable of derailing both career and
special education efforts when he proposed
that schools should confine their purpose to
cultivating cognitive competence or face failure. Ebel's writings suggested that education is an opportunity but not necessarily a
civic responsibility. He detested compulsory
attendance and purported "schools should not
accept responsibility for success of every
pupil in learning, since success depends so
much on the pupil's own efforts (p. 7)."

In conclusion, the literature reflects
that many persons have invested much energy
in esteeming cognitive excellence and while
collar professions. Career education is
viewed as a threat to the future pursuit of
these desirable goals. The influence of the
values as exemplified by Ebel (1972) in determining the future directions of education
represents a major barrier to the implementation of career education.

Pragmatic Considerations. The disadvan-
tages of career education primarily represent
social and conceptual barriers to career education. The following list presents some of
the more pragmatic obstacles to the implementation of career education.
1. Swanson (1972) reported that organizational problems represent a barrier to career education. The mobilization of the efforts of

educators at all levels toward a goal as comprehensive as career education is an enormous
task.
2.   Career education requires a massive program of inservice training. Swanson (1972)
reported that in addition to higher education
instructors there are over two million elementary and secondary teachers who will require inservice training.
3.   Career education needs legislative authorization at the state level in order to generate the funds needed for its implementation
(Swanson, 1972).

Facilitators of Career Education

Career education has graduated to a level
where today it is congruent with traditional
educational practices. The impetus for this
change has occurred as a result of the advantages inherent in the career education movement. These advantages are discussed under
the headings of feasibility and changing times.

Feasibility. The histories of special
education and vocational rehabilitation indicate the feasibility of career education for
the handicapped. The fact that only 21 percent of handicapped children leaving school
in the next four years will continue to higher
education or be fully employed is a sad com-
mentary of present efforts to prepare handicapped youngsters for gainful employment.
These statistics reflect a condition which
has led to a renewed interest in preparing
the handicapped for employment. For example,
Klinkhamer stated,

>The Bureau of Education for the
>Handicapped has adopted as one of
>its major goals that by the year
>1977, every handicapped child who
>leaves school will have had career
>educational training that is rele-
>vant to the job market, meaningful

to his career aspirations, and realistic to his fullest potential
(Lake, 1973b, p. 127).

For many handicapped youngsters career
education represents the interface between
employment and unemployment, between poverty
and livelihood, and finally between waste or
use of our nation's most valuable resource--
its people.

Changing Times. Career education has
numerous other advantages which fall under
the heading "Changing Times." Social, economic, and political considerations have set
the stage for several of these advantages
which are listed below.
1. A recent Gallup Poll revealed that 44 percent of the public sampled indicated that the
primary purpose of education is to prepare
students for better jobs (Gallup, 1972). This
finding suggests that many citizens are prepared to support a career education movement.
2. The career education concept is being
given top priority at the national level (Marland, 1971). The USOE is capable of generat-
ing interest, funds, and resources toward the
advancement of its priorities.
3. The number of unskilled jobs is rapidly
diminishing (Dunn, 1973). Shoemaker (1972)
reported that only five percent of people will
be in unskilled jobs by 1975. Due to technological advances, more skills are required
for job entry. Career education represents
a viable solution to the problem of preparing
pupils for entry into the modern job market.
4. Wells (1973) speculated that education
may be on the verge of experiencing a vocational education revolution. Muirhead (1973)
supported the notion that vocational education is on the upswing by acknowledging the
large number of career education programs in
existence.

Secondary Career Education for the Exceptional Student

At the secondary school level career education for handicapped individuals affords an opportunity for them to develop the prerequisite skills necessary for employment. A multitude of secondary programs exists, but each varies with respect to objectives and procedures. For this reason the basic characteristics to be described are those common to many approaches.

The success or failure of a career education program hinges to a great extent on the curriculum. Therefore, the curriculum components have undergone a vast amount of scrutiny by researchers (Capobianco & Jacoby, 1971; Goldstein & Heber, 1964). In a review of work study programs, Kolstoe and Frey (1965) reported that the following curriculum components are essential in secondary school programs.
1. A curriculum which encompasses academic and vocational experience to develop the mandatory skills for gainful employment.
2. A curriculum which ameliorates secondary handicaps, i.e., speech problems, physical handicaps, visual impairments.
3. A curriculum which emphasizes physical characteristics, i.e., physical fitness, personal hygiene.
4. A curriculum which develops the necessary skills for independent living, i.e., money management, use of public transportation.
5. A curriculum which promotes inter- and intrapersonal behavior, i.e., cooperation, self-confidence.
6. A curriculum which provides on the job training.

A primary objective of the career education curriculum is career preparation. The vehicle for this preparation is a curriculum which combines academic and vocational ex-

periences. High school programs generally
are of a three or four year term which allows
for the gradual convergence of academic and
vocational activities. It is expected that
each student will move through three distinct
stages during which he makes the transition
from general education to specific job training. The first stage is essentially an academic program. The program exists as a bridge
between the emphasis in the elementary school
on career awareness and the emphasis in the
secondary school on preparation for a career.
The school personnel facilitate career orientation and career exploration via academic
course work and indirect vocational experience,
i.e., films, field observations. The second
stage evenly divides course work between academic and career oriented activities. The
curriculum focuses on skill development and
academic material related to vocational preparation. In the last stage the student devotes
almost full time to specific job preparation
in which academic courses are only supplemental to the curriculum.

For exceptional children the curriculum
content needs to focus on the behaviors necessary for independent living in the world of
work. Classroom instruction study units are
used to supplement on the job taining. These
units generally include themes such as health
and grooming, money management, transportation, housing, job applications, and interpersonal relations. In certain instances these
factors may determine the employability of the
handicapped individual. For this reason the
objective and instruction technique for each
unit is described.

The objective of the health unit is to
develop in the student the health standards
which are acceptable to the community. The
instruction includes general cleanliness techniques and the proper use of soaps and cosmet-
ics. Basic grooming habits and hair styles

are demonstrated via films and in class experiences. Other health themes focus on the
effects of alcohol, drugs, and tobacco.

The objective of a money management unit
is to develop the student's ability to handle
financial affairs without dependence on another
individual. How to count and make change, the
importance of a budget, the difference between
cash and charge payments, and how to use a
bank are found in the curriculum. Since a
bank is such an integral part of society, the
students generally visit a banking institution, open an account, and practice depositing
and withdrawing money on the bank forms.

The proper use of public transportation
in order to arrive at and leave the work site
necessitates a unit on transportation. The
students are directed to familiarize themselves with alternative means of transportation. The proper use of buses, taxis, and
subways is enhanced through experience under
the school personnel's supervision.

Since housing may present a potential
problem, methods for securing suitable housing
are presented in the curriculum. The students
are shown how to check newspapers and public
advertisement boards for housing. Important
points related to housing such as cost, loca-
tion, shopping areas, and distance from public
transportation are brought to the students'
attention.

Job applications are frequently the first
contact between employer and employee. If a
student cannot master the task of completing
an application, the likelihood of securing a
job is greatly reduced. Therefore, students
are taught how to apply for a job and fill out
the forms. Practice sessions are used for
completing application forms and personal data
sheets.

Interpersonal relations with supervisors and work peers often determine vocational success or failure. For this reason the importance of cooperation is stressed through role-playing activities. During these sessions the role of supervisors, employers, and peers is illustrated.

In summary, the curriculum content emphasizes the development of behaviors necessary for independent living. Without these skills the student would experience difficulty obtaining and maintaining an independent life. Through the various activities of discussion, films, simulation, and role playing, the curriculum broadens the repetoire of student behaviors and increases the likelihood of successful career employment.

Throughout the career education process basic rehabilitation and education services are allotted which enhance the value of the program. These services are fully discussed in Chapter 13 and here will be briefly noted. A diagnostic evaluation focuses on the student's specific aptitudes, interests, and abilities which help to determine a realistic plan for job preparation. Career training furnishes formal training courses, on the job training, and related instruction which lead to eventual job entry. For exceptional youth job placement and follow-up are necessary ingredients for successful career adjustment. Job placement seeks to locate a suitable environment for optimum career adjustment. Follow-up aids in determining the extent of student adjustment. The provision of these services helps to insure the value of career education programs.

Although it is not frequent, criticism of career education programs has been voiced. In a discussion of career programs for the mentally retarded, di Michael (1961) concluded,

The programs assume that retarded
adolescents have little or no more
to gain from school, that experience
on a job is a better form of training for adult living than any curriculum the school has to offer, or
could possibly devise (p. 371).

The criticism of di Michael is not uncommon and reveals a soft spot in the career
education movement. Although certain programs
are worthwhile, a majority are stagnant which
depreciates their value to exceptional children. In career education today the emphasis
is on implementing only those programs with
a high potential for success and weeding out
those programs with limited value. For this
reason career education for handicapped children can be expected to reflect changes in the
near future.

Trends

In discussing trends it appears natural
to describe the utopian program and predict
the rate and manner in which identifiable
forces will mobilize and achieve the panacea.
Since trends in career education are linked
to a constantly changing social phenomenon,
its future directions must be forecast in a
very tenuous manner. At this stage in the
development of career education a model program for handicapped individuals has not been
identified. Thus, it appears profitable at
this juncture to examine the possible direction of forces which can create a catalytic
environment for the development of career education for the handicapped.

The Management Force. It is feasible to
predict that during the next 10 years the
emergence of quality career education programs
will be sporadic. This prediction is based
on the premise that the implementation of career education requires expertise in modern

management practices. This expertise is currently only sporadically available in the educational community (Stadt, Bittle, Kenneke, &
Nystrom, 1973). To effect career education,
management must mobilize interdisciplinary
resources to respond to a common goal which
in turn requires commitment to a specific educational philosophy. In order to establish
and maintain career education programs, Stadt
et al. suggested management by objectives as
a viable management approach. Management by
objectives requires (a) the establishment of
measurable objectives, (b) the identification
of each individual's responsibilities, and
(c) the development of a system to evaluate
each individual's performance. In essence,
Stadt et al. inferred that future career education programs will embrace the management
by objectives concept.

The Legal Force. Recent court decisions
should act as an impetus to professionals from
the various disciplines to cooperate in career
education endeavors. In essence, litigation
has set the stage for increased involvement
within the school and community environments.
This increased cooperation between disciplines
in the educational community should result in
career education programs which serve the handicapped child in a manner which does not require segregating him from the mainstream of
education. Thus, career education programs
10 years hence will reflect an integration of
handicapped youngsters into regular educational programs. Hehir (1973) has already described a program which features vocational
training for deaf students within a regular
vocational technical school.

The Economic Force. The corporate society's need for graduates with salable skills
will continue to increase. This factor will
result in increased participation by industry
in career education programs. The literature
already describes a multitude of training

programs for the handicapped which feature
the joint efforts of school-industry partner-
ships. In 10 years many career education programs for the handicapped will feature the
employer-based model that Marland (1972) has
described.

The Technological Force. The career
choice of many exceptional youngsters is restricted by the nature of their handicap.
The 15 occupational clusters identified by
the USOE represent over 20,000 jobs. These
jobs need to be reviewed in terms of their
relationship to specific handicaps if exceptional children are to be exposed to occupational information tailored to their unique
needs. This organization of occupational information as it relates to specific handicaps
may be greatly facilitated by the use of com-
puter assisted instruction. It is likely
that commercial curricula materials designed
for implementing career education for the
handicapped will flood the market. Due to
the capacity of computers to store and retrieve vast amounts of knowledge and the ability of commercial publishers to generate and
deliver curricula packages, it is probable
that the content available to career education programs for the handicapped 10 years
from now will be readily accessible.

Conclusion

Career education is a new concept to education and this "newness" necessitates a perspective. New concepts and new theories which
emerge in the social sciences generate a ground
swell of program descriptions, opinions, and
experience-anchored statements. A preponderance of career education literature is being
unveiled, but few definitive or data based
constructs can be teased out of this mass of
literature. Until research efforts deliver
information pertaining to the efficacy of the
various constructs, the direction of educa-

tional planning should be rooted within a framework of discretion and tentativeness.

REFERENCES

Capobianco, R. J., & Jacoby, H. B. The Fair-
    fax plan: A high school program for
    mildly retarded youth. In J. H. Roth-
    stein (Ed.), Mental retardation: Readings
    and resources. (2nd ed.) New York:
    Holt, Rinehart, & Winston, 1971.

di Michael, S. G. Vocational rehabilitation
    and the mentally retarded: A statement
    of issues. In J. H. Rothstein (Ed.),
    Mental retardation: Readings and re-
    sources. (2nd ed.) New York: Holt,
    Rinehart, & Winston, 1971.

Dunn, L. M. A historical review of the treat-
    ment of the retarded. In J. H. Roth-
    stein (Ed.), Mental retardation: Read-
    ings and resources. New York: Holt,
    Rinehart, & Winston, 1961.

Dunn, L. M. Children with mild general learn-
    ing disabilities. In L. M. Dunn (Ed.),
    Exceptional children in the schools:
    Special education in transition. (2nd
    ed.) New York: Holt, Rinehart, & Win-
    ston, 1973.

Ebel, R. L. What are schools for? Phi Delta
    Kappan, 1972, 54, 3-7.

Gallup, G. H. The fourth annual Gallup poll
    of public attitude toward education.
    Phi Delta Kappan, 1972, 54, 33-46.

Goldstein, H. Social and occupational adjust-
    ment. In H. A. Stevens & R. Heber (Eds.),
    Mental retardation: Review of research.
    Chicago: University of Chicago Press,
    1964.

Goldstein, H., & Heber, R.   Preparation of
mentally retarded youth for gainful employment.   In H. A. Stevens & R. Heber
(Eds.), Mental retardation: Review of
research.   Chicago: University of Chicago Press, 1964.

Hehir, R. G.   Integrating deaf students for
career education.   Exceptional Children,
1973, 39, 611-618.

Johnson, B. B.   Practical preparation for the
21st century.   Phi Delta Kappan, 1973,
39, 518-521.

Kolstoe, O. P., & Frey, R. M.   A high school
work study program for mentally retarded
subnormal students.   Carbondale, Ill.:
Southern Illinois Press, 1965.

Lake, T. P.   Career education and the handicapped child.   Exceptional Children,
1973, 39, 657-667. (a)

Lake, T. P.   Career education as a philosophy
and a practice: An interview with George
Klinkhamer.   Teaching Exceptional Children, 1973, 5, 124-127. (b)

Marland, S. P., Jr.   Career education.   Today's Education, 1971, 60(7), 22-25.

Marland, S. P., Jr.   Career education: Every
student headed for a goal.   American
Vocational Journal, 1972, 47(3), 34-36,
62.

Martin, E. W.   Individualism and behaviorism
as future trends in educating handicapped
children.   Exceptional Children, 1972,
38, 517-525.

Muirhead, P. P.   Career education: The first
steps show promise.   Phi Delta Kappan,
1973, 54, 370-372.

Olympus Research Corporation. Career educa-
     tion: A handbook for implementation.
     Salt Lake City, Utah: Olympus Research
     Corporation; and Baltimore, Maryland:
     State Department of Education, February,
     1972.

Shoemaker, B. R. Career education: A chance
     for change. American Vocational Journal,
     1972, 47(3), 27-31.

Stadt, R. W., Bittle, R. E., Kenneke, L. J.,
     & Nystrom, D. C. Managing career educa-
     tion programs. Englewood Cliffs, N. J.:
     Prentice-Hall, 1973.

Swanson, G. I. Career education: Barriers
     to implementation. American Vocational
     Journal, 1972, 47(3), 81-82.

Wells, C. E. Will vocational education sur-
     vive? Phi Delta Kappan, 1973, 54, 369,
     380.

Wolfe, H. E. Career education: A new dimen-
     sion in education for living. The New
     Outlook for the Blind, 1973, 67, 193-199.

Younie, W. J., & Rusalem, H. The world of
     rehabilitation: An atlas for special
     educators. New York: John Day, 1971.

12. FACILITIES FOR THE HANDICAPPED

From a historical perspective rehabilitation programs for the handicapped have ranged
from extermination and ridicule to acceptance
and treatment. The course of history illustrates that rehabilitation practices were
directly influenced by the philosophical and
social values in vogue at the time, as well
as the economical and political beliefs. In
a discussion of provisions for the handicapped,
Kolstoe and Frey (1965) stated,

> While political philosophy is often
> thought of as distinct from educa-
> tional philosophy, the close rela-
> tionship between political philosophy
> and treatment of the disabled seems
> inescapable (p. 3).

Influenced by political considerations, the
care of the handicapped has progressed through
distinct eras. The history has been documented in several sources (Dunn, 1973a; Kolstoe &
Frey, 1965; Oberman, 1965; Roberts, 1965) and
here is briefly outlined. Kolstoe and Frey
identified five eras of treatment.

Eras of Treatment

Era of Extermination. In primitive societies man's basic quest was one of survival.

Each member of society was expected to pull
his own weight and add to the community's
growth. Handicapped individuals who could
not care for themselves were a burden to society. For this reason, disabled children
were systematically eliminated from society.
For example, the Spartans of ancient Greece
expected the citizens of Sparta to be well
of body and mind. Those who were not physically fit became a liability to the community.
In order to rid society of the burden, defective children were sent away from the community and left to perish. In Rome, centuries
later, similar methods were in vogue and deformed children were left in open sewer drains
to die.

Era of Ridicule. Prior to the Middle
Ages an agrarian caste system developed around
the nobleman-serf relationship. In return
for safety and protection serfs worked the
farms surrounding the nobleman's manor. The
relationship proved to be beneficial to both
parties, and these mini-cities grew economically secure. Since the basic need of survival was neutralized, society grew lenient
toward the handicapped. The practice of extermination of the disabled was replaced with
ridicule, e.g., dwarfs acted as clowns and
imbeciles as court jesters (Dunn, 1973a). Although ridicule was a step above extermination, the handicapped were still relegated to
the lower depths of society.

Era of Asylum. The Middle Ages marked
the emergence of a social conscience. Led
by the Roman Catholic Church, society's view
of the disabled shifted toward a more humane
approach. In the churches the religious teachings declared that all individuals were "children of God" and worthy of life. It was recognized that the disabled were people who
needed to be cared for by society. In the
tradition of this attitude monasteries and
asylums were constructed for the handicapped,

and these individuals became wards of the church.

Era of Education. During the 18th century the monks who previously attended only
to the physical needs attempted to educate
the handicapped. This shift in attitude from
a custodial service to education symbolized
a first step toward rehabilitation. The new
concept of treatment slowly spread beyond the
walls of the asylums, and the populace became
aware of the ability to modify an individual's
behavior. This change was exemplified by the
work of Itard (1962). Itard found Victor, a
boy whose behavior was similar to that of an
animal, in the forests of Averyon. Five years
were devoted to teaching Victor and, although
the boy made progress, Itard gave up when Victor did not meet his expectations. Itard, however, provided further impetus to the new era
of education by instilling in his students
faith in the rehabilitation process. The Industrial Revolution was another significant
factor to the education movement. The need
for an educated populace became apparent as
society became more industrialized. No longer
were citizens allowed to be illiterate, including those who were disabled. Thus, another
reason for the birth of educational programs
for the handicapped developed from the economic
needs of society.

Occupational Adequacy Era. Out of the
education movement emerged a new type of treatment for the handicapped. Developed in the
1940s, vocational training programs directed
efforts to maximize the abilities of the individual for an occupational career. This
movement is still popular today as illustrated
by the proliferation of work programs for the
handicapped.

Facilities and Treatment Orientation

Rehabilitation facilities can be grouped
according to where the efforts for change are

directed, i.e., the handicapped individual
or the environment of the handicapped. Specifically, a rehabilitation program can attempt to change the behavior of the handicapped individual or modify the environment
to meet the needs of the handicapped. From
this perspective facilities may be classified
according to their treatment orientation:
(a) change environment, (b) remove from society, (c) change clients, and (d) combination programs.

Change Environment. Traditionally, work
programs for the handicapped have focused on
changing the client. A movement conceptually
alien to changing the client is one which
strives to change the environment to meet the
needs of the handicapped. In this case an
environment is created to afford the disabled
an opportunity to establish roots in a sensitive community. The handicapped are assured
the opportunity for a productive livelihood
which includes their own cultural life and
social contacts. Variations of this theme
include the following programs: Camphill Village, U.S.A.; Innisfree; Marbridge Ranch; and
Dan Torisky's program.

The Camphill Movement is the major program for adapting the society to the handicapped. Camphill villages have pioneered the
idea of community living in which mentally
retarded adults dwell in an environment designed to meet their needs. Popular in America, the movement is deeply rooted in European
philosophy.

Rudolf Steiner, an Austrian philosopher,
provided the guiding principle for the Camphill Movement. In his youth Steiner was deeply influenced by the philosophical writings
of Goethe. In formulating his own philosophy,
Steiner rejected the contemporary need for
"objectivity" and believed that psychic powers
must be used to restore a sense of humanistic
values to a materialistic world.

Steiner became interested in the life of the disabled during a resident tutorship. One of his charges was described as a sickly, retarded youth, whom others thought was incapable of cognitive development. Full of a naive sense of zeal, Steiner accepted the task of developing the youth's latent abilities. After a two year period of intensive tutoring, the boy was functioning on the same level as his peers. The child, with Steiner's help, went on to complete medical college and enter into private practice as a physician. This experience laid the groundwork for Steiner's later interest in the handicapped and the development of a new method for educating the mentally handicapped (Scientific Seer: Rudolf Steiner, 1969).

Dr. Karl Koenig, a Viennese pediatrician and an avid student of Steiner, applied the teachings of Steiner (Camphill Village, U.S.A.). The approach, known as Curative Education, emphasizes the innate qualities of each person and accepts the mentally retarded as individuals. Furthermore, Curative Education concentrates on abilities rather than dismissing the retarded individual as a defective organism. In 1939 Dr. Koenig founded the Camphill Movement in Aberdeen, Scotland. The school accepted children who were physically, emotionally, and mentally handicapped. The initial success of Camphill led quickly to expansion into England and the European continent.

The first Camphill village for mentally retarded adults in the United States was founded by Carlo Pietzner, a follower of Dr. Koenig. The philosophy of Camphill Village, U.S.A. is opposite that of other institutional settings. The staff-client dichotomy is absent and the emphasis is on establishing healthy interpersonal relationships. Each member of the village works according to his ability and receives according to his needs. All members of the community share the ownership and profits of labor as equal partners.

The entrance criteria for adult villagers specify that each member must be able to care for his own physical needs and not require medical or custodial care. In addition, those who can meet the social standards of the normal community are not permitted to be villagers. The staff consists primarily of European adults with supplemental help from local volunteers who function as temporary workers. Each staff member is a house-parent to a group of villagers and together they represent a family constellation. The village arrangement projects the image of a close commitment between the villagers and staff.

The goal of each village is economic self-sufficiency. Each member is to be self-supportive and contribute the excess of his labor to the welfare of the community. The community has its own livestock and vegetable garden. The surplus food and the products manufactured in the village are sold to the neighboring communities. Although the objective is to be self-sufficient, tuition is charged to the villagers' parents. In addition, outside donations are collected to reduce the operating costs. These communities are flourishing and 25 villages are operating in the United States, Europe, and South Africa.

Innisfree Village, located in the Blue Ridge Mountains near Charlottesville, Virginia, is modeled after Camphill Village, U.S.A. Innisfree, meaning inner freedom, was founded in 1971 by Heinz and Alice Kramp. The village was developed as an alternative to the inadequate public and private institutions, and it functions as a model for other community programs.

Innisfree was built on the concept that a natural environment will allow the handicapped individual to reach the zenith of his potential as a productive self-respecting member of a society. The founders refer to Innisfree as,

a place where a person can say, "I
am retarded, this is my way of life,
this is where I can function. I
live in a community where I need not
be told that I am a member--I know
I am a member, doing interesting
things, good work and having something that is mine (Innisfree Village, p. 10).

Innisfree Village melds the lives of
villagers and staff into one family. The retarded adults share homes with the staff members and their children. Each member is given
vocational instruction commensurate to his
skills and interests. The social life and
recreational facilities promote camaraderie
and develop a feeling of communal living.
Economically, Innisfree has self-sufficiency
as its goal, although currently it is dependent on tuition and outside resources.

Marbridge Ranch represents another example of a community designed to meet the
needs of the handicapped. The ranch mirrors
Western style living and the environment projects a wholesome atmosphere of communal living. The ranch provides the opportunity for
the handicapped to develop community roots in
a setting which offers employment, family living, and social exchange. The emphasis is on
developing personal relations, and little dis-
tinction is made between the staff and the
handicapped. The handicapped are taught ranch
skills suitable to their abilities. Each member of the ranch is expected to produce to
the fullest of his potential and to share with
the other members of the community.

Dan Torisky's program, as advertised in
national media, represents a large commercial
venture. Torisky conceived that state or national parks with their recreational and lodg-
ing facilities provided an excellent environment in which handicapped individuals can live

and develop. To staff the parks, he advocated employing an unusual group--the mentally retarded and physically handicapped. Under supervision, the handicapped were to maintain and service all aspects of the facilities. The supervisors were to check work standards and maintain an acceptable level of work.

Torisky envisioned the community as a viable alternative to the system of institutional care. He argued that many handicapped individuals living in institutions should not be there and that each member of society should be allowed to lead a productive life. To finance his idea, Torisky traveled through the state of Pennsylvania to secure potential support. Today, the dream of Dan Torisky has blossomed into reality as Otolsin State Park in central Pennsylvania and is staffed by handicapped individuals who are past inhabitants of the state institution.

Remove From Society. Institutions historically have functioned to remove the handicapped individual from society. The majority of persons placed in institutional care never leave the premises (Rhodes & Gibbins, 1973). In institutions few rehabilitation programs are employed, and the criticism of institutional care has been mounting. Fortunately, today there is a transition process directed toward rehabilitation.

Early attempts at institutional care were created to modify the behavior of the handicapped (Kolstoe & Frey, 1965). This attempt at humane treatment rapidly diminished and was replaced with removing disabled individuals from society. During the reign of Elizabeth I of England, the first poor laws were passed and institutions for the physically disabled were established. Although these institutions were created with high aspirations, these settings quickly became "hell on earth" for the physically disabled. Garrett (1969) emphasized

the deplorable conditions of institutions by
citing a public health service bulletin of
1965.

> Bethlehem Hospital in London ... came
> to be known as "Bedlam." It was no-
> torious for its deplorable conditions
> and practices. Violent patients were
> exhibited to the public for an ad-
> mission fee, while the harmless were
> sent into the streets to beg. Stripped
> of all human dignity, the patients
> were subjected to beatings, chains
> and other means of physical force (Men-
> tal Illness and Its Treatment: Past
> and Present, p. 32).

In America, the era of institutional care
began in 1818 when an asylum for the deaf and
dumb was started in Hartford, Connecticut.
In 1832 the Perkins School for the Blind in
Massachusetts was constructed and was the
first state supported institution. The first
institution for the mentally retarded was
opened in 1848 in Barre, Massachusetts. In
the second half of the 19th century the movement for institutional care was extensive and
expanded in the early 20th century. The expansion was followed by a change in treatment
philosophy from custodial care of the disabled
to rehabilitation through work experiences.
The disabled were trained, however, to work
in institutional jobs and not for employment
outside the institutions. This pattern of
self-perpetuation is still active today and
the conditions of the facilities are reminis-
cent of earlier times.

Burton Blatt, one of the prime movers to
facilitate change in institutional care for
the mentally handicapped, presented a pictorial
essay documenting current institutional life.
In describing the living quarters, Blatt and
Kaplan (1966) stated,

> In each of the dormitories for se-
> verely retarded residents, there is
> what is euphemistically called a
> day room or recreation room. The
> odor in each of these rooms is over-
> powering. After a visit to a day
> room we had to send our clothes to
> the dry cleaners to have the stench
> removed (p. 22).

Unfortunately, these conditions are too often
representative of the current institutional
care of the mentally handicapped.

In commenting on institutions, Mamula
and Newman (1973) identified three factors
created by institutional care which have im-
peded adequate treatment: (a) the mentally
retarded are viewed as sick and incurable;
(b) residential and community care functions
have been separated; and (c) large custodial
institutions have been developed and maintained.

The criticisms against institutional facilities are slowly having an effect on treatment procedures, and this is reflected in the
movement away from custodial maintenance to
vocational training. New vocational and educational programs are being adopted in a few
institutions (Blatt, 1970). In addition, community placement programs and halfway houses
are providing an alternative to large facilities (Mamula & Newman, 1973). In looking to
the future, Younie and Rusalem (1971) foresee
the following trends in institutional care:
(a) institutions will be located in communities closer to patients; (b) educational and
training services will be stressed; (c) re-
habilitated clients will be returned to the
community; and (d) there will be an emphasis
on prevention.

Change Clients. The client is viewed
in the third type of program as the object of

change. The orientation of these programs is
to prepare the handicapped for gainful employment in society. In essence, these programs
are at the heart of the rehabilitation movement. Two types of work programs exemplify
the client-change movement: work study and
vocational education.

Work study programs were developed to
blend academic course work with vocational
experience. These programs are located in
community-based residential facilities and
public school systems. The student population consists of youths who have experienced
problems functioning in the regular classroom
and remain as potential dropouts.

The principle which guides the work study
movement dictates that rather than forcing the
child to adapt to the traditional high school
program the educators should attempt to fit
the program to the individual child's needs.
The aim of the program is to develop the student's potential abilities for future employment.

In the first phase the student-client is
in an essentially academic school program.
The rehabilitation services consist primarily
of vocational diagnosis, vocational evaluation, and social and personal adjustment evaluation. During the second phase the student-
client receives an equal share of academic
and job oriented training. The rehabilitation activities include academic preparation,
prevocational training, and vocational training. In the third phase the student-client
devotes almost full time to job training with
supplemental academic instruction related specifically to job training.

In America, schools designed specifically
for the purpose of rehabilitation have had a
relatively short history (Oberman, 1965). In
1918, Massachusetts became the first state to

pass legislation providing funds to train disabled persons (Roberts, 1965). Other states
quickly followed the lead of Massachusetts
and enacted similar laws. In 1920, Congress
passed the Smith-Fess Bill (Industrial Rehabilitation Act) which became the first national law advocating vocational rehabilitation. The law provided monies to state governments interested in developing and maintaining
training programs for disabled workers. During the years following the Smith-Fess Bill,
numerous pieces of legislation (e.g., Barden-
LaFollette Act, 1943; Vocational Rehabilitation Amendment, 1954) advanced the development of services in vocational schools. The
impact of these funds has allowed vocational
schools to develop to the extent that today
they can furnish the full spectrum of rehabilitation services.

Vocational education exists as a part of
the total educational program combining academic development with vocational training.
For the mentally and physically handicapped,
the school's program prepares them for gainful
employment (Roberts, 1965). Each school is
to assist the handicapped individual with as-
sessing his vocational strengths and limitations. After the evaluation which documents
the extent of impairment, each client is
trained to develop vocational skills for employment in the competitive marketplace. Unlike other work programs, vocational schools
are committed to returning their clients to
the community. This commitment represents
the second objective of vocational schools--
to place each handicapped individual in a
position of employment where the chances for
successful adjustment are maximized.

To accomplish their objectives, vocational schools furnish a number of rehabilitation
services including evaluation, vocational
training, counseling, placement, and follow-
up. The provision of these services neces-

sitates the utilization of various professionals such as physicians, counselors, psychologists, teachers, special educators, and employers. The success of a program rests on
the ability of these professionals to function as a team.

The efforts of work study programs and
vocational schools, while laudable, have been
tarnished by internal conflicts. The scope
of training services, as previously cited,
entails the interweaving of various professional disciplines. Unfortunately, the necessary cooperation between professionals has
not been forthcoming and many vocational programs have stagnated. The following review
capsulizes many of the internal problems.

Wells (1973) reported that vocational
education has had to struggle to maintain its
niche in schools and has historically faced
not only an unfavorable image but also apathy.
This apathy has originated from both the school
and community. The bad image of vocational
education has had direct impact on the handicapped. Dunn (1973b) stated, "vocational and
technical schools have tended to bar low IQ
pupils because of their alleged tarnishing
effects on the status of these facilities
(p. 175)." The 1968 amendments to the Vocational Education Act of 1963 stipulated that
10 percent of the federal funds allocated
must be used to provide vocational education
to the handicapped. Even with such directive
legislation Wolfe (1973) indicated that during
the 1970-1971 fiscal year only a small percentage of these funds were used, and of those
used the blind received only a minute portion.
Hehir (1973) reported that occupational teachers exhibited negative attitudes and low ex-
pectation levels when confronted with the
prospect of teaching deaf students. Wrobel
and Colella indicated that special education
has been guilty of perpetuating its own autonomy and consequently diverging itself of

the mainstream of education (Lake, 1973).
Colella acknowledged that vocational education necessitates a melding of services but
claimed that the past has demonstrated that
professionals from special and occupational
education have failed to articulate their
mutual concerns and plan cooperative endeavors
beneficial to all pupils (Lake, 1973). Klinkhamer reported that vocational educators have
not wanted handicapped pupils in their programs (Lake, 1973). In a comprehensive review
of legislation concerning vocational education, Thompson (1973) had some interesting
comments in reference to Job Corps from a vocational educator's perspective.

> Contracts for the ... operation of
> Job Corps camps went directly to
> private companies. Vocational edu-
> cators were forced to sit on the
> sidelines and watch with some glee
> the disarray that often passed for
> education (p. 83).

From this perspective, "with some glee" does
not appear to represent an attitude commensurate with the development of the esprit de
corps needed to undertake the massive job of
vocational education.

The number of cooperative vocational rehabilitation-special education work study programs has diminished during the last few years.
Garrett indicated that the amount of federal
vocational rehabilitation funds expended an-
nually on research and demonstration projects
for the retarded has dropped from a high of
over three million dollars in 1965 to well
under one million dollars in 1970 (Dunn, 1973b).
Younie and Rusalem (1971) reported on a survey
which revealed the respective negative attitudes that the vocational rehabilitation counselors and the special education teachers had
of each other.

In summary, work study programs and vocational schools exist in order to rehabili-
tate handicapped youth. The facilities and
services provided represent the foundation
on which to develop a dynamic program. The
key to success, however, is the extent to
which the various participating disciplines
can constructively function together as a
team. Until now these disciplines have fos-
tered internal conflicts which have fractured
the rehabilitation process. Vocational schools
and work study programs, therefore, will become more productive as teamwork increases.

Combination Programs. The last type of
work program for the handicapped encompasses
the view that both the client and the environment can be changed. Sheltered workshops are
representative of the combination concept and
are considered,

> a nonprofit organization or institu-
> tion conducted for the purpose of
> carrying out a recognized program
> of rehabilitation for physically,
> mentally, and socially handicapped
> individuals by providing such in-
> dividuals with remunerative employ-
> ment and one or more other rehabil-
> itating activities of an education-
> al, psycho-social, therapeutic, vo-
> cational, or spiritual nature (Na-
> tional Association of Sheltered
> Workshops and Homebound Programs,
> 1961, p. 1).

Each sheltered workshop is unique to the
characteristics of the clients served, the
local community, and the administrators and
workers. However, sheltered workshops may
be grouped according to the eventual employment of the handicapped as either transitional, extended, or comprehensive (Gold, 1973).
A transitional workshop concentrates on the
development of vocational skills so that the

disabled worker will gain employment in the community. An extended workshop provides long-term employment to disabled individuals who cannot secure employment in competitive industry. The comprehensive workshop, which is the most common, provides services to both types of clients. The type of work found in sheltered workshops varies and generally is dictated by the abilities of the clients, the surrounding community, and the local industry. For the most part, each workshop adapts the work to local industrial needs and trains clients for employment in that industry. The specific work products can be categorized in three groups: (a) industrial subcontracts to local industry, (b) repair of products, and (c) manufacturing of new goods.

In order to attain the goal of employment for the handicapped, each sheltered workshop provides basic rehabilitation services: work evaluation, work adjustment, and work experience. Each client is evaluated in various vocational settings to assess his work limitations and capabilities. A work adjustment program is used to shape behavior conducive to long-term employment. The development of these behaviors is accomplished through work simulation tasks to accustom the handicapped individual to work schedules, rules, regulations, supervisors, etc. On the job work experience is used to increase the level of work skills needed for vocational employment. The work-oriented curriculum follows a sequential step-by-step progression of occupational skills. At each skill level the client is observed to see if his work production meets the required industrial standards. The curriculum covers the spectrum of employment opportunities ranging from unskilled assembly line tasks to highly complex skilled occupations. The purpose is to match as closely as possible the client's aptitudes to an appropriate occupation.

The number of services and facilities found in sheltered workshops demand a large budget. To meet the financial obligations sheltered workshops must draw economic support from a variety of sources. Economic self-support is possible but only by obtaining a large number of contractual agreements and having productive clients. However, self-sufficiency rarely is attained due to the need to provide expensive services. For this reason workshops canvass alternative sources of revenue including: federal, state, and local grants; community resources; and financial contributions. In addition, to reduce budget costs sheltered workshops solicit volunteer workers and the donation of free services.

Sheltered workshops represent an economic contradiction in our capitalistic system (Kolstoe & Frey, 1965). These nonprofit organizations with their emphasis on training and service have difficulty surviving in the competitive marketplace. Self-sufficiency, as cited previously, is a goal which for most workshops is unattainable. In order to approach economic solvency and avoid bankruptcy, workshops depend for the most part on industrial contracts. Although these contracts represent an economic blessing, they often are menial, unskilled jobs which pay relatively little to the handicapped (Gold, 1973). Since the existence of workshops is based on the utilization of work to develop skills in their clients, a variety of jobs are needed. The industrial contracts frequently foster only menial tasks and thus restrict the scope of vocational training available in sheltered workshops. To reverse the present unproductive conditions, Gold (1973) cited specific characteristics needed in future industrial contracts as: (a) the task should require the learning of a new skill; (b) adequate time must be allowed for production and training; (c) full-time man labor, rather than automation, should be emphasized; (d) a variety

of jobs should be provided; and (e) both the
shop and the client should profit. Effectiveness of sheltered workshops will be enhanced
as these contract characteristics are incorporated.

Architectual Barriers

Architectural barriers represent one of
the greatest handicaps to the amelioration of
efforts of disabled individuals. In construction of the physical world the environment has
been designed for the young and the healthy.
Forgotten have been the old, the mentally
handicapped, and the physically handicapped.
Moreover, in environments specifically assigned
as facilities for training the handicapped
these architectural barriers are ever present.
Simple obstacles such as narrow doorways, lack
of an elevator, inaccessible bathrooms, and
inadequate bathroom fixtures are invariably
blocking the handicapped from living a normal
life.

In a recent study of a typical university town only 27 buildings out of 200 sur-
veyed were found accessible to the handicapped
(Alpha Phi Omega, 1972). Everyday, normal
activities enjoyed by the majority such as
shopping, pursuing an education, and parking
a car become a chore. The ubiquitous problems
include narrow aisles, high curbs, narrow
rest room doors, steps, etc. Furthermore,
these barriers represent a major obstacle to
employment for handicapped citizens and, in
essence, deny the handicapped the right to a
normal life.

To reverse this process of architectural
discrimination some basic considerations are
suggested. In designing a facility it must
be considered whether the building will be
suitable for the various training and living
activities of handicapped individuals. The
furnishings should be adequately spaced and

comfortable, and the total building should
be accessible to the physically handicapped.
Other considerations are acoustics, lighting,
size, special services, etc. A guiding principle to remember is: If you would not design
it for yourself and your family, do not design
it for the handicapped (Ganges, 1970).

In summary, this chapter focused on the
rehabilitation facilities available to handicapped individuals. The facilities were divided according to the locus or object of
change, i.e., the handicapped individual or
the environment. Four types of facilities
were identified: (a) change environment,
(b) remove from society, (c) change clients,
and (d) combination programs. In the next
chapter a complete description of basic rehabilitation services found in these facilities is reviewed.

REFERENCES

Alpha Phi Omega. Architectural barriers in Charlottesville. Roanoke, Va.: Virginia Easter Seal Society for Crippled Children and Adults, 1972.

Blatt, B. Exodus from pandemonium. Boston: Allyn & Bacon, 1970.

Blatt, B., & Kaplan, F. Christmas in purgatory: A photographic essay on mental retardation. Boston: Allyn & Bacon, 1966.

Camphill Village, U.S.A. (Brochure). Copake, New York.

Dunn, L. M. An overview. In L. M. Dunn (Ed.), Exceptional children in the schools: Special education in transition. (2nd ed.) New York: Holt, Rinehart, & Winston, 1973. (a)

Dunn, L. M. Children with mild general learning disabilities. In L. M. Dunn (Ed.), Exceptional children in the schools: Special education in transition. (2nd ed.) New York: Holt, Rinehart, & Winston 1973. (b)

Ganges, A. G. Architecture. In J. Wortis (Ed.), Mental retardation: An annual review. New York: Grune & Stratton, 1970.

Gold, M. W. Research on the vocational habilitation of the retarded: The present, the future. In N. R. Ellis (Ed.), International review of research in mental retardation. Vol. 6. New York: Academic Press, 1973.

Hehir, R. G. Integrating deaf students for
    career education. Exceptional Children,
    1973, 39, 611-618.

Innisfree Village. (Brochure). Crozet, Vir-
    ginia.

Itard, J. M. G. The wild boy of Aveyron.
    New York: Appleton-Century-Crofts, 1962.

Kolstoe, O. P., & Frey, R. M. A high school
    work study program for mentally subnormal
    students. Carbondale, Ill.: Southern
    Illinois University Press, 1965.

Lake, T. P. Career education and the handi-
    capped child. Exceptional Children,
    1973, 39, 657-667.

Mamula, R. A., & Newman, N. Community place-
    ment of the mentally retarded. Spring-
    field, Ill.: Charles Thomas, 1973.

Mental illness and its treatment: Past and
    present. U. S. Department of Health,
    Education, and Welfare, Public Health
    Service Publication #1345, 1965. Cited
    by Garrett, J. Historical background.
    In D. Malikin & H. Rusalem (Eds.), Vo-
    cational rehabilitation for the disabled:
    An overview. New York: New York Univer-
    sity Press, 1969.

National Association of Sheltered Workshops
    and Homebound Programs, Publications
    Committee. Planning a workshop: A grow-
    ing responsibility. Washington, D. C.,
    1961.

Oberman, C. E. A history of vocational re-
    habilitation in America. Minneapolis:
    T. S. Denison, 1965.

Rhodes, W. C., & Gibbins, S. Community pro-
    gram for the behaviorally deviant child.

In H. C. Quay & J. S. Werry (Eds.), Psy-
chopathological disorders of childhood.
New York: Wiley & Sons, 1973.

Roberts, R. W. Vocational and practical arts
education: History, development, & principles. (2nd ed.) New York: Harper &
Row, 1965.

Scientific seer: Rudolf Steiner. MD, The
Medical News Magazine, 1969, 13, 245-
250.

Thompson, J. F. Foundations of vocational
education: Social and philosophical concepts. Englewood Cliffs, N. J.: Prentice-Hall, 1973.

Wells, C. E. Will vocational education survive? Phi Delta Kappan, 1973, 54, 369,
380.

Wolfe, H. E. Career education: A new dimension in education for living. The New
Outlook for the Blind, 1973, 67, 193-
199.

Younie, W. J., & Rusalem, H. The world of
rehabilitation: An atlas for special
educators. New York: John Day, 1971.

13. SERVICES FOR THE HANDICAPPED

The history of rehabilitation reveals a complete metamorphosis in thought and action. Changes in treatment of the handicapped have reflected an evolution in the underlying principles guiding the rehabilitation movement. In earlier periods the handicapped were ridiculed or removed from society, while today the attitude is toward helping the handicapped to help themselves. The principles which govern the current delivery of services date back to a 1958 seminar at Princeton, New Jersey (di Michael, 1969). Sixty-six national leaders in the fields of rehabilitation and psychology participated in the conference. Beatrice Wright (1959), the chairperson of the seminar, collected the conference statements and, as paraphrased by di Michael (1969), they are outlined as follows:

1. Every human being has an inalienable value and is worthy of respect for his own sake.
2. Every person has membership in society, and rehabilitation should cultivate his full acceptance.
3. The assets of the person should be emphasized, supported, and developed.
4. Reality factors should be stressed in helping the person to cope with his environment.

257

5.   Comprehensive treatment involves
the "whole person," because life-
areas are interdependent.
6.   Treatment should vary and be
flexible to deal with the special
characteristics of each person.
7.   Each person should assume as
much initiative and participation
as possible in the rehabilitation
plan and its execution.
8.   Society should be responsible,
through all possible public and private agencies, for the providing of
services and opportunities to the
disabled.
9.   Rehabilitation programs must be
conducted with interdisciplinary and
interagency integration.
10   Rehabilitation is a continuous
process that applies as long as help
is needed.
11.   Psychological and personal reactions of the individual are ever-
present and often crucial.
12.   The rehabilitation process is
complex and must be subject to constant reexamination--for each individual and for the program as a whole
(p. 13).

These principles direct the current implementation of rehabilitation services. Moreover, the list defines the goals of rehabilitation as: (a) to restore dignity and self-
worth to the handicapped, and (b) to provide
the handicapped an opportunity for a productive and independent livelihood. The impact
of these principles has charged vocational
rehabilitation with the responsibility of
preparing handicapped persons for employment.

Vocational rehabilitation traditionally
has focused on adults, but recent legislation
has authorized that services may be extended
to younger persons. The authorization to pro-

vide services to persons of all ages enables
vocational rehabilitation to complement the
career education concept over a longer span
of time by extending services to persons during all phases of career development, i.e.,
orientation, evaluation, training, employment,
and follow-up. A review of the history of vocational rehabilitation provides some insight
into how the field has expanded to the extent
that it currently is congruent with the career
education concept.

The Smith-Sears Act of 1918 was passed
to authorize services to disabled veterans
who were unable to return to their former
jobs. Two years later the Smith-Fess Act extended services to disabled citizens. Both
of these acts were viewed as a response to
temporary need, and it was not until the Social Security Act of 1935 that vocational rehabilitation was established as a permanent
service. One year later the Randolph-Shepard
Act established vending stands for the blind
in federal buildings. The Barden-LaFollette
Act of 1943 established that the mentally ill
and mentally retarded were eligible for vocational rehabilitation services (Younie &
Rusalem, 1971). In 1945 President Truman
designated a National Employ the Physically
Handicapped Week. Oberman (1965) indicated
that in 1954 Public Law 565 "added strength
to the existing State-Federal program and provided for extension and improvement through
special grants to the states that desired to
enter into new fields of rehabilitation (p.
316)." In 1965 Public Law 333 increased the
coverage of vocational rehabilitation services
to include social offenders and the disadvantaged. It also increased sheltered workshop
support and matching grant standardization
for training support. In conclusion, the
many federal statutes have enlarged the scope
of vocational rehabilitation to encompass many
disabled and disenfranchised groups.

The Disabled and Eligibility Requirements

Provisions for rehabilitation services are governed by federal and state laws concerning which population will receive support. State laws differ in specifying who is the beneficiary of services, although the federal statutes are more exact in documenting who will receive aid. Generally, the federal guidelines identify the following disabled groups as recipients of services (Younie & Rusalem, 1971).
1. Cardiac patients.
2. Cerebral palsied.
3. Disadvantaged.
4. Emotionally disturbed.
5. Hearing impaired.
6. Juvenile delinquent.
7. Mentally retarded.
8. Physically limited.
9. Visually imparied.

The eligibility requirements and the types of disabilities differ among the various states. However, enough similarity exists in eligibility standards to outline the following three basic criteria:
1. A disability must exist in the form of either a physical, mental, or emotional handicap which results in limitation.
2. The limitations caused by the disability must impose a vocational hardship on the individual.
3. A reasonable expectancy must exist that, as a result of the rehabilitation services, the individual will be able to enter gainful employment upon completion of the program.

In conclusion, disabled individuals who can satisfy the requirements are eligible for the full range of services available to them through vocational rehabilitation.

Basic Services

The services furnished by each rehabilitation agency differ according to the facilities and monies available to the agency and
to the needs of the clients and community.
The services, therefore, are not uniform but
vary from institution to institution. A number of basic services provide a framework for
establishing a model which follows the client
from intake to successful employment. The
model which is described below aims to help
the unemployed handicapped individual achieve
the state of gainful employment. The eight
stages of the model are: (a) intake, (b) diagnostic evaluation, (c) vocational evaluation, (d) guidance and counseling, (e) prevocational training, (f) vocational training,
(g) placement, and (h) follow-up. Each stage
is separately described with explanations outlining the objectives and procedures related
to each part.

Intake. The purpose of intake is to review the potential client's records to determine his eligibility for services and whether
admittance will be granted. Referrals for
intake interviews are received from various
community sources such as: (a) teachers,
(b) guidance counselors, (d) physicians,
(d) courts, (e) parents, (f) welfare agencies,
(g) employment offices, (h) social workers,
and (i) veteran groups. Present at the intake interview are the rehabilitation counselor, the potential client, and sometimes
the person who made the referral. The discussion focuses on whether or not the disabled
individual meets the eligibility criteria.

Diagnostic Evaluation. The objective
of the diagnostic evaluation is to ascertain
the extent of the disability and the imposed
limitations. Those conducting the evaluation
attempt to make a realistic, practical assessment of the client's present level of function-

ing and to predict future behavior. The areas
included in the evaluation are: (a) medical,
(b) psychological, and (c) social (McGowan,
1969; Roberts, 1965).

The purpose of a medical study is to determine the existence of an impairment which
places a limitation on the individual. Other
information to be gained includes the detec-
tion of any secondary disabilities and a current health status report. The evaluation
also may indicate if the disability can be
corrected through restoration. Medical reports should contain the diagnosis, prognosis,
limitations, and recommendations of the examining physician.

The psychological evaluation gives a
broad picture of the individual in terms of
social and emotional maturity and vocational
aspirations. The evaluation focuses on current and past behaviors (McGowan, 1969).
Counselor interviews and observations help
determine current behavior patterns. Psychological tests are frequently administered in
an attempt to measure potential performance
and actual achievement level. The psychological report should include a thorough comprehensive assessment of the client's psychological functioning and potential for future performance.

The social aspect of the evaluation centers on the past social history of the client.
The knowledge gained includes educational
level, work experience, family relations, home
environment, and overall life style. The importance of a detailed history is that it remains one of the best predictors of future
performance (McGowan, 1969).

Vocational Evaluation. Vocational evaluation measures the client's vocational assets
and limitations and places them in a frame of
reference which will aid in developing realis-

tic educational goals. The evaluation should
determine the specific work deficiencies which
must be compensated for in order to plan an
effective program. In essence, the purpose
of the evaluation is to match the client to
the proper vocational training program.

The evaluation is designed to describe
and/or measure many areas. Personal variables
observed are job interests, work attitudes,
responsibility, and aspirations. The physical
characteristics related to general job skills
are obtained through work simulation where
measures can be taken of manual dexterity,
visual acuity, speed, accuracy, and neatness.
The following outline illustrates many of the
areas in a vocational evaluation.

A. Prevocational Readiness for General Func-
    tioning in the Community.
    1.   Appearance.
    2.   Personal hygiene.
    3.   Neatness.
    4.   Care of property.
    5.   Personal finances.
    6.   Quality of work.
    7.   Use of phone.
    8.   Safety.
    9.   Independence.
    10. Self-controlled behavior.
    11. Self concept.
    12. Realistic goals.
    13. Use of transportation.
    14. Knowledge of existing employment in
         home community.
    15. Finding, applying for, and keeping a
         job.
    16. Ability to communicate to others.
    17. Consideration for others.
    18. Social acumen.
         a.   Peers.
         b.   Adults.
    19. Adaptation to new and different social
         groups.
    20. Ability to handle large or small mis-
         fortunes.

B. Prevocational Readiness to Work.
    1. Work attitudes.
    2. Adjustment to shop rules.
    3. Adjustment to changes in tasks.
    4. Ability to follow directions.
    5. Adjustment to work stresses.
    6. Adjustment to work demands.
    7. Ability to learn tasks or procedures.
    8. Reaction to supervision.
    9. Relations to co-workers.
    10. Ability to plan and complete work.
    11. Work satisfaction.

The evaluation report is based upon a composite of all factors in the evaluation--physical abilities, intellectual capacities, emotional factors, social adjustment, vocational abilities, and potential. A summary identifies specific skills, talents, and the client's production rate on job tryouts. Essentially, an evaluation report could contain one of five recommendations: (a) for prevocational training, (b) for on the job training, (c) for training at a special institution, (d) for continued education pursuits, and (e) not feasible for vocational rehabilitation.

Vocational Guidance and Counseling. From an administrative perspective, guidance and counseling facilitate the organization of the rehabilitation process. For the client guidance and counseling serve to interpret the relevant information concerning occupational training and placement into the decision-making process. Of additional importance to the client is the opportunity to voice problems and seek counseling related to adjustment or personal difficulties as well as occupational problems.

The services available to the client are: (a) personal information transfer, (b) educational and occupational data, (c) counseling, and (d) placement. After the evaluation report

has been processed and received by the rehabilitation counselor, an interview is scheduled between counselor and counselee. During
this meeting the counselor discusses the report with the client. The information covers
the counselee's interests, attitudes, abilities, and limitations, along with the recommendations of the rehabilitation team. During
the interview the counselor projects a realistic description of the present situation. A
second part of the interview allows the counselor to encompass the recommendations of the
evaluation report into a rehabilitation plan
which delineates educational and occupational
opportunities. The exchange marks the initial
process in matching the client to appropriate
job training. Furthermore, it allows the client an opportunity for self-evaluation and to
make a viable decision for future action.

    The counseling component exists to help
the disabled individual solve any personal or
social problems and to make a satisfactory
adjustment. To a strong individual the effect
of a disability can be disheartening, while to
a weaker person it can be "the straw that broke
the camel's back." The psychological effects
of a disability arise from: (a) the disability, (b) the client's attitude, or (c) the reaction of others (McGowan, 1969). The after-
math of a negative reaction to a disability
stands as a barrier to successful adjustment.
Counseling, then, exists to identify, interpret, and ameliorate those problems which
hinder the client's adjustment.

    Prevocational Training. The purpose of
prevocational training is to identify adjustment problems and to reduce these difficulties
through specific and individualized attention
to each area. The services focus on activities
of daily living necessary for good personal and
vocational work adjustment.

    Prevocational training, traditionally, is
included in secondary programs for the handi-

capped. Each student-client is observed, and
the discrepancy between adequate vocational
behavior and the client's on the job vocational behavior is measured. After evaluation a
prevocational training program for each student is designed to minimize the discrepancy.
Completion of prevocational training leads
into vocational training.

Classroom instruction uses a variety of
simulated and real work tasks which are germane to many occupations. Training areas may
include: health and grooming, money management, transportation, housing, telephone use,
job applications, interpersonal relations, and
care and use of equipment.

Vocational Training. The purpose of vocational training is to provide an opportunity
to the client to acquire skills and attitudes
necessary for gainful employment in his chosen
field. Each client is placed in a work environment where his behavior can be observed.
During this phase the focus is on skill development which concentrates on compensating
for work deficiencies. The actual training is
provided in various settings.

On the job training furnishes the opportunity for specific occupational development.
Supervision during training is essential in
order to promote a satisfactory training experience for the client. For this reason, the
counselor frequently visits the client and employer and helps to implement corrective measures.

Formal training courses and related instruction review essential work habits and
work skills. The nature of the occupation
defines the curriculum which generally is a
refinement of the earlier training. The following outline is an example of the job related instruction and skill refinement typical
of vocational training.

I. Job Related Instruction.
  A. Language and communication skills necessary to perform jobs.
     1. Studying manuals, instructional materials.
     2. Reading and following directions for specific projects.
     3. Knowledge of terms and their use.
     4. Ability to understand written or verbal instructions.
     5. Ability to understand written or verbal communications from management.
     6. Ability to communicate verbally or in writing to supervisors or co-workers about specific job clusters.
  B. Practical math.
     1. Ability to calculate, measure, or observe various parts of a mathematical operation.
     2. Ability to record date if necessary.
     3. Ability to read dials, instruments, or other measuring devices.
  C. Understanding the operation and repair of equipment from:
     1. Demonstrations.
     2. Schematics.
     3. Mechanical drawings or similar material.
  D. Ability to complete a project by following plans, schematics, mechanical drawings, etc.
  E. General scientific principles related to this training.
     1. Understand concepts and application.
     2. New developments in particular occupation.
  F. Use of instructional aids.
     1. Movies.
     2. Slides.
     3. Illustrations.
     4. Charts.
     5. Programmed material, etc.

G. Employment information regarding specific trade.
   1. Wages.
   2. Unions.
   3. Availability of work in locality.
   4. Hours.
H. Specific safety requirements of trade.
   1. Specific job.
   2. Others nearby.
   3. Whole plant or place of employment.
I. Meaningfulness of job in relation to:
   1. Other trades.
   2. Other jobs in same place of employment.
   3. Local community.
   4. State and wider geographic community.
J. Personal and social requisites of job or trade.
K. Consultations with skilled workers in the trade.
L. Visits to other job locations.

II. Skill Refinement.
   A. Use of tools specifically related to on the job training or vocational training.
      1. Development of fine dexterity.
      2. Ability to make fine discriminations in judgment and perception for tool selection.
      3. Constant practice to improve proficiency.
   B. Understanding the use of equipment.
      1. Theoretical.
      2. Practical.
      3. Safety aspects.
   C. Improving quality and quantity of work.
   D. Refinement of organized and neat work habits.
   E. Improve tolerance of particular physical stresses connected with trade or job, e.g.,

1. Standing.
2. Reaching.
3. Stooping.
4. Bending.
5. Balancing.

Placement. Job placement means placing
the client on a job commensurate with the rehabilitation plan and vocational training.
The goal of placement should afford the client
the optimum chance for vocational adjustment.

The rehabilitation counselor is responsible for locating potential placement sites.
The counselor, in canvassing the community
for potential employers, should present to
the employer an accurate description of the
client's disability and the rehabilitation
plan. After gaining the consent of the employer, the counselor is responsible for final
client placement.

Follow-Up. The purpose of follow-up is
to determine the extent of adjustment. The
counselor is responsible for the follow-up
interview and is to determine the client's
satisfaction with his work situation. At this
time contact with the employer is helpful to
explore sensitive areas for clarification.

Follow-up also serves to provide a realistic evaluation of the rehabilitation program and services. The information gained in
follow-up is beneficial for program planning,
updating, and revision.

The function of vocational rehabilitation
is not to lead handicapped individuals "by the
hand throughout life." It does not seek to
"pigeonhole" people but rather to aid them in
achieving a degree of independence and mobil-
ity through gainful employment so they may
have a broad base for self-determination in
their future growth and development.

Obstacles to Rehabilitation

In the discussion of the delivery of rehabilitation services, it was inferred that
the process is a smooth transition from service to service. Unfortunately, vocational
rehabilitation is not characterized by smooth-
ness, for the road to rehabilitation is marred
with many unforeseen obstacles. A selected
few of these obstacles are discussed below.

The disabled individual, although the
recipient of the services, may present obstacles which hinder the program. For example, the client may not appear for a diagnostic evaluation, be habitually tardy to
training classes, or appear for a placement
interview in unkempt, shoddy dress. The family of the disabled also may undermine the
best efforts of a rehabilitation counselor.
For example, a young client may not be transported to his appointments, the family may
move from community to community, or the family may feel antagonistic to any community
worker. A rehabilitation program without full
community support will have difficulty in
meeting budgetary obligations and delivering
adequate services. Other problems which may
arise are: (a) inability to travel, (b) un-
realistic aspirations, (c) lack of emotional
stability, (d) inadequate communication skills,
and (e) poor work motivation (Younie & Rusalem,
1971). Any of these obstacles may restrict
the rehabilitation effort; however, through
the skills and determination of the rehabilitation team, especially the counselor, each
obstacle can be overcome.

The Rehabilitation Counselor

Throughout the discussion tangential reference has been directed toward the rehabilitation counselor. In Chapter 3 a discussion
focused on the personality characteristics of
the counselor and how in the growth process he

can influence the client's life style. Here
the rehabilitation counselor is reintroduced
with a view to his role, his task as a team
member, and his specific functions.

The rehabilitation counselor represents
a link between the world of the physically,
mentally, and emotionally handicapped and
the world of work. As a counselor, he can
help the client to confront his disability,
to understand his abilities and limitations,
and to engage in a program leading to a more
productive life.

The rehabilitation counselor functions
as a viable member of the rehabilitation team.
Depending on the community and the handicapped
individuals served, the rehabilitation team
is comprised generally of: physician, nurse,
psychologist, psychiatrist, occupational therapist, social worker, teacher, employer, volunteer personnel, and the rehabilitation counselor. The task of the counselor is to coordinate the services of the other team members into a unified plan. The counselor, as
the team coordinator, is visible throughout
the entire rehabilitation process. For example, in the early stages of diagnostic evaluation, the counselor with the rehabilitation
team interprets, analyzes, and synthesizes
all vocationally significant data regarding
the student and relates them to occupational
requirements. Also, within the framework of
the team structure, the counselor develops
the rehabilitation plan and discusses it with
each individual client.

In order to secure employment, the rehabilitation counselor is responsible for development of job opportunities within the
community. Communication is imperative between the employer and the agency. Therefore,
the counselor frequently meets with employers
to explain the educational and rehabilitation
program, the abilities and disabilities of the

client, and to perform public relation work.
In terms of placement the counselor is responsible for ensuring that the work is suitable
for the client. He places clients in part-
time jobs, visits the job site at frequent
intervals to determine progress, and evaluates
the clients' adjustment.

In essence, the counselor functions within the total spectrum of the rehabilitation
process. As a team member he coordinates
services and evaluates progress and thus represents a mainstay to the client.

Services for Exceptional Children

In directing energy toward disabled and
exceptional individuals, the professions of
rehabilitation and special education embrace
similar goals. Unfortunately, lack of communication and knowledge of other services
have thwarted efforts to work in unison. Duplication of effort and inadequate delivery
of services have resulted from this lack of
teamwork. Educators and rehabilitation counselors frequently have recognized their lack
of teamwork and have initiated joint programs.
Younie and Rusalem (1971) provided the rationale in stating, "The justification for
rehabilitation teamwork is that the combined
impact of participating exceeds the sum of
their individual efforts (p. 28)." In essence, the rehabilitation effort gains strength
and effectiveness when the two professions act
as a team. For this reason a discussion of
services for the handicapped would remain in-
complete without a description of the facilities and services available to exceptional
children.

Dunn (1973) identified 12 alternative
plans for serving the exceptional child. To
the rehabilitation counselor these services
represent potential sources of aid for students in vocational education. Dunn catego-

rized these services into four subgroups:
(a) day school plans, (b) residential or boarding school facilities, (c) hospital instruction, and (d) homebound instruction.

Day School Plans. Since almost 90 percent of exceptional children attend day schools,
a great number of services are furnished in
the day school setting. For this reason, Dunn
(1973) subgrouped day school services into
nine categories.

Special education instructional materials
and equipment service are provided for students who can function in the educational
mainstream. The supportive service is for
materials or equipment, such as a braille
reader for a blind child or a special desk
for an orthopedically handicapped student.

Special education consultants to regular
teachers afford indirect service to the exceptional child. The consultant's service
is directed to the regular teacher. For example, the consultant may demonstrate diagnostic teaching or suggest alternative methods of instruction with a student.

Direct service to exceptional children
is found with itinerant or school-based tutors. The tutors spend a majority of time
in individualized or small group instruction
with students who have a special need. The
remaining time is spent in a consultative
role with the regular teacher.

In resource programs the exceptional
child remains enrolled in a regular class but
receives direct instruction from a special
education teacher. The special education
teacher provides instruction and coordinates
her efforts with those of the regular classroom teacher.

Children who need more direct special
education instruction are enrolled in part-

time special classes. The coordination of
services between the regular and special education class enables the child to receive
special services yet participate in the educational mainstream.

Self-contained special classes are designed for children who experience difficulty
functioning in the regular classroom. Generally, the classes represent a homogeneous
group of children with the same type of exceptionality. Although the students take part
in some school-wide activities, i.e., physical
education, art, and music, these classes are
segregated from the mainstream of education.

In the combination of regular and special
day schools, exceptional children are bussed
to a central school and share the facility
with children from the immediate vicinity.
The exceptional children are brought together
in order that essential educational classroom
services can be provided.

Children who experience a great difficulty in regular classes may receive their
total educational instruction in a special
day school. The school population usually
includes one type of exceptionality. For example, special schools have been designed for
the severely emotionally disturbed.

A relatively new plan is found in the
diagnostic and prescriptive teaching centers.
Children are brought to these facilities to
receive instruction for a short period of
time. During this period a team of educators
and diagnosticians evaluates the child's performance and develops a remedial plan. The
child then continues at his regular school
where his instruction is based on the remedial
teaching strategy.

Residential or Boarding Schools. Approximately 10 percent of exceptional children re-

ceive services in residential or boarding
schools (Dunn, 1973). Boarding schools are
considered to provide services that are un-
available in local systems. The students
generally are those who cannot function in
a regular class setting and are in need of
the higher quality of service. Residential
schools are similar to institutions where
the main task is to remove the child from
the mainstream of society in order to provide
the intensive services required to rehabili-
tate him.

Hospital Instruction. Children confined
to a hospital or convalescent home are eligible for special education services from their
local school systems. If the period of hos-
pitalization disrupts education, a teacher
is assigned to tutor the child.

Homebound Instruction. Homebound instruction represents the most segregated of
special education services. The students who
receive this service are chronically ill or
convalescing from an illness or accident.
The instruction is furnished by either an
itinerant teacher or the regular classroom
teacher. Since the child is isolated from
the mainstream of education, a recent attempt
has been made to minimize the number of children on homebound instruction.

The decision concerning the proper assignment for a child is influenced by many
variables. Dunn (1973) identified the characteristics of the child, his school, his
parents, and the community as directly influencing the decision-making process. Some
of the child's variables are: (a) type and
degree of disability, (b) motivation factor,
(c) academic performance, and (d) behavioral
characteristics. Factors included under
school variables are: (a) adequacy of regular class program, (b) alternative special
education facilities, and (c) competence of

special educators. The parental and community factors include: (a) parental support, (b) home environment, and (c) community services.

Although these factors influence the assignment decision, Dunn (1973) called for "normalization" as a guiding principle in the placement decision. Normalization states that the child should be integrated as much as possible within his school, home, and community. In effect, the programs which segregate the child from his environment should be implemented only as a last resort.

Conclusion

This chapter focused on services common to rehabilitation facilities. The services which were discussed included intake, diagnostic evaluation, vocational evaluation, guidance and counseling, prevocational training, vocational training, placement, and follow-up. The services exist to facilitate positive behavioral growth on the part of the handicapped. Also discussed in the chapter were provisions and services for exceptional children.

The realm of rehabilitation and special education services was presented as an overview. What remains is an analysis of the two predominant views which influence teaching, i.e., humanism and behaviorism. These two methodologies encompass the spectrum of strategies for teaching handicapped individuals. The next chapter is directed to the important issue of effective teaching.

REFERENCES

di Michael, S.   The current scene.   In D.
    Malikin & H. Rusalem (Eds.), The voca-
    tional rehabilitation of the disabled.
    New York: New York University Press,
    1969.

Dunn, L. M.   An overview.   In L. M. Dunn
    (Ed.), Exceptional children in the
    schools: Special education in transi-
    tion.   (2nd ed.)   New York: Holt, Rine-
    hart, & Winston, 1973.

McGowan, J.   Referral, evaluation, treatment.
    In D. Malikin & H. Rusalem (Eds.), The
    vocational rehabilitation of the dis-
    abled.   New York: New York University
    Press, 1969.

Oberman, C. E.   A history of vocational re-
    habilitation in America.   Minneapolis:
    T. S. Denison, 1965.

Roberts, R. W.   Vocational and practical arts
    education: History, development, and
    principles.   (2nd ed.)   New York: Harper
    & Row, 1965.

Wright, B. A. (Ed.)   Psychology and rehabili-
    tation.   Washington, D. C.:   American
    Psychological Association, 1959.

Younie, W. J., & Rusalem, H.   The world of
    rehabilitation: An atlas for special
    educators.   New York: John Day, 1971.

14. HUMANISM AND BEHAVIORISM[1]

Whenever an individual assumes the responsibility of helping a handicapped person attain a meaningful life style which is characterized by occupational competence and social adjustment, a dilemma emerges. First, an individual must deal with his feelings toward the client, and secondly he must understand how these feelings influence his acquisition of the skills which are required to help a handicapped person. In other words, educators and counselors readily ask the question, "What is the relationship between my feelings and the delivery of rehabilitation services?"

This dilemma concerning feelings and services is vividly illustrated by a scene from a movie about Roy Campanella and his adjustment to a disabling condition. Campanella was a great baseball player whose baseball career was abruptly ended when he became severely paralyzed as a result of a car accident. Although he was a skeptical and de-

---

1. Adapted in part from: Payne, J. S., & Mercer, C. D. Effective teaching may not be enough: Behaviorist and/or humanist teachers. Thought Patterns in Education, 1973, 1(3), pp. 12-15. Reprinted by permission.

pressed patient, his personal therapist,
through concerted efforts, was able to obtain Campanella's confidence. The two worked
arduously for months developing Campanella's
self-help skills. It was obvious that the
two people grew very close to each other and
that Campanella depended on his therapist to
assist him in the activities of daily living,
e.g., eating and dressing. Although a strong
affective bond developed between them, the
time arrived when the therapist was confronted
with the dilemma created by his personal feelings and their relationship to the delivery
of services. For example, one day at lunch
time the therapist assisted Campanella into
a wheelchair and transported him to the dining
room. Campanella, somewhat dismayed, asked,
"What are we doing here?" The therapist told
him it was time that he learn to eat unassisted
in the dining room. Campanella pleaded for
the therapist to stay and assist him with his
meal, but the therapist matter-of-factly walked
away and from a distance agonizingly watched
his patient struggle to feed himself. Campanella spilled his peas, dropped his milk, and
angrily shoved his plate on the floor. After
leaving the dining room, the therapist emphasized that it was necessary for Campanella to
develop a broader perspective concerning his
therapy and focus on caring for himself unassisted. The therapist pointed out that disabled individuals could not indefinitely depend on assistance from others and also make
an adequate adjustment to natural environments, e.g., home, work, etc. In this example it is obvious that the therapist had to
deal with his intense feelings concerning his
patient yet simultaneously structure services
in a manner which seemed therapeutically best.

Although it is apparent that feelings
exist throughout the rehabilitation process,
their importance and role remain in question.
Two predominant schools of thought, humanism
and behaviorism, consider the role of feelings

from opposing viewpoints. A humanist considers feelings as an integral part of the
rehabilitation process. On the other hand,
the behaviorist sees little relevance in considering feelings. This dichotomy presented
by the behavioristic and humanistic viewpoints
is similar to the previously cited attitudes
found in the areas of business management and
rehabilitation counseling.

In business the two most popular administrative approaches are Theories X and Y, which
in philosophy and application are opposing
viewpoints. An administration based on Theory
X is described as a structured, controlled
environment in which the manager assumes an
authoritarian posture. On the other hand, an
administration based on Theory Y is characterized by an unstructured, democratic, and trust-
ful atmosphere.

In the realm of counseling, the most common therapeutic techniques are labeled directive and nondirective, and these techniques
parallel behaviorism and humanism respectively.
Directive counseling demands that the counselor assume a directive, structured, and organized posture. On the other hand, the nondirective counselor focuses on the affective
domain of the client and utilizes reflective
techniques, e.g., the therapeutic sessions
are often unstructured and the client's verbal
responses direct the treatment. In summary,
the different philosophical viewpoints salient
to administration theories and counseling reflect a basic division which may be examined
within the humanism-behaviorism domain.

In education a similar schism exists concerning teacher training. Certain advocates
call for an extremely directive, behaviorally
oriented teacher, while others recommend a
more humanistic position.

The remainder of this chapter focuses on
an examination of some of the current discus-

sions which are occurring among educators concerning the training of teachers as behaviorists and/or humanists. Many individuals discussing this issue seldom get beyond the descriptive or definition stage because they get
bogged down in semantics or are very opinion-
ated. A discussion which briefly defines humanism and behaviorism and identifies the cor-
responding issues related to teacher effectiveness is presented in order to facilitate
an understanding of how these philosophical
viewpoints pragmatically effect education.

Definitions

Some individuals view the philosophical
viewpoints of humanists and behaviorists as
diametrically opposing positions. The humanist is defined as a warm, sensitive individual
who assists students in their development
through a nurturing process which improves
self-worth, self-image, and self-esteem. The
humanist believes that as children find their
"true" selves they begin to grow. Much, if
not all, of the learning is child directed
rather than teacher directed. The behaviorist,
on the other hand, is looked upon as a technician who sets goals for the learner and assists him in attaining these goals through environmental manipulation, i.e., controlling
various stimuli and reinforcers. By describing the humanist and the behaviorist in this
manner, it is theoretically possible to have
a humanist who is warm, sensitive, and views
the learner as the center of learning at one
extreme of the continuum, while at the other
extreme have a behaviorist as a distant technician who views the learner as being almost
incapable of learning without the careful
manipulation of environmental events. Although most people operate somewhere between
the two extremes, the dichotomy is helpful
in exploring various questions and issues
which are commonly discussed among educators
today.

Issues

The first question is, "Which of the two
extremes makes the best teacher?" To answer
this question it is helpful to define the
"best" teacher. Is the "best" teacher a leader or educational superstar whose existential
problems focus on peace, love, freedom and/or
society's well-being? To be honest, it is
difficult, if not impossible, to define the
"best" teacher. It is apparent that a prospective teacher can enter a teacher training
institution and learn all about himself, feelings, and children. He can learn about different types of educational programs but, if
he fails to develop the teaching competencies
necessary to facilitate learning, he often
will fail as a teacher and quickly terminate
his teaching career. It also is obvious that
a future teacher can enter a teacher training
institution and learn about teaching processes,
curricula, and various techniques and after
graduation enter the teaching profession and
actually do harm to children. When consideration is given to these two facts about teacher
training programs, it behooves educators to
analyze what is necessary for the teacher to
know in order to survive in the classroom instead of concentrating on what it takes to be
the "best" teacher. If a teacher cannot survive, he may be an outstanding person but will
not be around long enough to facilitate learning in children. However, if these teachers
remain in the classroom, it is possible for
them to have an impact in the school and community by applying their exceptional qualities
of creative excellence, special talents, and/or
charisma.   .

So what is necessary for an individual
to be able to hold a teaching position? To
begin with, a teacher must know how to set up
and implement a teaching strategy or a remedial
instruction program. He must know what to
teach and where to locate resources which im-

improve his curricula content. Finally, the
teacher must develop classroom management
skills and alternatives for teaching various
concepts. If the prospective teacher pos-
esses these competencies, he will survive as
an _effective_ teacher yet may be characterized
as an educational technician. Children will
learn from him; however, it is possible for
children to learn from a technician without
enjoying it. It is even possible for children to learn things which are actually detri-
mental to them. The ultimate purpose of an
educational technician is to change the learner in some way.

> The child who is exposed to a first
> grade teacher should be different at
> the end of first grade than he was
> at the beginning. The worst thing
> that could happen to a teacher would
> be to expose himself, his talents,
> and his skills to a child and the
> child remain unaffected.
> Basically educators have evolved
> from a field of conservatives. In-
> stead of desiring to change kids, to
> excite them, they have had a strong
> fear of the possibility of hurting
> the children to the extent that they
> have been content to maintain the
> status quo. The dominance of a strong-
> er desire not to hurt anybody over
> the desire to stimulate has led us
> into an era of ineffective education.
> Effective education changes kids; ef-
> fective teachers change kids.
> Now for the kicker--effective
> communication systems change kids but
> the ability to change _does_ _not_ _neces-_
> _sarily_ _connotate_ _change_ _for_ _the_ _good._
> Thus, education must strive to be ef-
> fective, yet be effective in a posi-
> tive way; that is, have _positive_ ef-
> fects on children. This directional
> influence of education on children

lies, to a large extent, in the hands
of the teacher, not the child, parent, school system or the President
of the United States (Stainback, Payne,
Stainback, Payne, 1973, p. 3).

Considering the current emphasis on "accountability," only effective teachers will
hold jobs. All teachers must be effective.
If a teacher cannot justify his existence, the
day is coming soon when he will be dismissed.
However, educators are foolish if they believe
that behavioral change is the ultimate in
teaching.

Although the contribution behaviorists
have made to education in relation to behavioral change, accountability, behavioral objectives, etc. should not be minimized, it is
important that these contributions be placed
in a proper perspective. This perspective
involves considering the behavioral contributions as forming the core of initial survival
skills necessary for holding a job.

Most humanists have difficulty handling
the concept of learning as behavioral change
because, when they view behavioral change as
only coming about through some type of manipulation, they must ask, "Who has the right to
manipulate another person?" The humanists
ask this question because they conceive that
most meaningful learning is intrinsic, while
the manipulation of environmental events is
considered an imposition on the learner. The
humanists realize that people can be manipulated but this manipulation of people is not
an honorable thing. However, as one studies
what a humanist strives for, i.e., self-actualization, the question concerning manipulation becomes answerable within the humanist's
framework. As a learner grows and develops,
the goal is to become himself--his real self.
This usually is referred to as becoming a
self-actualized person. A self-actualized

person is a person who is sensitive, has full
and vivid experiences, indulges in self-inquiry, is honest, and has trust in himself.
In short, this person is a man among men. He
knows himself as well as his fellowman.

According to Maslow (1971), the self-
actualized individual is a most healthy person and is "ought-perceptive," i.e., he seems
to be less "ought-blind," more understanding
of situations, and capable of making value
decisions. Maslow stated,

> If we want to answer the question how
> tall can the human species grow, then
> obviously it is well to pick out the
> ones who are already tallest and study
> them. If we want to know how fast a
> human being can run, then it is no
> use to average out the speed of a
> "good sample" of the population; it
> is far better to collect Olympic
> gold medal winners and see how well
> they can do. If we want to know the
> possibilities of spiritual growth,
> value growth, or moral development
> in human beings, then I maintain that
> we can learn most by studying our most
> moral, ethical or saintly people (p. 7).

This line of reasoning seems to be apropos to
the question, "Who has the right to manipulate
other people?" Ironically the humanists (ones
who are most bothered by the question) have
the best answer to this question. The answer
is the "self-actualized" individual. Thus,
the behaviorist or technician may be the most
effective teacher; however, the direction of
the effectiveness, be it honorable or dis-
honorable, lies within the bailiwick of the
humanist. Hence, it appears that the most
effective and best teacher is the humanist
with technical skills and, even better, is a
humanist who uses technical skills for the
betterment of people and their environment

In order for a teacher to be a superstar
and/or leader in the teaching profession, he
must have humanistic qualities and behavioral
qualities. He must be a self-actualizing person and possess teaching techniques necessary
for the enhancement of learning. According
to the behaviorist, these techniques can be
accomplished best by being objective. Objectivity to the behaviorist is as important as
the proverbial M&M itself. If objectivity is
taken away, the entire technical framework of
a behaviorist has been destroyed. Self-actualized individuals seem to value affectiveness, but most behaviorists claim that too
much affectiveness (or feelings) interferes
with objectivity. According to Maslow (1971),
objectivity may best be achieved by individuals possessing humanistic qualities. Maslow
stated,

> My work with monkeys, I am sure, is
> more "true," more "accurate," in a
> certain sense, more objectively true
> than it would have been if I had dis-
> liked monkeys. The fact was that I
> was fascinated with them. I became
> fond of my individual monkeys in a
> way that was not possible with my
> rats. I believe that the kind of work
> reported by Lorenz, Tinbergen, Good-
> dall, and Schaller is as good as it
> is, as instructive, illuminating, true,
> because these investigators "loved"
> the animals they were investigating.
> At the very least this kind of love
> produces interest and even fascina-
> tion, and therefore great patience
> with long hours of observation. The
> mother, fascinated with her baby, who
> examines every square inch of it again
> and again with the greatest absorp-
> tion, is certainly going to know more
> about her baby in the most literal
> sense than someone who is not inter-
> ested in that particular baby. Some-

thing of the sort, I have found, is
true between sweethearts. They are
so fascinated with each other that
examining, looking, listening, and
exploring becomes itself a fascinat-
ing activity upon which they can
spend endless hours. With a nonloved
person this would hardly be the case.
Boredom would set in too rapidly (p. 7).

However, if an obsession with the affective
realm develops and concerns predominantly focus on love, fellowship, and friendliness,
Maslow stated,

> But finally, and perhaps most impor-
> tant of all, if we love or are fas-
> cinated or are profoundly interested,
> we are less tempted to interfere, to
> control, to change, to improve. My
> finding is that, that which you love,
> you are prepared to leave alone. In
> the extreme instance of romantic love,
> and of grandparental love, the be-
> loved person may even be seen as al-
> ready perfect so that any kind of
> change, let alone improvement, is re-
> garded as impossible or even impious
> (pp. 17-18).

Therefore, if observation is important to education and learning, a combination of humanism
and behaviorism may be the only answer when
talking about developing "best" teachers, su-
perstars, and/or leaders. Thus, educators
need to be concerned about not training either
of the two extremes.

It is not sufficient for a teacher to be
nice, affective, and well liked. He must be
able to justify his existence and this is commonly demonstrated through the measurement of
quality and quantity of student learning. A
teacher can survive and be effective and show
large learning increments in his children, but

upon close examination it might be discovered
that he is a mediocre teacher. To be "best,"
he must stimulate self-inquiry. He must stimulate children to the point that they get involved in thinking. The behaviorist talks
about learning as behavioral change but seldom
talks about thinking. The "best" teacher must
be concerned about thinking. To facilitate
thinking it is helpful if the educational leader is a self-actualizing person. However, he
needs to possess technical skills and competencies for the enhancement of learning in
addition to thinking. In measurement the degree of sophistication to quantify self-inquiry has not been obtained. However, if a
person looks closely enough it is possible
to see self-inquiry in terms of growth, becoming, and thinking, and, if it can be seen,
by the behaviorist's definition, it can be
measured.

The basic question now is, "If the 'best'
teacher needs the ingredients of both the humanist and the behaviorist, how is he best
developed?" Should teacher trainees be taught
humanistic qualities first and then later behavioristic qualities, or should they be taught
the technological skills first and the affective skills later, or can the two be developed
simultaneously? This is a difficult question
to answer, but at this time it appears that
the two cannot be developed simultaneously
because on the surface the two are so diametrically opposed that a future teacher would
have difficulty comparing and contrasting the
two for the betterment of himself. Also, if
an individual is very humanistically oriented
before entering a teacher training program,
it is possible that he will refuse to learn
technical skills for manipulating students.
In other words, he will refuse to develop
survival skills. Unfortunately, if a teacher
trainee is obsessed with things such as worth,
self-image, ego, self-actualization, unfolding,
and nurturing, he is frequently unable to ben-

efit from a competency-based training program.
He is primarily concerned with <u>acceptance</u> but
not with growing, changing, or stimulating.
If a future teacher enters a teacher training
program and has grown on the humanistic scale
toward the extreme of acceptance to such a
degree that he refuses to set educational goals,
it is possible that this individual must be
content with being a nice, angelic, mediocre
teacher. In order to build a teacher who can
enhance learning by the attainment of specified goals in addition to developing self-inquiry in his students, this individual must
have technical skills and competencies to do
so and cannot operate on intuition or remain
predominantly in the affective realm. This
teacher must develop the skills to prod, push,
challenge, parry, love, admire, observe, and
adore. The education of young children is so
important and youth is such a prized commodity
that educators cannot afford to hire, promote,
or train extremists. From a teaching perspective the most extreme humanistic teacher acceptable would be a "lover with technique" and
the most extreme behavioristic teacher acceptable would be a "warm machine."

In essence,

Average Teachers	Tell
Good Teachers	Demonstrate
Excellent Teachers	Explain
Gifted Teachers	Inspire

REFERENCES

Maslow, A. H. The farther reaches of human nature. New York: Viking Press, 1971.

Stainback, W. C., Payne, J. S., Stainback, S. B., & Payne, R. A. Establishing a token economy in the classroom. Columbus, Ohio: Charles E. Merrill, 1973.

BIBLIOGRAPHY

Alpha Phi Omega. *Architectural barriers in Charlottesville*. Roanoke, Va.: Virginia Easter Seal Society for Crippled Children and Adults, 1972.

Bereiter, C., & Engelmann, S. *Teaching disadvantaged children in the preschool*. Engelwood Cliffs, N. J.: Prentice-Hall, 1966.

Bissell, J. S. *Planned variation in Head Start and Follow Through*. Washington, D. C.: Department of Health, Education, & Welfare, 1972.

Blatt, B. *Exodus from pandemonium*. Boston: Allyn & Bacon, 1970.

Blatt, B., & Kaplan, F. *Christmas in purgatory: A photographic essay on mental retardation*. Boston: Allyn & Bacon, 1966.

Boyd, W. N. Vocational rehabilitation of the mentally retarded. *Canada's Mental Health*, 1964, 12, 17.

Brazziel, W. Two years of Head Start. *Phi Delta Kappan*, 1967, 48, 344-348.

Caldwell, B. The rationale for early intervention. *Exceptional Children*, 1970, 36, 717-727.

Camphill Village, U.S.A. (Brochure). Copake, New York.

Capobianco, R. J., & Jacoby, H. B. The Fairfax plan: A high school program for mildly retarded youth. In J. H. Rothstein (Ed.), *Mental retardation: Readings*

291

and resources. (2nd ed.) New York: Holt, Rinehart, & Winston, 1971.

Chaffin, J. D., Haring, N. G., & Hudson, F. I've just found a job. Kansas Teacher, 1965, 74, 30-35.

Chaffin, J. D., Haring, N. G., & Smith, J. O. A selected demonstration for the vocational training of mentally retarded youth. Kansas City, Kansas: University of Kansas Medical Center, 1967.

Cicirelli, V. G. The impact of Head Start: An evaluation of the effects of Head Start on children's cognitive and affective development. Vol. 1. Springfield, Va.: Clearinghouse, 1969.

Clark, G. The man who tapped the secrets of the universe. Waynesboro, Va.: The University of Science and Philosophy, 1973.

Cohen, J. S. Community day work in an institutional vocational training program. American Journal of Mental Deficiency, 1962, 66, 514-579.

Cohen, J. S. Employer attitudes toward hiring mentally retarded individuals. American Journal of Mental Deficiency, 1963, 67, 705-713.

Cohen, J. S., & Williams, C. F. A five phase vocational training program in a residential school. American Journal of Mental Deficiency, 1961, 66, 230-237.

Coleman, J. S. Equality of educational opportunity. Washington, D. C.: United States Government Printing Office, 1966.

Coleman, R. W., & Provence, S. Environmental retardation (hospitalism) in infants living in families. <u>Pediatrics</u>, 1957, 19, 285-292.

Cook, D. L.   The Hawthorne effect in educational research. <u>Phi</u> <u>Delta</u> <u>Kappan</u>, 1962, 44, 116-122.

Deiulio, A. M., & Young, J. M.   Career education in the elementary school. <u>Phi</u> <u>Delta</u> <u>Kappan</u>, 1973, 54, 378-380.

Delamar, W.   Graves and behavior in the work system. Unpublished manuscript, May, 1972.

Dennis, W., & Najarian, P.   Infant development under environmental handicap. <u>Psychological</u> <u>Monographs</u>, 1957, 71(7).

Deutsch, M.   The disadvantaged child and the learning process. In A. H. Passow (Ed.), <u>Education</u> <u>in</u> <u>depressed</u> <u>areas</u>. New York: Columbia University, 1963.

Dick, F.   The Sylvania work-study program. In D. Y. Miller & R. H. Danielson (Eds.), <u>Work-study</u> <u>for</u> <u>slow</u> <u>learners</u> <u>in</u> <u>Ohio</u>. Columbus, Ohio: Columbus Blank Book Co., 1965.

di Michael, S.   The current scene. In D. Malikin & H. Rusalem (Eds.), <u>The</u> <u>vocational</u> <u>rehabilitation</u> <u>of</u> <u>the</u> <u>disabled</u>. New York: New York University Press, 1969.

di Michael, S. G.   Vocational rehabilitation and the mentally retarded: A statement of issues. In J. H. Rothstein (Ed.), <u>Mental</u> <u>retardation</u>: <u>Readings</u> <u>and</u> <u>resources</u>. (2nd ed.) New York: Holt, Rinehart, & Winston, 1971.

Dubrow, M.   On the job assistance. In The Woods Schools, <u>Outlook</u> <u>for</u> <u>the</u> <u>adult</u>

retarded. Langhorne, Pennsylvania: The
Woods Schools, 1960.

Dunn, L. M. A historical review of the treatment of the retarded. In J. H. Rothstein (Ed.), Mental retardation: Readings and resources. New York: Holt,
Rinehart, & Winston, 1961.

Dunn, L. M. An overview. In L. M. Dunn (Ed.),
Exceptional children in the schools:
Special education in transition. (2nd
ed.) New York: Holt, Rinehart, & Winston, 1973. (a)

Dunn, L. M. Children with mild general learning disabilities. In L. M. Dunn (Ed.),
Exceptional children in the schools:
Special education in transition. (2nd
ed.) New York: Holt, Rinehart, & Winston, 1973. (b)

Ebel, R. L. What are schools for? Phi Delta
Kappan, 1972, 54, 3-7.

Festinger, L., & Katz, D. (Eds.) Research
methods in the behavioral sciences. New
York: Dryden Press, 1953.

Forgays, D. G., & Forgays, J. W. The nature
of the effect of free environmental experience in the rat. Journal of Comparative Physiology and Psychology, 1952, 45,
322-328.

Fraenkel, W. A. The mentally retarded and
their vocational rehabilitation: A resource handbook. New York: National
Association for Retarded Children, 1961.

Freedman, D. G., King, J. A., & Elliot, O.
Critical period in the social development of dogs. Science, 1961, 133, 1016-
1017.

Gallup, G. H. The fourth annual Gallup poll
of public attitude toward education.
Phi Delta Kappan, 1972, 54, 33-46.

Ganges, A. G. Architecture. In J. Wortis
(Ed.), Mental retardation: An annual
review. New York: Grune & Stratton,
1970.

Garber, H., & Heber, R. The Milwaukee Project:
Early intervention as a technique to pre-
vent mental retardation. Stoors, Conn.:
The University of Connecticut Technical
Paper, 1973.

Gilhool, T. K. Education: An inalienable
right. Exceptional Children, 1973, 39,
597-609.

Gold, M. W. Research on the vocational habilitation of the retarded: The present,
the future. In N. R. Ellis (Ed.), International review of research in mental
retardation. Vol. 6. New York: Academic Press, 1973.

Goldstein, H. Social and occupational adjustment. In H. A. Stevens & R. Heber (Eds.),
Mental retardation: Review of research.
Chicago: University of Chicago Press,
1964.

Goldstein, H., & Heber, R. Preparation of
mentally retarded youth for gainful employment. In H. A. Stevens & R. Heber
(Eds.), Mental retardation: Review of
research. Chicago: University of Chicago Press, 1964.

Graves, C. W. The deterioration of work standards. Harvard Business Review, 1966,
44, 117-126.

Graves, C. W. Levels of existence: An open
system theory of values. Journal of
Humanistic Psychology, 1970, 10, 131-155.

Graves, C. W.   Levels of human existence and
     their relations to management problems.
     (Brochure). Management Center, Institute
     for Business and Community Development,
     University of Richmond, 1972.

Gray, S. W., & Klaus, R. A.   An experimental
     preschool program for culturally deprived
     children. Child Development, 1965, 36,
     887-898.

Gray, S. W. & Klaus, R. A.   The early train-
     ing project for disadvantaged children:
     A report after five years. Monographs
     for the Society for Research in Child
     Development, 1968, 33(4).

Gysbers, N., & Moore, E.   Guiding career ex-
     ploration: Any teacher can. Instructor,
     1972, 81(6), 52-56.

Harlow, H.   Total social isolation: Effects
     on Macaque monkey behavior. Science,
     1965, 148, 666.

Hawkridge, D., Chalupsky, A., & Roberts, A.
     A study of selected exemplary programs
     for the education of disadvantaged chil
     dren. Palo Alto, Calif.: American In-
     stitutes for Research in the Behavioral
     Sciences, 1968.

Heath, R.   The reasonable adventurer. Pitts-
     burgh, Penn.: University of Pittsburgh
     Press, 1964.

Hebb, D. O.   The organization of behavior.
     New York: Wiley, 1949.

Heber, R.   (Ed.) Special problems in voca-
     tional rehabilitation of the mentally
     retarded. U. S. Department of Health,
     Education, & Welfare, Vocational Reha-
     bilitation Administration, Rehabilita-
     tion Service Series No. 65-16, 1963.

Hehir, R. G.   Integrating deaf students for
    career education.   Exceptional Children,
    1973, 39, 611-618.

Hershey, G. L., & Lugo, J. O.   Living psy-
    chology.   London: Macmillan Company,
    1970.

Hess, R. D., & Shipman, V. C.   Early experience
    and the socialization of cognitive modes
    in children.   Child Development, 1965, 36,
    869-886.

Hewett, F. M.   A hierarchy of educational tasks
    for children with learning disorders.   Ex-
    ceptional Children, 1964, 31, 207-214.

Hoppock, R.   Occupational information.   (3rd
    ed.)   New York: McGraw-Hill, 1967.

Hoyt, K. B., Evans, R. N., Mackin, E. F., &
    Mangum, G. L.   Career education: What
    it is and how to do it.   Salt Lake City,
    Utah: Olympus, 1972.

Hunt, D. E.   A conceptual systems change model
    and its application to education.   In
    O. J. Harvey (Ed.), Experience, structure
    and adaptability.   New York: Springer,
    1966.

Hunt, J. McV.   Intelligence and experience.
    New York: Ronald Press, 1961.

Innisfree Village.   (Brochure).   Crozet, Vir-
    ginia.

Itard, J. M. G.   The wild boy of Aveyron.
    New York: Appleton-Century-Crofts, 1962.

Johnson, B. B.   Practical preparation for the
    21st century.   Phi Delta Kappan, 1973,
    39, 518-521.

Kagan, J.   On class differences and early de-
    velopment.   In V. Denenberg (Ed.), Educa-

tion of the infant and young child. New
York: Academic Press, 1970.

Karnes, M. B., Hodgins, A., & Teska, J. A.
An evaluation of two preschool programs
for disadvantaged children: A traditional
and a highly structured experimental
school. Exceptional Children, 1968, 34,
667-676.

Kirk, S. A. Early education of the mentally
retarded: An experimental study. Ur-
bana, Ill.: University of Illinois Press,
1958.

Klinkhamer, G. E. The implications of career
education for visually handicapped students. The New Outlook for the Blind,
1973, 67, 207-209, 215.

Knezevich, S. J. Administration of public
education. New York: Harper & Brothers,
1962.

Kokaska, C. A tool for community adjustment.
Mental Retardation, 1964, 2, 365-369.

Kolstoe, O. P., & Frey, R. M. A high school
work study program for mentally subnormal
students. Carbondale, Ill.: Southern
Illinois University Press, 1965.

Kruger, D. H. Trends in service employment:
Implications for the educable mentally
retarded. Exceptional Children, 1963,
30, 167-172.

Lake, T. P. Career education and the handicapped child. Exceptional Children,
1973, 39, 657-667. (a)

Lake, T. P. Career education as a philosophy
and a practice: An interview with George
Klinkhamer. Teaching Exceptional Children, 1973, 5, 124-127. (b)

Lambie, D. Z., & Weikart, D. P. Ypsilanti
    Carneige infant education project. In
    J. Hellmuth (Ed.), Disadvantaged child.
    Vol. 3. New York: Brunner/Mazel, 1970.

Levens, D. A look at project Head Start.
    Childhood Education, 1966, 42, 481-483.

Likert, R. The human organization: Its man-
    agement and value. New York: McGraw-
    Hill, 1967.

Mackie, R. P. Special education in the United
    States: Statistics, 1948-66. New York:
    Teachers College Press, Columbia Univer-
    sity, 1969.

Mamula, R. A., & Newman, N. Community place-
    ment of the mentally retarded. Spring-
    field, Ill.: Charles Thomas, 1973.

Marland, S. P., Jr. Career education. To-
    day's Education, 1971, 60(7), 22-25.

Marland, S. P., Jr. Career education: Every
    student headed for a goal. American
    Vocational Journal, 1972, 47(3), 34-36,
    62.

Marland, S. P., Jr. Career education: A
    report. The Bulletin of the National
    Association of Secondary School Princi-
    pals, 1973, 57(371), 1-10.

Management Center Staff. Clare W. Graves'
    theory of levels of human existence and
    suggested managerial systems for each
    level. Unpublished manuscript, Institute
    for Business and Community Development,
    University of Richmond, 1971.

Martin, E. W. Individualism and behaviorism
    as future trends in educating handicapped
    children. Exceptional Children, 1972,
    38, 517-525.

Maslow, A. H. Toward a psychology of being.
    (Rev. ed.) Princeton, N. J.: Van Nos-
    trand, 1968.

Maslow, A. H. The farther reaches of human
    nature. New York: Viking Press, 1971.

McGowan, J. Referral, evaluation, treatment.
    In D. Malikin & H. Rusalem (Eds.), The
    vocational rehabilitation of the dis-
    abled. New York: New York University
    Press, 1969.

McGregor, D. The human side of enterprise.
    New York: McGraw-Hill, 1960.

Mental illness and its treatment: Past and
    present. U. S. Department of Health,
    Education, and Welfare, Public Health
    Service Publication #1345, 1965. Cited
    by Garrett, J. Historical background.
    In D. Malikin & H. Rusalem (Eds.), Vo-
    cational rehabilitation for the disabled:
    An overview. New York: New York Univer-
    sity Press, 1969.

Miller, D. Y., & Danielson, R. H. Summary.
    In D. Y. Miller & R. H. Danielson (Eds.),
    Work-study for slow learners in Ohio.
    Columbus, Ohio: Columbus Blank Book
    Co., 1965.

Muirhead, P. P. Career education: The first
    steps show promise. Phi Delta Kappan,
    1973, 54, 370-372.

Myers, M. S., & Myers, S. S. Adapting to the
    new work ethic. Business Quarterly, 1973,
    38(4), in press.

Nash, R. J., & Agne, R. M. Career education:
    Earning a living or living a life? Phi
    Delta Kappan, 1973, 54, 373-378.

National Association of Sheltered Workshops
    and Homebound Programs, Publications

Committee. Planning a workshop: A growing responsibility. Washington, D. C., 1961.

Oberman, C. E. A history of vocational rehabilitation in America. Minneapolis: T. S. Denison, 1965.

Oklahoma Rehabilitation Service, Division of the State Board for Vocational Education. Bridging the gap between school and employment. A cooperative program of special education-vocational rehabilitation, 1964.

Olympus Research Corporation. Career education: A handbook for implementation. Salt Lake City, Utah: Olympus Research Corporation; and Baltimore, Maryland: State Department of Education, 1972.

Omwake, E. B. From the President. Young Children, 1969, 24, 130-131.

Orton, R. E. Comments on the President's January message. Young Children, 1969, 24, 246-248.

Page, E. B. Miracle in Milwaukee: Raising the IQ. Educational Researcher, 1972, 15, 8-16.

Payne, J. S. Kansas vocation rehabilitation and special education cooperative project. In J. D. Chaffin, L. Edwards, & F. Hudson (Eds.), Workshop on cooperative development of vocational rehabilitation services to the handicapped in public schools. Lawrence, Kansas: University of Kansas, 1966.

Payne, J. S., & Chaffin, J. D. Developing employer relations in a work study program for the educable mentally retarded. Education and Training of the Mentally Retarded, 1968, 3, 127-133.

Payne, J. S., & Mercer, C. D.　Head Start.
　　In S. E. Goodman (Ed.), Handbook on con-
　　temporary education.　Princeton, N. J.:
　　Xerox Corp. R. R. Bowker Co., 1974.

Payne, J. S., Mercer, C. D., Payne, R. A., &
　　Davison, R. G.　Head Start: A tragicom-
　　edy with epilogue.　New York:　Behavioral
　　Publications, 1973.

Peck, J. R., & Stephens, W. B.　Success of
　　young adult male retardates.　Coopera-
　　tive Research Project No. 1533.　Austin:
　　University of Texas, 1964.

Perry, W. G., Jr.　Forms of intellectual and
　　ethical development in the college years.
　　New York:　Holt, Rinehart, & Winston,
　　1970.

Peterson, R. O., & Jones, E. M.　Guides for
　　jobs for the mentally retarded.　Pitts-
　　burgh:　American Institute for Research,
　　1964.

Pines, M.　Revolution in learning.　New York:
　　Harper & Row, 1966.

Pinneau, S. A.　A critique on the articles by
　　Margaret Ribble.　Child Development, 1950,
　　21, 203-228.

Pinneau, S. A.　The infantile disorders of hos-
　　pitalism and anaclitic depression.　Psy-
　　chological Bulletin, 1955, 52, 429-452.

Pinner, J. I.　New York State employment ser-
　　vice's experience in placing the mentally
　　retarded.　In The Woods Schools, Outlook
　　for the adult retarded.　Langhorne, Penn-
　　sylvania:　The Woods Schools, 1960.

Retarded Youth: Their school rehabilitation
　　needs.　Research and Demonstration Proj-
　　ect 681 sponsored by Minneapolis Public

Schools, Federal Vocational Rehabilitation Administration, March, 1965.

Rheingold, H. L. The modification of social
responsiveness in institutional babies.
Monograph of the Society for Research in
Child Development, 1956, 21(2).

Rheingold H. L. The effect of environmental
stimulation upon social and exploratory
behavior in the human infant. In B. M.
Foss (Ed.), Determinants of infant behavior. New York: Wiley, 1961.

Rhodes, W. C., & Gibbins, S. Community program for the behaviorally deviant child.
In H. C. Quay & J. S. Werry (Eds.), Psy-
chopathological disorders of childhood.
New York: Wiley & Sons, 1973.

Ribble, M. A. Infantile experience in relation to personality development. In J.
McV. Hunt (Ed.), Personality and the behavior disorders. New York: Ronald
Press, 1944.

Richmond, J. B. Beliefs in action. Childhood Education, 1967, 44, 4-7.

Riesman, D., Glazer, N., & Denney, R. The
lonely crowd. New York: Doubleday,
1953.

Roberts, R. W. Vocational and practical arts
education: History, development, & principles. (2nd ed.) New York: Harper &
Row, 1965.

Roethlisberger, F. J., & Dickson, W. J. Management and the worker. Cambridge, Mass.:
Harvard University Press, 1939.

Schein, E. H. Organizational psychology.
(2nd ed.) Englewood Cliffs, New Jersey:
Prentice-Hall, 1970.

Scientific seer: Rudolf Steiner. MD, The
    Medical News Magazine, 1969, 13, 245-
    250.

Scott, T. B., Dawis, R. V., England, G. W., &
    Lofquist, L. H. A definition of work
    adjustment. Minnesota Studies in Voca-
    tional Rehabilitation, 1960, 10(30).

Scott, J. P., & Fuller, J. L. Genetics and
    the social behavior of the dog. Chicago:
    University of Chicago Press, 1965.

Shoemaker, B. R. Career education: A chance
    for change. American Vocational Journal,
    1972, 47(3), 27-31.

Shostrom, E. L. Man, the manipulator, New
    York: Bantam Books, 1968.

Shriver, R. S. After Head Start--what? Child-
    hood Education, 1967, 44, 2-3.

Skeels, H. M. Adult status of children with
    contrasting early life experiences. Mono-
    graphs of the Society for Research in
    Child Development, 1966, 31(3).

Skeels, H. M., & Dye, H. B. A study of the
    effects of differential stimulation on
    mentally retarded children. Convention
    Proceedings American Association on Men-
    tal Deficiency, 1939, 44, 114-136.

Sluckin, W. Imprinting and early learning.
    London: Mcthuen, 1964.

Spicker, H. H. Intellectual development through
    early childhood education. Exceptional
    Children, 1971, 37, 629-640.

Spitz, R. A. Hospitalism: An inquiry into
    the genesis of psychiatric conditions in
    early childhood. Psychoanalytic Study
    of the Child, 1945, 1, 53-74.

Stadt, R. W., Bittle, R. E., Kenneke, L. J., & Nystrom, D. C. Managing career education programs. Englewood Cliffs, N. J.: Prentice-Hall, 1973.

Stainback, W. C., Payne, J. S., Stainback, S. B., & Payne, R. A. Establishing a token economy in the classroom. Columbus, Ohio: Charles E. Merrill, 1973.

Strickland, S. P. Can slum children learn? American Education, 1971, 7(6), 3-7.

Swanson, G. I. Career education: Barriers to implementation. American Vocational Journal, 1972, 47(3), 81-82.

Taylor, F. W. The principles of scientific management. New York: Harper & Brothers, 1913.

Thompson, J. F. Foundations of vocational education: Social and philosophical concepts. Englewood Cliffs, N. J.: Prentice-Hall, 1973.

Thompson, W. R., & Grusec, J. Studies of early experience. In P. H. Mussen (Ed.), Carmichael's manual of child psychology. New York: Wiley, 1970.

Thompson, W. R., & Heron, W. The effects of restricting early experience on the problem-solving capacity of dogs. Canadian Journal of Psychology, 1954, 8, 17-31.

Townsend, R. Up the organization. New York: Alfred A. Knopf, 1970.

Uxer, J. E. Career education and visually handicapped persons: Some issues surrounding the state of the art. The New Outlook for the Blind, 1973, 67, 200-206.

Venn, G. Career education in perspective: Yesterday, today, and tomorrow. The

Bulletin *of* *the* *National* *Association* *of*
Secondary *School* *Principals*, 1973, 57(371),
11-21.

Warren, F. G. Ratings of employed and unemployed mentally handicapped males on
personality and work factors. *American*
Journal *of* *Mental* *Deficiency*, 1961, 65,
629-633.

Weikart, D. P., & Lambie, D. Z. Early enrich-
ment in infants. In V. Denenberg (Ed.),
Education *of* *the* *infant* *and* *young* *child*.
New York: Academic Press, 1970.

Wells, C. E. Will vocational education survive? *Phi* *Delta* *Kappan*, 1973, 54, 369,
380.

Wispé, L. G. Evaluating section teaching methods in the introductory course. *Journal*
of *Educational* *Research*, 1951, 45, 161-
186.

Wolfe, H. E. Career education: A new dimension in education for living. *The* *New*
Outlook *for* *the* *Blind*, 1973, 67, 193-199.

Wolff, M. Is the bridge completed? *Child-*
hood *Education*, 1967, 44, 12-15.

Wright, B. A. (Ed.) *Psychology* *and* *rehabilita-*
tion. Washington, D. C.: American Psychological Association, 1959.

Wright, J. S. The Washington D. C. school
case. In M. Weinberg (Ed.), *Integrated*
education: *A* *reader*. Beverly Hills,
Calif.: Glencoe Press, 1968.

Yando, R. M., & Kagan, J. The effect of teacher tempo on the child. *Child* *Development*,
1968, 39, 27-34.

Younie, W. J., & Rusalem, H. The world of
    rehabilitation: An atlas for special
    educators. New York: John Day, 1971.